GOLD, MUD A[...]

THE INCREDIBLE TOM RICHARDS: FOOTBALLER, WAR HERO, OLYMPIAN

Greg Growden has been the chief rugby union writer for The Sydney Morning Herald and the Sun-Herald newspapers since 1987. He has covered all four World Cup tournaments, well over 100 Tests, and more than 15 Wallaby overseas tours. He is the author of three books- two with ABC Books: *A Wayward Genius- the Fleetwood Smith Story* (1991), ranked by acclaimed British author Frank Keating among the 100 best sporting books of the 20th century, and *With the Wallabies* (1995). However, his main claim to fame is being the only international rugby writer to have the main race at a Wentworth Park greyhound meeting named after him.

GOLD, MUD AND GUTS

THE INCREDIBLE TOM RICHARDS: FOOTBALLER, WAR HERO, OLYMPIAN

GREG GROWDEN

ABC BOOKS

Published by ABC Books for the
AUSTRALIAN BROADCASTING CORPORATION
GPO Box 9994 Sydney NSW 2001

Copyright © Greg Growden 2001

First published July 2001

All rights reserved. No part of this publication may be reproduced,
stored in a retrieval system or transmitted in any form or by any means,
electronic, mechanical, photocopying, recording or otherwise,
without the prior permission of the Australian Broadcasting Corporation.

National Library of Australia
Cataloguing-in-Publication entry
Growden, Greg.
    Gold, mud 'n' guts: the incredible Tom Richards:
    footballer, war hero, Olympian

ISBN 0 7333 0976 3

1. Richards, Tom, 1887–1935. 2. Rugby Union football players–Australia–Biography.
3. World War, 1914–1918–Australia–Biography. I. Australian Broadcasting
Corporation. II. Title

796.333092

Designed and typeset by Kerry Klinner
Colour separations by Colorwize, Adelaide
Set in Sabon 10/14 pt
Printed and bound in Australia by
Griffin Press, Adelaide

5 4 3 2 1

CONTENTS

ONE:	THAT DAY	7
TWO:	CLIMBING THE TOWER	13
THREE:	CHASING CHICKENS AND BIGGER BIRDS	25
FOUR:	VELDT AND VIOLETS	35
FIVE:	THE TOUR	49
SIX:	OLYMPIC GOLD	69
SEVEN:	WALLABY WANDERLUST	89
EIGHT:	STARS AND BARS	99
NINE:	OUR COUNTRY'S FINEST	111
TEN:	SCALING THE SPHINX	123
ELEVEN:	GALLIPOLI	137
TWELVE:	THE FRONT	161
THIRTEEN:	THE HONOUR	179
FOURTEEN:	HAPPY EVER AFTER?	197
FIFTEEN:	THE BREAKDOWN	211
	AFTERWORD	227
	ACKNOWLEDGMENTS	232

ONE

THAT DAY

TOM 'RUSTY' RICHARDS took a small, battered, leather-bound notebook out of his side pocket, and wrote: "I don't feel the coming danger any more than I have felt anxious the night before an International football match."

He stopped, fidgeted, once again checked his supplies — bully beef, biscuits, a full water bottle for two or three days. He turned towards the sunset over Lemnos harbour, to be dazzled by the "lovely deep red coloured orb disappearing between the purple hills and the dense rose-pink sky".

He was on his way to Gallipoli, savouring the last moments of 24 April 1915.

As soon as night fell, his fellow Australian troops perched on the deck of the *City of Benares*, attempted to hide their nervousness and uncertainty of what to expect the following morning by making jokes, mimicking each other's voices, taking cheeky digs at the officers around them. It enabled them all to relax, to stop thinking about what was to come.

The sea was calm, indicating the onset of a clear day on the morrow. Somewhere at the other end of the ship, a group of soldiers, accompanied by mouth organ and concertina, played softly: "Nearer My God to Thee" then "Lead Kindly Light." Eventually everyone fell into a restless slumber, including Tom.

There were constant interruptions. After leaving Lemnos around 1am, "there was a wholesale roaring and spitting of big guns, our warships being particularly aggressive".

This didn't bother Tom, but several others around him were getting nervous. After endless restless months lolling around Egypt, causing havoc around the Pyramids, Sphinx, the local brothels and villages, here was the brutal reminder that this was no longer an extended holiday. They were now actually soldiers. The high value of human life had suddenly diminished.

"The roar of guns did not bother me much," Tom wrote before once more going through his gear to ensure his camera was in perfect working order, so that he could take a photographic record of the landing. Rusty had already proven himself to be Australia's greatest Rugby forward, the only Australian Test representative to play for the famous British Lions, the only Wallaby to travel almost continuously around the world, but he wanted to write, to take photographs, to be a travelling adventurer, and to have a lasting record of his part of history.

He diligently worked on cleaning his lens and the exterior of the camera, trying to protect it wherever he could against the damaging effects of seaspray and sand. All around him was the echoing, booming sound of guns roaring, and the spit of shrapnel.

He was still some distance from shore, but from the repeated flash of lights, he knew that from about 4.30am the landing of Gallipoli had started. By 6am, with the first rays of light and with the harsh Turkish landscape rising straight up in front, he could see the Australian troops clambering up the most inhospitable of rock faces, stopping in his tracks and collapsing, others looking for protection from the Turkish troops, who were hitting them from above with a rain of bullets. Everything seemed to be in slow motion, but at the same time everything appeared so frenzied, with general mayhem on the beachfront, as the Australians fortified themselves for the long haul.

"No bugle call to wake us this morning," Tom wrote, "but most of us were astir before the sun rose, a brilliant and pleasing red glow. It was just the same as the sunset last night—a stage setting with the flashes and booming of the cannon to enliven matters."

At 8.30am the call was for those on Tom's craft to transfer onto the torpedo boat *Scourge*. They were going to be part of the second wave, landing a mile north of the beach originally chosen for the invasion. The moment coincided with a loud crash. A shell had flown over the top of the No 13 transport, and had "stirred up the water to a height of perhaps 60 feet, within 150 yards of us. This brought home to me the grim reality of war, but to my surprise I was not much troubled and took seven photos before landing up over our knees in water from the rowing boats into which we were transferred from the *Scourge*.

"As we were landing, a shrapnel shell burst 150 yards away and threw a shower of bullets into the water — rather a pretty display!"

Tom hit the beach running. As a member of the 1st Field Ambulance, 1st Australian Division, it was his job to follow the soldiers up the Gallipoli cliffs and bring back the wounded. Before following the tribe, he turned, aimed the camera at those coming in behind him, those in front of him. He wanted a permanent record of this most extraordinary day. It was also the longest day of his life. Within minutes of clambering up the cliff, he thought he was "done for". He was hiding behind a shrub. A Turk, only thirty metres away, put him in his rifle sights, and blasted away. The shrub exploded, leaves and twigs splintering everywhere.

The Turk was about to take a second aim when someone, somewhere, shot him.

That night Rusty buried himself away in a dugout on the cliff-face, found a candle, and stimulated by what he had seen and felt, wrote into the early hours, explaining what had gone on around him. Even he, who had already had an astonishing life, struggled to comprehend how the world had suddenly turned upon itself and, it seemed, gone completely mad.

"Twenty minutes (after landing) with stretchers we were climbing the steep, rough hills looking for wounded, but it was about 1pm when I got my first case, and from then until 6pm I had fully 20 dressings to do. The wounded were in splendid spirits and told me that in landing this day, the Turks were right down on the beach, but were soon driven back over the terrible ridges for a distance of two miles, but alas, our fellows got knocked about badly before this.

"Seeing that the Turks had been pushed back and three guns taken, it was surprising to me to find only a few dead and wounded Turks, while our officers and men were knocked about.

"In a fairly well sheltered valley I waited for an hour within a short distance of the attacking party. The word was continually being sent back that help was badly needed on the left flank. A whole battalion of men were sent in, but it was too late. The Turks had brought about a successful counter-attack and driven our men back, chiefly by the use of machine guns and shells. Showers of these shell bullets were falling all around our positions and it fairly made us shake.

"Machine guns were being pushed forward by the New Zealanders. They only just passed our little party when a captain got a bullet through his calf, and a lieutenant got a shattered forearm. Both came under my treatment.

"A fellow came along and asked me to go up and fix up his pal, whose foot was shot. With a stretcher Watts and I went only 100 yards along the valley. The bush was too thick and water-worn track so rough that we discarded the stretcher and proceeded on all fours up to the firing trenches upon which our fellows had been driven back. Here was a poor fellow with his heel and sole of foot blown away, and although in great pain he was what might be considered cheerful. I cut his boot off and dressed the foot. Bleeding was then not heavy.

"Now the trouble was to get him away with rifle fire pinging overhead and through the bushes within a foot of us. This safely done, the way out was awful, but my patient skipped down the steep side on his hands and seat, while I went forward holding the limb. In the bottom of the gorge I got him onto my back and made good progress, but as the foot started to bleed heavily I had to put a ligature onto the artery at the thigh.

"Finally two hours had passed before we got back to the boats taking wounded aboard the transports, and he bore up wonderfully well right throughout. In his belt was a large sum of money, which he said amounted to 100 pounds. When we got back I was pretty well finished. It was a hard job for me, but truly terrible for the patient.

"When he was waiting he got out a sovereign and made me take it.

It was a remarkable day right enough and a day in which it was easy to pick out the wasters, also the brave men. I am delighted with our Australian troops; the way they take the gruel is splendid.

"At times there was a shortage of ammunition and reinforcements were badly wanted but seeing they had landed everything under shell fire I should say they did very well.

"The Turks seemed to do most damage with their shrapnel shells, not so much damage perhaps as fright, as really they are uncanny damned things. Our warships kept up a stready fire throughout the day but I fear they were missing their marks badly.

"It was heart-rending to hear the plaintive and the only too ominous call of 'more ammunition wanted on the left'. What a doleful story these words really unfold. Also the call for reinforcements that came back from mouth to mouth to dire troubles that were being experienced on the other side of the hill.

"'Reinforcements- hung up on the right!' What a significant sentence, especially when uttered by the parched lips of a wounded man. Reinforcements were hurrying forward, sweating and panting, loaded with their equipment and a box of ammunition between two."

He could write no more. The candle was about to go out. It had started to rain. He was exhausted, and knew he had to be up at first light, for another day of searching for casualties and bodies in the endless crevices of this living hell. He also had to keep his head down so that he did not become another statistic.

On 25 April 1915 the first of 8,141 Australians, including several Wallabies, were killed in the Dardanelles campaign. But Tom 'Rusty' Richards, the great survivor, lasted that day, and more.

TWO

CLIMBING THE TOWER

He was of tough mining stock. But even Rusty would flinch when confronted by his deeply religious father as he sneaked into the house via the back door late on Sunday winter afternoons.

It was the most frightening of sights. His father, still in his dress as a Methodist minister, would be glowering, drawing himself up to his full height, and swishing a cane.

Tom and his three brothers would skulk in front of him, pushed by their father into a straight line, as he bellowed: "John, have you been playing football on the Sabbath?"

"Yes father."

Swish.

"William, have you been playing football on the Sabbath?"

"Yes father."

Swish.

"Charles, have you been playing football on the Sabbath?"

"Yes father."

Swish.

"Tom, have you been playing football on the Sabbath?"
"Yes father."
Swish.

The sting was immense, rising steadily up the arm and making the whole body throb with pain.

The four brothers would be bowed double, rubbing their hands in the hope of quelling the numbness. But there was no respite. Their father would push them back into the same straight line, and twice, thrice, would go through the ritual of asking them a simple question, getting the affirmative, and then crashing the cane down on their right hands.

Then they were told to bend over and their posterior was given the same treatment.

Eventually their father would leave the room in frustration, disgusted that, week in week out, his most important day was disturbed by the necessity to unleash such aggression on his sons. If flicking the cane was not disconcerting enough for John Richards Senior, the irritation was amplified by his knowledge that he was not getting through to them.

All he had taught them from the Bible had been in vain. They were heathens, prepared to damn him for the most puerile of pursuits ... football, and on a Sunday.

The boys were brutally thrashed, but never complained. They were already attuned to the harshness of life.

They were adventurers, travellers from the beginning. Their father left England in search of riches, always restless, always chasing the big strike, the easy fortune.

He was born and raised in Cornwall, but became restless when hearing of the big money being made on the Australian goldfields. After turning 21 in 1868, he headed for Melbourne, and the Victorian fields, revelling for several years in the lively pace of Ballarat and Bendigo. After a decade wandering throughout Victoria, John Richards eventually made enough money from his diggings to impress one of the local beauties- Mary Ann Davis- known throughout the area as "The Belle of Ballarat".

After eloping, they married in April 1879. Then they were off, heading north, and three years later found themselves in a tin settlement called Vegetable Creek near Tenterfield in northern New South Wales.

Mary, eleven years younger than her fossicking husband, was the doting mother; John the one-day-a-week Bible basher; on the other six days the most committed of miners.

Commitment did not lead to financial success, however, and the family lived in the most primitive of surroundings. John Jr was the first to arrive, followed by Bill, Charles and — on 29 April 1882 — Tom, who in turn was followed by Bert and Mabel. Tom, who became known as Rusty, was born in a small village called Rose Valley.

As Rusty wrote years later: "I first saw light of day on this impulsive, whirling sporadic sphere in the unpretentious home of a tin miner ... Vegetable Creek was just a rough mining camp, scattered for miles around with bark and galvanised iron humpies hastily constructed in the makeshift way of expectant, ruthless, nomadic mining men, ever ready to rush away on to something new, something larger or more attractive, full of optimism and gloriously stout hearted."

Endless articles and books have claimed that Tom was born anywhere between 1883 and 1887. Not one has had his birthdate right, which is understandable because it appears that not even Rusty knew it. Even C.E.W Bean's *Official History of Australia in the War of 1914-18* states that Rusty was born on 8 April 1883. Rusty's birth certificate, in the possession of the author, confirms that he was at least one year older than he actually said during his footballing days. For many decades, it was a common trait of Australian sportsmen to pretend that they were younger than they actually were, believing it would improve their longevity in the sport. On numerous occasions, especially when he was a Wallaby and during the early years of World War I, Rusty made out he was at least twelve months younger. His personal diaries confuse the matter, as sometimes the ages match, and sometimes they don't. Several diary entries, especially during the war, indicate that he had even convinced himself his birthday was on 8 April.

But Rusty's stay in Vegetable Creek, which now boasts the more elegant name of Emmaville, was short. He was only one year old when his nomadic father went off by himself to the far reaches of Queensland, where he had been told all he had to do was simply turn up to become a millionaire by nightfall.

Gold fever had gripped everyone. And the latest strike had

occurred in far-off Charters Towers. John Richards had to be part of it, and he didn't hesitate to leave the rest of the family behind.

This restless attitude is understandable, almost excusable; ridiculously large fortunes were being made by the most inexperienced of miners.

Tom's father had heard all the stories. Ten years previously local pastoralists Hugh Mosman and John Fraser, a prospector George Clarke, and their ten-year-old Aboriginal servant Jupiter had been riding towards some minor diggings when in a brief thunderstorm, their horses took fright and fled. The following morning before breakfast, Jupiter had gone off to round them up. Suddenly the early quiet was broken, when Jupiter, his hand clasping a grey stone, rushed back to the camp, calling: "Boss! Boss! Look!"

Mosman took the stone and to his near-disbelief realised that it was gold. Jupiter had discovered the outcrop of the North Australian reef, and for several days the four of them strolled around the area, picking up gold from the surface. From the surface of one reef, they picked up quartz that yielded 1600 ounces.

Shortly after Mosman had galloped to Ravenswood to apply for claims, a frantic rush to the area began. Within days 500 prospectors had arrived from everywhere, including the Cape River, Townsville, Bowen, and at least one hundred prospecting areas had been pegged out. One of the first arrivals managed to find 400 ounces of gold, including one nugget thirty centimetres long and fifteen centimetres wide, weighing 123 ounces. Within a year, 91,265 ounces had been discovered.

A few years later, thanks to Jupiter's discovery, this area known as Charters Towers had become Queensland's second largest city and easily the richest in the state, surpassing even Brisbane. Within two months the first hotel, the Reefer's Arms, was operating and by the turn of the century more than ninety hotels were catering for the parched among its 32,000-plus citizens, who had settled within seven kilometres of the spot where Jupiter and Co had pitched camp.

Charters Towers boasted stately homes, a cosmopolitan population, the best shopping in the state, racing, entertainment, dance houses, electric lights, telephones, a railway station: even its own stock exchange. As they would say in northern Queensland: "If you haven't been to Charters Towers, you haven't been anywhere."

The town was naturally the strongest of magnets for the most restless, including, of course, John Richards. He arrived in early 1883, setting up camp near the centre of town, before the rest of his family joined him.

It was no easy task, especially as Vegetable Creek was more than 1000 kilometres south, and the northern train from Sydney went no further than Tamworth. Mary Richards and her children had to travel in a waggonette drawn by three horses abreast, with a Chinese driver and three other Chinese passengers. The Richards clan hardly travelled in comfort, negotiating old, rocky bush tracks, and managed to travel only forty-five kilometres on the first day, finishing up in the small settlement of Bolivia.

"Here there was only very rough accommodation to be had. It was a trying, sleepless night; at intervals there were loud explosions of crackers, accompanied by the crashing and beating of cymbals, also the noisy shouts and cheers from the local and visiting Chinamen, who were celebrating their New Year in the proper traditional spirit," wrote Tom Richards years later. The squeaky, shaky waggonette reached Tenterfield the following day and the Queensland border on the third, where they were at last able to change their mode of transport, taking the train from Stanthorpe to Brisbane.

Then the small coastal boat from Brisbane to Townsville, giving young Tom his first taste of the sea — "a taste that has never relaxed to this day," as he wrote almost fifty years later. "Ships and trains have called and beckoned me on and on ever since those infant days. I can still hear the calling and coaxing and feel the tempting spell."

When reaching Townsville, it was back to the train and a 130-kilometre trip to their destination. Even then there were further hurdles, as about twenty kilometres from Charters Towers the Burdekin River was in flood, forcing all the passengers to be forded across in open boats. Tom wrote: "On the other side my father was waiting to take us home. Home was built of bark, the floors were earthen; no water supply, no garden, not even a fence; but as far as home were judged in those early pioneering days, our place was well within the accepted standards of what a home should be."

It was primitive, frugal, but all around, there were distractions to entice Tom and his brothers.

"Gold-mining was booming. The township contained 12,000 people (some 30 men to every woman) with new arrivals every day. It's gold that hurries the world along, both in thoughts and in action, and there were stories of this fanciful, romantic, and alluring metal in and for miles around Charters Towers. Men grew from poverty to riches in a single day. Some were thrifty, and careful with their newly acquired wealth, but many were restless and wasteful.

"Charters Towers was a law-abiding and law-respecting town until it came to the regulation of drinking hours and gambling restrictions. Then the latent forces within those hard-working, rugged miners asserted themselves. There were 36 hotels, all doing a tremendous business. A brewery soon sprang up. In the hotel backyards, two-up was played. Amongst the cases and empty boxes, 'hazards' were played with dice; in the backrooms poker was the all popular game, and in the billiard rooms pool was played for high stakes.

"Some of the largest schools, where bets oftimes ran into hundreds of pounds, were found amongst the mine mullock-heaps on Sunday mornings. Saturday nights were the great promenade nights. Thousands of people walked and stood about Gill and Mosman Street.

"In laneways and under cover were shooting galleries and 'Yankee sweat' tables where a dart was shot at a spinning wheel with numbers on, and the bets laid on the numbered mat either won or lost according to the registration on the wheel. Sweeps were drawn at regular intervals, when two shilling tickets would win hundreds of pounds. One sweep of shilling tickets was drawn every Saturday night, with 100 pounds as first prize.

"Crowds lined the hotel bars until closing time at 11pm. This did not mean that the hotel were closed to business. The crowds just dwindled away, but there was drinking going on until one and two o'clock in the morning."

It was a hard-working, hard-drinking town, with an edge because of the flotsam and jetsam that had been attracted by the lure of supposed instant wealth.

Tom's father was often distracted in search of gold, his mother somehow trying to keep a ramshackle house in order, the children whenever possible getting a rudimentary education from the town's hastily arranged school. It was basic stuff, with too many distractions for any of the Richards to become scholars. They learned to read and write, but not much more.

A more important chore was helping the family feed itself. John Richards did not get rich on the goldfields; he found occasional small pickings to feed the family, but little more. The Richards family did not move up the social ladder, did not buy one of the stately mansions or have the money to spare to play around on the stock exchange. They struggled.

The pressure was soon applied on all the sons to leave school in their early teens. There was no place in this family for shirkers or slackers.

Rusty started with fire, working for the blacksmiths Brennand and Andrews in the centre of town. It was tough work, and the ultimate initiation to the ardours of life. His first chore was as the assistant to a drunken farrier. This man, by the name of Bradford, employed young Rusty to sneak off and get bottles of beer for him so that he could top himself up with booze for most of the day, and make this hellish job almost bearable. As Bradford spent so much on drink, the business had to compromise, "having to beat horse-shoes out of old waggon tyres," wrote Rusty many years later.

"It was jolly hard work for a youngster, but it was worth 17s6d a week, and there was a lot of fun to be got out of it by practical joking, which I was extremely fond of. I worked for ... Bradford for 7s6d a week which I did not always get, as he was a drunkard though a good tradesman. He used to coax me sometimes to go and get bottles of beer for him. I went willingly enough if it were counter lunch time, otherwise I often refused him."

Rusty eventually had to move on because the booze-soaked Bradford had nothing left to pay his apprentice.

There was no alternative but for Rusty to follow his father and brothers into the mines. His father was enthusiastic, believing that such a tough life would lead his son away from silly distractions.

Instead it proved the opposite, putting father and son on a collision course.

"Mining brought me into touch with men who had travelled, and who had talked and argued about Rugby football," Rusty explained. "The work in the mines was hard, but not unpleasant where the ventilation was good, but in some of the deep levels, up dead end slopes and rises, the heat was terrible. I worked in places with sweat clogging in my boots and oozing through the lace-holes, amidst sickening fumes of exploded gelignite and floating screens of dust.

"I have often wondered how a human frame could stand such abuse, bullocking and heaving, sweating and swearing."

He needed an outlet. It came in the form of the NSW Rugby Union team that visited Charters Towers in 1897, when Rusty was fifteen. According to Rusty, this visit "sowed the seed of Rugby in my heart", firing his youthful imagination "with ambition for the glory and the glamour of a footballer's life".

While Charters Towers was a world away from the Rugby heartlands of Sydney and Brisbane, it was inevitable this outpost would become a footballing mecca. Gold had lured to the town countless English gentlemen, steeped in the traditions of the British Rugby game, as well as many excellent players from Brisbane in particular, who were all after a better life. So strong was the competition in Charters Towers around the turn of the century that it even became a way for these alleged gentlemen to add a little extra to their purses. As the *Rockhampton Bulletin* complained in 1892: "One has only to note the many famous players who have migrated to Charters Towers during the past 12 months to see that if professionalism does not exist there, appearances are exceedingly deceptive."

A fair comment, considering that playing in the local competition at the time were such legendary figures as New Zealander Jimmy Anderson, a longtime Queensland player, state representative back Willie McCallum, and H.C (Harry) Speakman.

Speakman, the father of Charters Towers football, was a member of the first British Lions team, which had toured Australia and New Zealand in 1888. He was one of the great performers of this thirty-five-match extravaganza that was marred by dramas and tragedies.

The organiser was the high-profile English professional cricketer Arthur Shrewsbury, who even lured the noted M.C.C Test cricketer A.E. Stoddart, to stay on after the 1887-88 Australian cricket tour, double up and play for the first British Rugby touring team.

Stoddart, rated as the finest three-quarter in the country, duly obliged, and became its leader after the original captain Bob Seddon drowned while sculling in the Hunter River near Maitland.

The tour was close to being cancelled but after several meetings the Brits decided to stay. They travelled to Brisbane where they played Queensland before the city's largest ever Rugby crowd. By this time Speakman had established himself as a top-class inner back.

At the end of the tour Speakman, lured by the local womenfolk and the lively pace of Australian life, remained in Brisbane. Within a few years he was coaching the northern Queensland representative team, playing in Charters Towers and nurturing all the young talent around him, including the Richards brothers.

As Charters Towers was virtually the third most powerful Rugby stronghold in the country, touring teams were lured to the top of Queensland in pursuit of top-quality competition. Reputable Brisbane club sides would leave with their reputation in tatters when they discovered that Speakman and Co were simply too formidable.

Crowds were large. One match against Mount Morgan lured 4500 fans with a gate of more than 200 pounds.

It was inevitable that the mighty New South Wales team would soon trek towards the Towers, lured by the lights, the glamour, the wealth, and the convincing football opposition.

New South Wales won the first game 21-19. Rusty wanted to be there, but because of his father's dire warnings he went to Sunday school instead.

A week later was the return match. "The town was aglow with excitement," Rusty wrote.

"My schemes and plots to see the game all fell before father's stern discipline, so I went to Sunday school as usual. Later my heart stirred within me and hope gleamed as my brother Bill asked my teacher to excuse me.

"Outside I saw that Bill had my hat in his hand. We did not speak or look behind, but ran until I became exhausted. Bill, being older and stronger, faithfully waited for me. When we arrived the crowd was enormous — buggies, cabs, carts, and men on horseback lined the hard playing area."

All around him were Rusty's heroes. "Big Freddie Henlen of Sydney kicked off. My soul was at its full height of bliss. 'Jupp' Gardiner was in the forwards, 'Dicken' Brown at five-eighth and George Outram at centre. Little Miller, on the wing, had a bandage around his calf and a sorry limp until the ball came his way; then he was so fast that our Bob Thompson took off his boots and ran barefooted to catch him.

"Joe Glenwright at full back went low and hard, tackling like a demon to the dismay of many NSW players. The Towers forwards, with big Billy Tregear, Steve Daddow and 'Dad' Benham courageously and fearlessly leading the heroic struggle, were wonderful. I learned that memorable afternoon that force alone cannot prevail over concentrated and well-timed movements. The scores were 18 to 3, and success was not ours."

After the game, Bill and Rusty tried to sneak back into Sunday school, but the class had long departed. The only alternative was to return home and confront their father. He knew straight away, what the pair had been up to, and thrashed both of them.

The Methodist church in Charters Towers, of which Mr Richards was a key member, was so influential that for some time it even attempted to have Sunday sport in the town stopped, going as far as applying to the local court for an injunction to restrain the footballers. As most of the miners worked Saturdays, all sports, including cricket and football, were played on the Sunday on a rough, ugly field, which even had a reef outcropped across it, protruding in some places like the edge of a chisel.

When the injunction was sought the president of the Charters Towers Rugby Union, a legal luminary named John Marsland, attempted to overcome the problem.

On the Friday before an important representative match he lodged an application for a gold mining lease on the Athletic Reserve, the main football ground. Consequently, until the application was heard by the Warden's Court which usually took at least thirty days, Marsland was basically the owner of the ground.

Therefore the Athletic Reserve was temporarily private property, and the footballers could merrily continue trying to maim each other on the reef. The church groups gave up, enabling the football club to get the funds to dig up the ground, remove the dangerous reef and build an oval as good as anywhere in Queensland. Soon Rusty, inspired by that one representative march, was the chief organiser in a team of youngsters called the Waratahs, who were almost unbeatable in their first season, tallying 300 points to the opposition's 10. Then Rusty, who the next season moved to the Natives club, was forced to play under the assumed name of Brown to avoid the notice of his father, now superintendent of the Methodist Church.

"My father had nothing but horror for my desire to play football," Rusty recalled. "He was of hardy, God-fearing Cornish stock. There were no half-measures about his religious beliefs- only a hereafter of burning pits, sulphur fumes, and scorching flames for those who strayed even a hair's breath from the 'narrow path'.

"My mother had too much work on hand keeping house for five husky, hungry boys to bother about the hereafter. Her greater concern was keeping seats in the many pairs of trousers, in washing, starching and ironing those little white sailor suits in which we all looked so clean and nice on Sundays.

"Mother had to bake bread, clean, scrub and make melon jam on the 30 latitude line north of the Tropic of Capricorn."

Sundays soon became the big day in the Charters Towers calendar.

"At daylight each Sunday cock-fighting for large stakes was well patronised. Disputes and differences that occurred during the week were settled with bare fists before breakfast, also on Sundays. The afternoons were devoted to cricket and football matches, foot-racing and horse-racing.

"Kangaroo-hunters, with horses and packs of dogs, found thrilling sport, while shooting parties brought in good bags of wild ducks and turkeys, pigeons and sometimes geese.

"Churches of all denominations and creeds provided spiritual entertainment; even the Chinese had their joss-houses open. Sunday was the great day for both Sabbath observer and Sabbath desecrator alike. Later on we secretly learned to play football on Sunday morning. Gravel-rashed knees, hips, and elbows had to be cautiously treated and carefully nursed. There was no sympathy. Limping or complaining, we had to help one another, and stuck it out for the good of the cause nearest our hearts."

Rusty was on his way.

THREE

CHASING CHICKENS AND BIGGER BIRDS

AN ESCAPE ROUTE eventually appeared. The discovery of gold in the Transvaal region of South Africa lured Rusty's father away. Yet again, he left the rest of the clan behind. With the whip-wielding tyrant on the other side of the world, the way was clear for the Richards boys to enjoy Sunday football. With the gate opened, Rusty charged through, playing and training for the Rugby game with an unstinting, overriding passion.

His physique was impressive. He was tall, athletic and well built, with determination in his eyes. He had the most piercing of stares, his dark brown eyes showing that he was someone not to mess around with. They were the eyes of a sportsman, observing, noting and comprehending everything. His demeanour was stern. He rarely smiled. He was a serious, focused young man.

He was involved in heavy menial work, plying his trade and building up his upper body as a coach-builder at 17s6d a week and then going into the mines, where he earned a weekly wage of 3 pounds, working deep below the ground in the shafts under Charters Towers.

He ran kilometres every day to get himself into condition as a football player, and was rewarded at the age of twenty when selected as a loose forward for Charters Towers against Townsville and Ravenswood. Unlike most of his teammates, he did not base his footballing diet around alcohol. The Charters Towers players were notorious for their drinking exploits, to the extent that even when they travelled away, they took with them their own so-called 'Towers brew', refrigerating the casks with onion skins. Rusty generally abstained and became one of the few not to harbour a hangover at kick-off.

Within just one season, Rusty was a representative player. He was raw. But from the start through Rugby he saw endless opportunities, a way of improving himself, and a ticket to the real world. Rugby was an international sport, and if he was good enough it would take him away on the most magical of carpet-rides.

Rusty was a serious lad, but he had his dreams. A resolute teenager who was persistent in pursuit of his goals, he always fantasised. He was paranoid about his lack of education. He read avidly. He always wanted to improve himself. He read more and more, even tackling major works he had difficulty in understanding. But he persevered, believing this would lead to enrichment. He knew the borders were limitless. He always wanted more.

He set down his plan. He was about to play his first representative game of Rugby, and knew exactly what to do. He had trained his mind and body.

His philosophy was basic. If he wanted to escape the mines of Charters Towers and the tedious, sapping work as a coachbuilder, he had to be sighted on a football field.

He wrote: "It seemed to me that the loose forward game, attractive and spectacular, offered immense possibilities for development; so I concentrated my studies upon a strongly individual style, learning to regulate my ideas according to my own lights and to cultivate 'attraction', so that, wherever I might roam, I would command immediate notice.

"I wanted a versatile, conspicuous, and yet a safe, hard and effective style, and to fit myself to fulfil any emergency position on the field."

Rusty's training methods were intensive, "from drawing diagrams of positions and field tactics to making my younger brother strengthen up my abdomen and solar plexus muscles with swinging punches". He practised diving tackles along the ground and over obstacles to toughen and harden himself up.

"I pushed between two posts for scrum work, jumped at a swinging rope, or lay on the floor with arms extended, lifting and moving a chair back further and further to improve reaching and lineout work.

"Running and passing, catching and handling a large waterlogged coconut along the beach at Magnetic Island [eleven kilometres off Townsville] was a most valuable exercise. Running and leaping, stepping and jumping over the boulder-strewn headlands taught me valuable lessons in quick starting, propping and turning, variation of pace and surefootedness. Skipping, club-swinging, dumb-bell and Swedish exercises were indulged in before going to bed and immediately upon getting up again."

As well, he and several of his mates made a habit of running around the hill at the back of Charters Towers, chasing wild goats on the rocky outcrop. Asked what he was up to, Rusty would reply: "Training for football, sir!"

He also had the ideal mentor. His elder brother Bill was making enormous strides as a footballer. Bill, who possessed a memorable bushy, black handlebar moustache, was tall and skinny, but like Rusty, possessed excessive, raw strength. He was a fearless miner, renowned for using his teeth to clench the detonator when preparing the charges in preference to the pinch pliers provided. Bill thought using his mouth was safer.

He excelled in local club matches, especially renowned for his enthusiastic play around the rucks and lineouts. He was a natural choice for north Queensland representative teams, after memorable performances for Charters Towers against the tough men from Mt Morgan.

In 1903, with Bill and Rusty appearing for the Natives' Club in Charters Towers and travelling far and wide for intertown matches against Townsville and Ravenswood, they were both selected for Country Week in Brisbane. Bill was picked for the emerald-green-jerseyed Country A team alongside other formidable Charters Towers notables such as Bob Thompson, Syd Davey and former Sydney centre Mark Dind. Rusty played with Country B.

Rusty was immediately involved in selection controversy. While his Country B team only lost one match in the week, with the precocious twenty-one-year-old standing out for his expressive back row play, he was surprisingly overlooked for the Queensland team to play New South Wales at the end of the carnival.

Bill was more fortunate, getting the first of many Queensland jerseys. Tom was overlooked by the sole selector Fred Lea, who instead gave the spot to an over-the-hill former Sydney forward Sammy Sampson, who was managing the Northern representative team to Brisbane but had been persuaded out of retirement to play with Country B.

Lea's shock omission of Bob Thompson, known throughout the region as "the Physician," was also a telling reason for Queensland changing the selection process in future years, reverting to a panel of selectors, rather than letting one person have all the power. Rusty took the decision on the chin, explaining: "My determination to succeed wiped out any feeling of disappointment."

His omission was nothing compared to a near-death experience in the mines, which came close to thwarting his football career well before it had really begun.

Soon gaining a reputation in the mines for his willingness to work, Rusty was, with a group of mates, descending the 600-metre vertical shaft, where they spent most of the day digging and exploring.

Ever keen to push everything to the limit and test the danger zone, Rusty would descend the shaft, standing on the rim of the steel bucket. Rusty argued that "it was quite comfortable, and the bucket could be readily prevented from spinning and bumping".

On most days it was safe until one morning, as Rusty passed an opening 100 metres down at the Kelly's Queen Block mine, a pointed batten from the side of the shaft caught the leg of his trousers. As the bucket continued to descend Rusty was wrenched off, and found himself precariously suspended over the shaft.

The bucket whooshed to the bottom of the shaft, with Rusty suspended upside down, and nothing to grab onto. He thought he was gone, realising that if the trouser ripped, he would plunge 560 metres to his death. He yelled for help. "I could hear my mate calling," Rusty recalled. "But the upward current of air prevented him from hearing my replies.

"It was an awful predicament for both of us. Eventually I heard the knocked line pull 'four' and then 'one', an instruction to the engine driver to haul up slowly. The taut wire rope rubbed and lashed at my side, and I wondered if ever that bucket would reach me — it appeared to come so slowly!

"My mate eventually reached me and favoured going home, claiming that we had had enough excitement for one day. But we worked on and completed a satisfactory day's labour." Rusty took all this as a warning, a last chance, and from then on attacked everything, especially his football, with relish.

His elder brother Bill was soon an established member of the Queensland lineup, playing the first of his five Tests for Australia in July 1904, against the visiting Great Britain team. Unbeknown to this shy Charters Towers stringbean with wide, innocent eyes, he became embroiled in one of the most dramatic and controversial series ever to involve an Australian Rugby team.

Making his debut alongside Bill Richards that same day at the Sydney Cricket Ground before 34,000 spectators was the man who would become renowned as Australia's greatest all-round athlete: Reginald 'Snowy' Baker.

During an extraordinarily diverse career, which ended in Hollywood appearing in silent movies and teaching celluloid heroes how to ride stallions, he competed in twenty-nine different sports, five internationally: boxing, polo, swimming, diving and Rugby. He achieved greatest renown as a boxer, winning the New South Wales and Victorian amateur middleweight and heavyweight titles on the same night. Several years later, he reached the 1908 Olympic Games middleweight final in London, losing in a highly controversial decision to the famous J.W.H.T. Douglas, of English cricket 'Johnny Won't Hit Today' fame.

Baker's pugilistic skills were also useful on the Rugby field, especially when picked as the Australian halfback for the opening Test of a series that would grab the headlines for all the wrong reasons.

The 1904 Lions team was the first fully representative team to tour Australia, with numerous characters including their volatile captain, the dour Scot David Bedell-Sivright, who had the nickname 'Darkie' not for his complexion but for his underhand playing methods, and another unsavoury forward in Blair Swannell.

The first Test was a rugged affair, with Australia down a man in the first half when their winger Charlie White was heavily tackled, breaking a rib. Shortly after, Snowy Baker nearly had his head kicked off when burrowing at the bottom of a ruck. Great Britain won the fights and the football 17-0.

Bill Richards went home to bathe his many wounds, especially the deep and long boot marks crisscrossing his back. Great Britain headed to Newcastle, and an unexpected walkoff.

Before the second Test in Brisbane Britain played Northern Districts and had the match well in hand when early in the second half the referee Hugh Dolan ordered the visiting front rower Denys Douglas Dobson from the field, claiming he had used abusive language. A seething Bedell-Sivright reacted immediately, signalling to his men and leading them all from the field.

After a half-hour delay and endless meetings between the British team management and the referee, with the tourists demanding that Dobson be allowed to continue playing, the game was resumed without Dobson. Britain won 17-3.

Bedell-Sivright was criticised for his actions, censured by the authorities for authorising a walk-off. But the British captain repeatedly argued his innocence, claiming that Dobson had not used an offensive expression, (alleged to be "What the deuce was that for?") and that the referee had been facing away from the play at the time.

The drama continued when Queensland met the Lions before the second Test, where Bill Richards was at least lucky to avoid the swinging boot of Swannell. Richards's teammate Alex McKinnon wasn't so fortunate, being stomped on by Swannell, and had to leave the field with a badly lacerated head. Swannell was roundly booed by the Brisbane crowd, earning their ire even more a few weeks later when he wrote a letter to *The Referee* newspaper defending his "dirty play."

Bill Richards missed the second Test, which the British side won 17-3, but returned for the third in Sydney, where he was moved from the lock position to the front row, duelling directly with the infamous Dobson.

Bill Richards was one of Australia's star forwards, coming close to scoring early in the second half, but the team's overall poor handling cost them dearly and they suffered yet another embarrassing loss, this time by 16 points. Once more, it was an unsavoury Test, involving brawls and incidents. Bill Richards returned to the goldfields, where he was regarded as a hero for being the first true-blood Towers representative to appear for Australia. Bedell-Sivright also remained, spending a year as a jackeroo and working as a stock-rearer, as did Swannell, who settled in Sydney. Swannell later played a critical role in Rusty's development.

The other prime name of that tour, Denys Douglas Dobson, made one more headline appearance. Several years later, he was killed by a charging rhinoceros in Nyasaland, prompting one of his cheekier colleagues to remark that he always had a weak fend.

In 1905 Bill and Rusty headed for Brisbane, the elder brother to represent Queensland in the hope of gaining selection in the first Australian team to tour New Zealand, while his sidekick tagged along in the hope of being granted a trial game. The issue of whether to finance Bill's trip to Brisbane even went as high as the Queensland Rugby Union executive committee, where a member objected to the expense of bringing one of Australia's finest forwards from the goldfields for the interstate matches.

Fortunately this miserly person was overruled and the Richards brothers were beckoned from afar, with their expenses covered by the QRU, enabling Rusty to play for the Queensland Second XV in the midweek match at the Exhibition Ground. Rusty ran onto the field, with "definite instructions" from his captain to mark one of the New South Wales forwards. He wrote: "I did my best, but I soon found that this forward was no ordinary fellow. He was a regular tornado, a real destroyer, out to demolish everything around him. He rushed into the lineouts all head, knees and elbows. He was an 'untamed darling' and they kept throwing the ball to him. Oh, but he was a fair demon."

For his first major representative match, Rusty was handed an enormous responsibility. His target was the famous New South Wales captain Harold Judd, probably Australia"s most prominent forward, rated as good as any from New Zealand or Britain.

But Judd, later a critical figure in the great Rugby League —Rugby Union split of 1907 when he struggled to get compensation from the New South Wales Union afer breaking his leg, was not Rusty's only problem.

Stan Wickham, the illustrious Australian captain and expressive wing-three quarter, proved as elusive, in the process teaching Rusty an important lesson.

Richards said that early in the match, he made a diving tackle at Wickham, "and felt certain to bring him down.

"But to my astonishment I only touched him with one hand. This experience was new to me, and set up a problem to be solved. Close observation disclosed that most dodgy runners mislead the tackler by feinting to move to the right and draw the tackler over to that side, when suddenly they charge towards the left-hand side and easily evade the tackle.

"To meet this ruse I had to draw on my patience and stand firm when a man was coming at me, and not be led astray by the preliminary drawing attempts of the runner, and I found that tackling was much simplified."

To improve this technique, he headed to the most unexpected spot: the chookyard at the back of the Richards shanty. While the chickens merrily clucked away, he crouched in the background, motionless. After minutes of silence came a flurry of feathers.

As Rusty explained: "I practised catching fowls, by not rushing up to them, but by just waiting patiently until they came within grabbing distance. I can catch fowls with anyone." However, the lesson was learned too late. Judd and Wickham had stood him up, and Rusty missed Queensland and Australian selection.

Bill was luckier, being one of nine Queenslanders selected in the twenty-three-man squad for New Zealand. As happened in so many future Wallaby tours of New Zealand, the selections were immediately criticised for being biased towards New South Wales, with the Queenslanders crying that they had been unfairly forgotten. In fact they did have a point, especially as the three selectors, including captain Wickham and Judd, all hailed from Sydney. The animosity between the two states was also not helped just before the team headed for Wellington with cries that the team should be re-selected, and two more New South Wales players included.

The QRU wouldn't budge. They also didn't budge when New South Wales attempted to get centre Eddie Mandible added as an extra player. Despite QRU resistance, Mandible still went on the tour, as an official 'spectator', but wasn't allowed to be selected.

It is hardly surprising that it was not the most harmonious of away Australian tours, with the group dividing into two distinct camps, strictly on New South Wales/ Queensland lines, as they travelled through Wellington, Nelson, Christchurch, Dunedin, Palmerston North, Hawera, Rotorua and Auckland, winning four of their eight matches.

On the tour, most Queenslanders received a raw deal, Richards playing just three matches, which thankfully included the only Test of the tour, won by the All Blacks 14-3, despite New Zealand's best players having left for a tour of England a few weeks earlier

The ill-feeling among the Australian players was shown when in the Test Swannell, who became one of the first International players to appear for two different nations, was kicked in the left eye by a New Zealand forward. It was a blatantly ferocious act, but not one Australian teammate came to Swannell's rescue as he lay writhing in the Dunedin slush, not even his supposed friends Judd, Alec Burdon or 'Butcher' Oxlade.

This had a lot to do with the memories of how roughly Swannell had played in previous tours of Australia with British representative teams, when he took delight in kicking players when they were down. They were also not impressed that whenever anyone complained of his spiteful tactics, he would reply in verse.

In the official photograph taken near the end of the tour, Richards stands proudly in the middle row, boasting the best moustache of the group. Immediately below him is Swannell, with an enormous shiner, a closed left eye, and the most pained of expressions. Even in a group shot, he appears the ostracised party.

Swannell's personal habits also did not endear him to his teammates. His clipped English tones irritated many, while his personal hygiene left a lot to be desired. He always turned up to club matches in a filthy once-white sweater, with badges and dates of all countries represented on it. His prized possession was an also once-white pair of football breeches, which he refused to wash, and which he wore in every match.

He also bored many with his past tales of bravery, which included sealing off the coast of Labrador, enlisting as a trooper in the Boer War, and fighting among the insurrectionists in the Republic of Uruguay.

As the first Wallaby captain H.M 'Paddy' Moran wrote in his autobiography *Viewless Winds*, the "feared" Swannell was "for a number of years, a bad influence in Sydney football" as "his conception of Rugby was one of trained violence.

"He had no enlightened ideas about sport, and used to teach schoolboys all sorts of tricks and tactics that were highly objectionable. In appearance he was extremely ugly but, like Wilkes in the eighteenth century, he could talk his face away in half an hour. He was popular with the fair sex; men, generally, disliked him."

These were tough times, but both Bill and Rusty were not waiting around too long to become comfortable in such surroundings.

The wanderlust had begun.

The high veldt beckoned.

FOUR

VELDT AND VIOLETS

TOM'S FATHER ONCE MORE summoned his family in 1905 and the clan responded to the call, picking up their meagre belongings near the end of the year to farewell one gold field for another. The trip took several months, veering through Melbourne, across the Indian Ocean past Madagascar before ending in the harsh veldt land of South Africa.

But Rusty was hardly idle during the trip. Although aware that his slowly flourishing Rugby career in Australia had stalled, he realised that South Africa offered as many opportunities. In fact, he was heading towards a more deeply entrenched Rugby culture. From the early 1860s the game had taken root in the Cape district and spread from there, soon becoming the game for the white man — both the English settler and the proud Afrikaaner. The British game appealed to the expat, who made certain it was introduced to the important schools in the country, while its expression of power and strength attracted the more belligerent Afrikaaner, who were looking for a sporting outlet. The British regiments fighting in the early Kaffir and Zulu wars played Rugby when they weren't being speared by the natives, and even during the Boer War a halt was called to hostilities so that a Rugby game could be played between opposing forces. By 1891, British teams were visiting frontierland to play the best South Africa could muster.

Soon South Africa was vying with New Zealand as *the* Rugby nation. As with New Zealand, within only a few years, Rugby was South Africa's premier sport, its overriding religion. South Africa was the ideal place for Rusty to hone his skills. But he wanted to be prepared before seeking a local club in his new home town of Johannesburg.

On the boat, Rusty kept himself in shape with endless boxing bouts. Soon he was getting pestered by the ship's bosun, a wild, freckle-skinned Irishman, who according to Rusty, was "a hard-fighting, hard-swearing, hairy-breasted salt of the old school" who "was the pride and terror of the crew, and ruled them by the power of his fists and his flow of lurid language".

Not before long, irritated by the Richards brothers entertaining the passengers with lively bouts on deck, the bosun challenged Rusty to a fight. "Knowing his reputation I hesitated for a moment, but could find no reasonable excuse; so at five o'clock, with my friendly old eight ounce gloves, I went along, to find a full complement of officers, passengers and crew waiting to see the fun."

The money was on the bosun, who "looked with scorn at my heavily-padded gloves and produced a new, wicked looking six-ounce set of his own. The crowd gathered round. The crew, especially the stokers with their half-washed, soot-grimed faces, beamed with satisfaction at the confident stance of their doughty champion. For myself, they had only a furtive look of sympathy. This husky, red-headed son of Ould Ireland was deep-chested and vicious to look at, but I doubted if he was as bad as his reputation.

"He quickly broke through my defences with a left hook to the chin. In closing with him a weighty right uppercut flashed through, missing me by the narrowist margin. They were two splendid punches, and I wondered how much more his repertoire contained. Caution was necessary.

"He had long, strong arms, and I made my initial mistake in closing with him instead of using footwork and a straight left, as my feet were quicker and faster than his; but try as I might I still found difficulty with that left hook and awful uppercut. The spectators held their breath in suspense when the uppercut was threatening.

"The next moment they cheered in relief at the bosun was compelled to break ground. I was now holding my own fairly well; but he was a difficult man to hold off — those left hooks seemed to come from any angle. Eventually he came over, shook hands, and said: 'Well done laddie, that was great. Be here again tomorrow afternoon, please.'"

Before the return bout Rusty spent hours in front of a mirror, picturing his opponent's every move, and building up a system of attack and defence that would "override and outwit his two punches". The next day, "to the amazement of the dazed and silent crew, they saw their all-powerful and destructive bosun disarmed and hopelessly beaten by long straight lefts and a right to his 'middle mark' which baffled and bewildered him". Rusty was left alone for the rest of the voyage. The bosun buried himself in the cellar of the boat, humiliated by the young upstart who had easily knocked the wind out of him.

When they reached the goldfields, Rusty had no difficulty in getting work around Johannesburg and Pretoria. With the rest of his family he settled in the Johannesburg suburb of Jeppestown (near where Ellis Park is now situated) soon accompanying his father and brothers down the deep shafts, mining some of the richest deposits in the world.

Around him was a cosmopolitan mix. The thousands of blacks, already at the bottom of the social heap , did the dirtiest, most demanding of jobs in the mines, while huge numbers of transients from all over the world were trying to get rich quick. Few succeeded, most toiled for virtually no reward.

To provide some diversion from this heartbreaking and backbreaking work, Rugby clubs flourished in the goldfields, with the Mines team, which the Richards brothers joined in late 1905, one of the strongest in the nine-strong Johannesburg club competition. In the team, made up of hardy miners, the two young Australians were surrounded by Cornishmen and there were several reputable British players, including their captain and halfback Jim Davey- a gold miner and bootmaker who several years later toured Australia with the English representative side.

Through Davey's fine initiative, especially an innate awareness when to attack from loose scrums and lineouts. Rusty's second year with the Mines in 1906 involved unbeaten premiership success. He was soon selected to play for the Johannesburg representative team in its annual match against Pretoria, and then in a 'Colonial-born' against 'Home-born' (British players) selection trial match.

It was the perfect time to be noticed in South Africa. At the end of 1906 the South African team would for the first time travel overseas for a twenty-nine-match tour of the United Kingdom, including Tests against Scotland, Ireland, Wales and England. This was the first true recognition that South Africa had come of age as a premier Rugby nation. Adding to the Rugby fever in the country was the fact that the first Springbok touring party would be chosen from the best twenty-eight players in the provincial Currie Cup competition to be played over two weeks in Johannesburg in July. Not realising that to be eligible for the tour a player must have lived in South Africa for seven years, Rusty planned to use the Currie Cup to become Australia's first Springbok. First, he had to make the Transvaal team, which was to play seven other provincial sides, to determine the best XV in the country.

In the final Transvaal trial, Rusty discovered he was the only man in his team who could not speak Dutch.

"The conversation, both in the dressing room and on the field, was entirely in that tongue. It was novel, but very worrying, and left me disjointed and forlorn. I badly wanted to win my Transvaal cap and blazer, but found it difficult to get a grip of the game.

"At half-time brother Bill came into the dressing room. His mission was not a peaceful or sympathetic one. He swore in no uncertain terms, condemning me and any chance of selection I ever had. In the second half I played my own game in my own way, listening to nobody; I did not heed the strange language at all."

That night he succeeded in being picked in the twenty-five-man Transvaal Currie Cup squad, eventually playing in two Currie Cup matches — against Orange River County and Border — each time in victorious lineups alongside his old club captain Davey. It was the ultimate Rugby initiation, playing with and against African Dutch, Boers and English, on hard grounds 'devoid of grass'.

After finally being informed he was not eligible for the South African team, Rusty joined thousands of people on the final night of the tournament, waiting outside the main newspaper office for official confirmation of the touring party. The names were even flashed onto the screen of the Empire Theatre.

All this did was confirm his belief that the only life for him was a travelling life pursuing his footballing interests.

As the Springbok tourists headed for Southampton aboard the SS *Gascon*, soon getting up to mischief by throwing all the deckchairs overboard, Rusty had made up his mind. He wasn't going to be left behind. He would follow the Springboks to England.

"I always felt that if a team is worth playing with it is also worth playing against. A sudden desire to play against touring Springboks on English soil flared within me, and I hurriedly decided to visit Britain on my own, test my mettle against their footballers, look over the problem of how forty millions of people could live in prosperity on an area of ground one-eighth the size of Queensland- which had puzzled me from childhood- but, above all, I wanted to play against those Springboks.

"So off I went from Durban, bound for the Mother Country."

Again he made a name for himself on that trip across. A fellow passenger, W.M. Early, recalled many years later in the *Sydney Mail* that on the White Star steamer "two of the finalists in the obstacle race were running neck-and-neck as they approached the last obstacle, a number of lifebuoys hung about four feet from the deck, through which the runners had to climb while the bo'sun played a saltwater hose on them. Instead of climbing through, one contestant made a dive clean through his buoy almost without touching and slid past the finishing post like a seal. The diver was Tom Richards."

Rusty disembarked in Plymouth and headed for Bristol, realising that with three English internationals in their lineup, here was his best chance to appear against the Boks in competent company. Bristol, surprised that such a luminary had arrived on their doorstep, immediately offered him a training spot. He stood out, astonishing his new-found friends with his ball skills, especially his ability to leap high and bring the ball down in his fingers, while his pass to England's star centre Harry Shewring was first-rate. The Bristol club secretary Jimmy Oats rushed up, wanted all his particulars, but Rusty had to be vague, considering that his luggage was still on the boat.

Within days, Rusty was travelling England with the illustrious Bristol team, providing steel to their back row play. The games were not exactly brilliant, but the atmosphere was memorable. "The first game I saw in England was one of the strangest games of Rugby. In the first half a severe hailstorm drove the referee from the field without notifying the players, who also knocked off playing, one after the other, and scampered for shelter to the grandstand. When play was recommenced the ball, while in a scrummage, punctured, and both referee and players stood around amazed for some moments before a new ball was sent for."

As fascinating were the after-match banquets. After the Exeter match: "the whole team sat around one large table, in the centre of which enormous plates were covered with either grilled steak, chops, or bacon and eggs. Never had I imagined food so rich and luscious.

"I passed my plate along so often that the fellows laughed, looked amazed, and then envious. Those immense plates were replaced by blackberry and mulberry pies and bowls of thick cream. It was wonderful. I ate so freely that the fellows lost restraint and cheered in admiration of my appreciation of their English fare."

With a bellyful of cider, Rusty was the life of the party on the train journey home, agreeing to teach the Bristol players an Australian war-cry.

Soon the carriages were echoing with the chant of:

Terrah woomba, terrah woomba

Bulla Bulla

yah, yah, yah

Richards explained that the English translation of the Aboriginal words was:

Can we fight, can we fight

yes, yes, yes

This gibberish impressed everyone, with the *Bristol Times* explaining that Richards "found his colleagues apt pupils, and the rehearsals in the saloon was a great success". The *Bristol Evening News* thought the war-cry would "strike terror into the hearts of even Welsh footballers".

Rusty's onfield prowess also immediately commanded column space. He was described as "a typical New Zealander in his style of play, handling the ball like a three-quarter and untiring in the open". The *Evening News* said he was "decidedly the stamp of player that the club needs — quick and clever in following up, deadly in tackling, and keenly alert to guard against danger when other men have got out of position".

All were impressed with his determination. The *Bristol Times* explained: "With clean cut Colonial features and a resolute expression it has been an interesting study to watch his facial contortion when the Bristol line has been crossed. His lips sometimes 'arched' in a manner, which indicative of his feelings, foreboded a desperate effort to equalise as soon as the ball was again set going."

Such good reviews, as well as Richards's outstanding form for Bristol, made him a natural selection for Gloucestershire County, which in a few weeks were to play the Springboks. But Rusty had to lie low, knowing that as he had been in England for less than nine months, he was not eligible for this representative lineup. Rather than lie, he decided to avoid the question of his residency. Eventually the Bristol secretary "agreed to accept the explanation that I had been in England for a 'considerable period' and promised that he would not ask me about my qualification again".

One Monday morning a postcard arrived. It read: "Will you play for Gloucestershire against the South Africans at Gloucester on Saturday, the 3rd November, 1906 at 3 o'clock? Train leaves Bristol at 12.50. Please reply as soon as possible. Dinner after the match. C.E. Brown (Hon Sec)."

Rusty arrived at the Bristol railway station hours before midday, determined not to miss his big chance.

He dressed early, and was one of the first in the Gloucestershire team to take the field against the Springboks, who were embarking on their twelfth match of the tour. At the first lineout, two Springbok players idly looked across at their opponents, standing just a metre away, and then did a shocked double-take. Surely not!

But there he was, their old Transvaal teammate, in uncharacteristic colours. The Transvaal pair 'Opa' Reid and Andrew Morkel yelled aghast: "What are you doing 'ere?"

"Doing my best," replied the cheeky Australian.

It was no surprise that for the rest of the afternoon, Gloucestershire won most of the South African lineout throws. The visitors had forgotten that in the opposition ranks was one player who understood Afrikaans. The code was broken. Up front the game was close, but out wide South Africa were near unstoppable, scoring five tries for a conclusive victory.

Still Richards was in heaven. He recalled nearly thirty years later that in the match "there was not a happier man on the field than myself, because I was proud that I had fulfilled my mission. When I spoke to the Africans, they wondered where I could have dropped from."

The *Cambria Daily Leader* was impressed with Richards, even if way astray with their facts — they said he was a New Zealander who had been a prominent front-ranker with the Wellington Club — explaining that he was considered by the critics to be one of the best forwards on the ground.

Then came humiliation. While South Africa went up country in readiness for their International against Scotland, Richards remained in the Gloucester side to play Devonshire. Here he earned the ire of the Exeter crowd.

"One of our backs had to leave the field and I went out to the wing, and was almost at once drawn infield by a dodgy runner who seemed likely to go through. When he saw me leave my wing exposed he passed to Scott, who scored unopposed.

"I was humiliated and humbled. Supporters on and off the field asked me where I learned to play football, and other nasty questions. To leave one's position is unpardonable in England; a delinquint is regarded either as inexperienced or a fool, and they won't excuse either.

"The match went down in the records as Richards' failure, and I had it recalled years afterwards."

Despairing, Richards took off, deciding it was time to be a spectator and learn from the terraces. He was an avid watcher at the South Africa—Wales Test in Swansea, and then went on to London for the England International, a match marred by torrential rain with the spectators "a heaped-up pile of wet humanity".

He was also growing sick of the damp, the cold, the continual English greyness. A lifeline came in a whisper he heard at the Bristol club.

South Africa were here, as were New Zealand, and the rumour was that in a year or so Australia were also going to be on their way to the Mother Country for their first full-scale tour of the Home Unions. Rusty wasn't eligible for South Africa, England would have probably picked him if he had stayed around long enough, but the chance of representing his own country in foreign climes, which he now had some knowledge of, was too alluring. He had already seen a great deal of the world, but still felt distinctly Australian — even if by now the rest of the family were elsewhere. He thought there was no alternative but for him to return home in the hope of being selected in the first serious Australian touring party.

He also knew that Australian Rugby was on the way up. It had even been referred to in the first serious Rugby book, entitled *The Complete Rugby Footballer* by All Black captain Dave Gallaher and W.J. Stead, with the authors explaining that "the prospects of the game in NSW and Queensland, as we can say from intimate personal experience, are of the highest positive character. The game is going ahead in these quarters very rapidly, it is in a thoroughly healthy state …"

Rusty paid a quick visit to his family in Johannesburg, and by 1907 he was back on home territory: Charters Towers, via Kalgoorlie where he spent a short time in the mines. His brother Bill had also had enough of the harsh Transvaal environment, moving back to northern Queensland to regain his spot in the Australian team, playing in two of the three home tests against New Zealand. His versatility was demonstrated once again: after already representing Australia in the second and front row, he played his last Test in the back row. Sadly his international career did not involve any joy of victory, with his five appearances coinciding with five Australian losses. But at least Bill had the experience of playing in his last Test with the most dashing player of the time — Harold 'Dally' Messenger, who made his international debut at the Gabba that year.

Richards's hopes of any more appearances were dashed because of the politics of the time. Being a Queenslander put him on the wrong side of the tracks. The Australian selectors chose one player each from Queensland and New South Wales. When the Test was played in Brisbane, the Queensland selector Poley Evans had the casting vote, ensuring that Richards was a starting member in the Second Test side.

In Sydney, the New South Wales selector Jimmy McMahon reigned supreme. For the first Test, Richards only got a cap as a replacement for forward Jack Barnett, while for the third Test he, like so many other Queenslanders, was overlooked.

The relationship between the two states was tenuous and volatile, with New South Wales, the far more powerful Rugby state, treating Queensland as an inferior orphan. After a combined Australian team, with Richards on the bench, had been beaten in the first Test by twenty points, the NSW Rugby Union passed a motion stating that if New Zealand won the second Test, the concluding match against Australia should be cancelled and a match against New South Wales substituted.

The NSWRU argued that as New South Wales had already beaten the tourists, they stood a better chance of containing New Zealand than if they had any Queenslanders messing up the mix. Not for the first or last time, the Queensland Rugby Union almost had apoplexy when told of the actions of their southern counterparts. They complained to New South Wales that such suggestions were "extremely detrimental to the interests of Australian Rugby and calculated to endanger the pleasant relations existing between our two nations".

Peace was restored. Or so Queensland thought, until the third Test team was announced. McMahon had wreaked his revenge. Not one Queenslander was selected; the Australian team was simply the New South Wales lineup in different coloured jerseys. In the end, the QRU could not complain too much, especially when this third Test team gave Australia's finest performance in their opening decade of international football by drawing 5-all with the almighty Blacks.

Bill Richards disappeared from the scene and young Rusty, watching it all with great interest, took note. He knew everything was against him making that Australian touring team. As a Queenslander he would have to be twice the player of any of his opponents, especially as he was told that the bulk of the 1908-09 Wallaby party to tour Great Britain would be New South Welshmen, with a small minority invited from Queensland to make up the numbers. If he wanted to make that tour he would have to be something special. Appearing for Transvaal, Bristol and Gloucester were insignificant compared to his next task. He had to basically convince everyone in Sydney that he was the most indispensable football player in the country. It was a big task, but Rusty knew he was up to it.

During the day, Rusty was burrowing away in the Charters Towers mines. Before and after work, his only purpose was preparing himself for the selection trials. It was an arduous physical regime.

"I worked hard at the Day Dawn Consolidated mine and trained enthusiastically, learning to fall over fences and obstacles so as not to hurt myself, and thereby toughen my muscles and strengthen my sinews.

"I wanted to prepare my body to resist the knocks, bumps and jolts that do so much to break down a player's condition, particularly in the last portion of a vigorously played game. I also put into operation a system of going as long as possible without water, refraining from drinking at meal-time so that the salivary glands would be developed to a point that would give a maximum of saliva, which, in preventing a dry mouth, would also aid physical vitality.

"Nobody in Charters Towers, not even my closest associates, knew that my objective was that year's Australian team."

He once even travelled to Townsville, believing that extensive sprint training along the beach could only help his stamina. Instead he almost ended up in gaol. One day, strolling along Townsville wharf, he noticed an old physician friend of his, Bob Thompson, standing at the front of a boat about to berth. Thompson asked him if he could take a parcel ashore. Rusty complied, and later realised to his horror that he had just smuggled ashore almost two kilograms of opium.

Considering his broad experience, Rusty was a natural captain for the north Queensland team that headed for Brisbane and Country Week. The team was laughed at, consisting of a collection of 'rough-looking' characters, but they overcame all, snaring nine spots in the Country team to play Metropolitan at the end of the tournament. Rusty was again skipper, playing in the second row alongside the infamous hard-drinking Jack Egan, who would arrive at games with his football gear rolled up in an old squatter's swag. These hard-living, rough-as-guts bushies swept the city slickers aside 16-3.

Considering their dominance, Country were expecting a large representation in the Queensland team to play New South Wales, from which the Australian touring team would be selected. But like New South Wales's dominance over Queensland, the Brisbanites exerted similar authority on their less powerful rural mates, offering only six spots in the state team. Fortunately Rusty snared one of those, but many who deserved state representation missed out, which almost led to Country breaking away from the QRU and forming their own union.

Rusty had passed step one but was aware a lot still had to go his way. Due to the recent selection bungles and animosity between the two states, New South Wales decided it would solely pick the touring team, and if need be invite several Queensland players to join the squad on the proviso that they wear the NSW colours with the Waratah emblem while away. Rusty didn't care, as long as a position in the team came with a berth on the ship.

First he had to convince the Queensland selectors to pick him in the right position during the four-match series. "One of the Queensland selectors advised me that if I wanted a place in the Queensland team I would have to play in the second row of the scrum. I told him that I would be pleased to play in whatever position they cared to choose for me, but while I was captain of the country side I would continue to play in the position that would serve my team best, and that was as 'breakaway.'"

Rusty meticulously planned to be in front of the two Australian selectors, Jimmy McMahon and James Henderson, for most of the match. His prime motive was to antagonise, upset and hover around the New South Wales halfback Freddy Wood. Richards realised that Wood was the 'kingpin' of the New South Wales game plan, "and so I set myself out to exploit a simple scheme for my own advantage, and, naturally, for my team's benefit as well".

The Queenslanders tried to unnerve their opponents with an Aboriginal war-cry before the start of the game. New South Wales had apparently rehearsed one, but according to one newspaper report opted against it, because "the vocalists of the side (or the captain) had not sufficient confidence to risk a comparison".

As expected, New South Wales dominated the series, but there was one Queenslander they could not handle. This was Rusty. In the first match in Brisbane, won by NSW 13-8, Richards was applauded for his brilliant open play, and it was said that among the Queenslanders he played the best forward game on the ground. The second game, again in Brisbane, ended in a 9-all draw, with the most memorable moment being Rusty, playing at No 8, hitting NSW forward Paddy McCue with a legal but devastating tackle. McCue was so dazed by the tackle that for one of the few times in his career he had to leave the field for attention.

With important positions at stake the series soon became heated. Rusty wrote, "I must confess that I thought the methods of several NSW forwards unnecessarily vigorous. On one occasion the ball came along slowly between an opposition forward and myself. He had a distinct advantage in distance, yet he did not make use of it until I dashed in to sweep the ball away, when this fellow rushed in, kicking venomously.

"I missed one boot, but he knocked me under the chin with his knee and splintered my teeth. This style of maliciousness was new to me, and it made me wonder what English critics would think if exhibitions of this nature occurred while the Australians were playing over there."

The series then headed to Sydney, where it attracted enormous attention. The interest was shown by the first Sydney Cricket Ground match luring 20,000 people, compared to the 7,000 who were next door at the Agricultural Ground watching the Australia—Maoris, NSW—Queensland Rugby league doubleheader.

Again Rusty excelled, described by the *Sydney Morning Herald* as "the most dashing of the Queensland forwards". But Rusty left the best until last. The crowd at the fourth game, again at the SCG, was down to 13,000, with more than 10,000 staying away because of a tram strike. They missed one of the greatest tries scored at the famous ground; a try that is still discussed as one of the best in the game's history.

Those who made it to the ground were in a cheeky, rebellious mood, spending most of the first time heckling the New South Wales centre Dan Carroll. As The *Referee* explained: "Carroll, who is an officer at the head office of the Tramways Department, had been assailed by a few ill-mannered individuals on the hill with the words 'Carroll the Scab' presumably because he had done his duty." Carroll shut them up shortly after when he scored the game's first try.

Queensland, although dominated, eventually responded through Richards, and the most extraordinary of athletic acts. Richards picked the ball up about five metres from the New South Wales line, fended off one defender, and had only the NSW fullback Jack D'Alpuget to beat. The *Referee* wrote: "As D'Alpuget bent for the tackle, he [Richards] sprang in the air over the fullback and came down with his outstretched hands holding the ball in goal, and his legs in the air on top of the fullback — a beautiful try."

It was a near replay of a similar leap that the great Dally Messenger had made to score against the New Zealanders the previous year. Messenger had since gone to League, and Rugby had wasted no time in finding an alternative.

Rusty had been the star of the Queensland team, and that final leaping try had sealed it. He was on his way to England. The official Rugby Union letter arrived from the secretary. Rusty wrote, "Mr W.W

Hill did not have long to wait for my acceptance, and naturally I was overjoyed at the success of my long, deeply and silently laid plans to become a member of this team."

Rusty's life was about to change dramatically.

FIVE

THE TOUR

THEY HAILED FROM EVERYWHERE, their occupations and pastimes diverse. They were a cross-section of Australian manhood, portraying the burgeoning, diverse life of a new country.

There were pastoralists from Wellington, Sydney clerks, Newcastle surgeons, university layabouts, Queensland station owners, humble miners, northern New South Wales train-drivers, Condobolin bank clerks, 'gentlemen of leisure', rough-as-guts waterfront warehousemen, Glebe butchers, inner-city plumbers who tried to con the Fleet Street press into believing they were owners of "a large station in Woolloomooloo", public servants, clay potters, insurance brokers, graziers, cattle salesmen. They boasted such nicknames as 'Big Dog', 'Giraffe', 'Emu', 'Banger', 'Bull', 'Daisy McIntyre', 'Bowser', 'Monkey', 'Boneta', 'Parky', 'Possum'. There were twenty-nine in all, and only four Queenslanders: Rusty; 'Peter the Prophet' Flanagan, a waggish forward with Dubliner links; fullback Phil Carmichael, a striking figure who played with a woollen cap tucked around his ears and the genteel-sounding Charles Esmond Parkinson, a whippy Brisbaneite, who played at three-quarter.

There would have probably been even less Queensland representation if five players, all from the Sydney University club, had not knocked back tour offers at the last minute because of studies. The final squad were aged between nineteen and twenty-eight , weighing between 9st10lb and 14st 2lb, rising between 5 ft 1 inch and 6 feet 2 inches.

In charge was a manager, Jimmy McMahon, who had a NSW Lancers background. The official tour visitor E.S. Marks was a high-ranking sporting official who wanted to interview Baron Pierre de Coubertin in the hope of convincing him of the value of holding future Olympic Games in Sydney. The 'official' journalist E.E. 'The General' Booth was a 1905 All Black representative back who went on the tour after missing out on the assistant manager's position.

The captain H.M. Moran was a 'miserable, stooped, poring, introspective sort of fellow', who became the first doctor in Australia to use radium to combat cancer, and wrote books that covered a range of subjects from homosexuality to an allegiance with Italian Fascist leader Benito Mussolini.Even British Rugby writers were astounded by how pale and unathletic Moran looked. Laurence Woodhouse wrote in the *Daily Mail* that when introducing Moran to friends as the Australian captain, they would take the reporter aside and ask: "Surely that delicate-looking man does not play Rugby football?"

The itinerary was mind-boggling. After a six-week cruise on the R.M.S *Omrah*, which went via Melbourne, Adelaide, Fremantle, Colombo, Guardafui, Suez, Port Said, Naples, Marseilles, Gibralter, Plymouth and finally Tilbury, the team faced a never-ending playing schedule that crisscrossed Great Britain for thirty-one matches, involving Internationals against England and Wales. There was two preliminary matches as they travelled around Australia, and five at the end in USA and British Columbia. And that was without playing Scotland and Ireland, who both deemed the Australians below them, claiming that they were professionals. Australia's crime? The players received three shillings a day out-of-pocket expenses.

They were Australia's pride, but not all Australians were behind them. One of their old teammates, Blair Swannell, gave them no hope, confidently expecting that they were about to be roundly embarrassed on the other side of the world.

Swannell thought the Australian backs lacked "devil, initiative, or whatever you like to call it". The Australian forwards "cannot wheel, and seemingly won't learn". They wouldn't do as well as the All Blacks or Springboks, because of their "lack of knowledge" and "lack of use of many of the finer points of the game". He added, "Unless the wheels of their football machinery are greased with the oil of hard work; the Australian team- good though it is, will not do as well as it might, or reflect the credit on Australia that it should."

This did not deter the NSW Rugby Union, who spent a great deal to ensure that the first national touring team did everyone proud. The tour was expensive, with original budgeting around the 8,600 pound mark, 3,000 pounds more than the recent New Zealand tour of Britain and 2,500 more than the sum South Africa spent to travel around the Home Unions. The prime reason was that the Australian team was to travel first-class to England. To pay for that, as explained in the NSWRU's 1909 annual report, an advance of 2,969 pounds was made.

The players attended endless club and civic receptions before they left. They received gold sovereigns, sets of pipes, travelling bags, gold watches, framed photographs of mates left behind, purses overflowing with coins. Even in Melbourne, the opposition Victorian Football League tendered a formal reception for the Australian team. Eight days before leaving, the players were guests of honour at a dinner at the Sydney Town Hall, where for the first time players broached the subject of what they should actually call themselves. The name 'Rabbits' was suggested, which was apparently popular. Meanwhile, Miss Estelle Mabel-Ward sang 'My Heart is Weary', and Sullivan's 'The Lost Chord', while the State Military Band chimed in with stirring renditions of 'Auld Lang Syne', 'Advance Australia' and 'God Save the King'.

There were a multitude of speeches, including one from the politician, the Honourable C.W. Oakes MLA, who babbled on and on about his old friend, the Australian captain. The only problem was that the honourable politician couldn't remember the skipper's name. In the end, he whispered loudly to his offsider asking for the identity of the mystery man. The offsider was as bewildered.

Outside it was teeming with rain. Eight days later, Sydney was still awash. But this fortnight-long rain did not deter more than 4000 waterlogged supporters to head for Circular Quay to farewell the team.

The ship was to leave at 1pm, but was held back until 6.15pm so that the players could attend the Anglo-Welsh match against New South Wales at the SCG, hear a round of farewell speeches in the Members' Pavilion after the game and then be driven through Darlinghurst and along George Street in open coaches in pouring rain with overflowing street gutters. So great was the crowd at the wharf and such was the chaos caused by a brass band playing endless selections that several of the players struggled to push their way through the throng and get onto the ship in time. They somehow smuggled on board a carpet snake named Bertie.

Eventually the R.M.S *Omrah* steamed towards the Sydney Heads, with a small group of enthusiasts waiting for them at Lady Macquarie's Chair to call out a few 'cooees'. As they passed through the Heads and turned for Melbourne those on board heard heard faint cries of 'bon voyage.' Those players still on the deck muttered, "They have the Eastern Suburbs accents." Not even Rusty was overlooked. Although he didn't have any friends in Sydney: "I was not entirely forgotten, however, and my heart jumped for joy when Herb May, a football rival from Charters Towers, called me to the gangway and presented me with a sovereign case and his good wishes."

Seasickness hit several of the landlubbers early, with Josh Stevenson, Charlie McMurtrie and Ed McIntyre hiding in the bowels of the Omrah, alongside 4000 crates of frozen rabbits and 1500 bales of wool, in the early days of the trip. Rusty, a seasoned ocean traveller, handled it all with aplomb.

Business and pleasure was easily mixed. Before the tour, team captain H.M. 'Paddy' Moran had organised a blackboard to be placed on the ship on which training sessions, tactics, team policy and theories would be planned and discussed. Moran also brought with him the latest textbook on syphilis, as he was worried that some of his players might contract venereal disease.

Moran took his responsibilities as captain seriously, treating the job as meticulously as one would expect from a highly intelligent medical intern. He knew the dangers of being idle and ensured that his players were up by 6am for a series of exercises that included walking, running, skipping, leapfrog and boxing.

Breakfast became a very important meal, with the already fatigued players often having three helpings of steak and eggs to build up their energy for the rest of the day.

Before lunch, Moran would have the players around the blackboard for several hours, explaining his strategies and working out various game plans before the forwards went off for scrum practice. It all happened again late in the afternoon. At 8pm each night there were lectures on the game. Lights were out at 11pm.

Moran and his cohorts kept the players' minds and bodies alert. There were countless competitions — progressive euchre tournaments, bull board, peg quoits, deck billiards, deck quoits, bucket quoits, dominoes, draughts, cards, skipping competitions, egg and spoon races, potato races, whistling competitions, cock fighting, threading the needle, chalking the pig's eye, slinging the monkey, spar boxing, cricket, cigarette races, sack races, apples in the tub.

Rusty, who was trying to hide the fact that he had fractured one of his ribs when playing in the first tour match in Melbourne because he was afraid of being sent home, competed in everything so the team officials would not realise that there was something wrong with him. Despite the pain, Rusty won the peg quoits and deck quoits competitions and the sack race. He also won the prize for best all-round performances.

There was even a limerick competition, which attracted 40 entries, including one from fullback William Dix, who hailed from Armidale.

It went:

> Richards, a man we all know,
> In sports makes an excellent show
> You'll find sure enough
> In all sports he's tough
> For he tries when he hears the word go.

It didn't win the prize. McMurtrie did, together with a mysterious Miss Grey, who had earlier doubled up to win the cigarette race with South Sydney five-eighth Arty McCabe.

The team even spent time working on a war-cry devised by the Newtown club president Dr Hall Bohrsmann. The players would stand in one straight line across the deck and bellow:

> Gau gau, John Bull, whir-r-r.
> Win-nang, a-lang, thur
> Mui-an-yal-ling
> Bu-rang-a-lang-yang
> Yai! Yai! Gun yib lang yang. Yai!

They had no idea what it all meant, but it was apparently all about being great men, that it was great to meet you, and may the bigger man win. The players weren't convinced, but followed instructions. They knew who was in charge at sea. The law of the land didn't exactly exist.

This was a team with no social barriers, but for some a rise in standards led to disconcerting moments. Rusty might have been one of the victims. As Moran explained in his autobiography *Viewless Winds*, he was very anxious that "all the men should accustom themselves to the social habit of dressing for dinner, so the first night out I took upon myself the task of inducing them all to put on what was then called by some of them their 'tuxedo'. My friend, the miner, was very reluctant, but finally submitted under friendly pressure.

"When he came, as arranged, to my cabin just before dinner, he had on a suit of 'tails', over a coloured shirt and he was wearing a celluloid collar. Tactfully I disrobed him and fitted him out with a shirt, collar and tie of my own. It was then that I discovered that he had come on this long tour with only a couple of coloured shirts and one or two celluloid collars.

"He was very self-conscious, but together he walked down to the dining saloon, though he stopped for a while opposite the large mirror on the landing to look at the full length image of himself. He was a little frightened of what the others might say, although nearly all of them had dinner coats on. The man with me, alone, was wearing 'tails.'

"I fear he did not enjoy that dinner. The jokes made disturbed him nearly as much as the rather high collar he was wearing. An hour or two later I was sitting on the deck when he passed by in company with another player; he had changed into a sweater. The tails were then and there discarded for ever. What happened to them I never discovered."

Rusty was not named in Moran's account, but according to some members of the Richards family he was the one targeted by his captain. The other possibility was the reserve scrum half Josh Stevenson, who had worked as a wheeler in a Newcastle coal mine. The miner eventually retired to more relaxed shipwear, which was appropriate when the ship crossed the equator, as the players were visited by King Neptune and his tribunal, to be "lathered with paint, shaven with a razor a yard long (the razor being wiped on the victim's hair repeatedly), then after the administration of a pill as large as a cricket ball, they were 'dumped' into a large tank of water, there to fight with the red-whiskered demons of the deep".

That night brought another lecture from Moran, this time with disturbing photographs of venereal disease. Moran realised that the following morning with the ship anchoring in Colombo, he could have a mass revolt on his hands. The players, who had been at sea for several weeks, could be lured straight to the Ceylon brothels.

"Just before we reached Colombo I assembled them all on the top deck, which had been reserved for us, and gave a vivid description of the dangers that waited in ambush for any philanderer," Moran wrote in *Viewless Winds*.

"I had the manager's authority for saying that any sufferer would, without further ado, be packed home. Then I passed round for perusal my textbook open at one of the most unpleasant pictures."

The tactic worked. No one strayed, no one veered towards a prostitute. Instead in the words of Moran, the team was taken to see "some miserable sleepy broken-down women perform the Can-Can and other dances that were mildly indecent and not even faintly seductive". Adding to the displeasure was the fact that the players had to pay three times the normal rate for warm beer.

Rusty's memories of Colombo were somewhat more vibrant. Moran called the locals "nasty little men" but Richards showed greater compassion, explaining in a letter to friends in Charters Towers that the players "watched with considerable interest the Cingalese who, in their quaint boats called catamarans, came to the side of our ship to sell their various wares.

"They were not allowed on board so they made their deals and sent the goods up on a rope, the money going down in a bag on the other end of the rope. It was very funny to hear them ask seven shilling for a native made inkstand, and after a lot of haggling it changed hands for 2 and 6."

When eventually on land, Rusty, with six other players (and Moran nowhere in sight), were surrounded by locals, all wanting to be their guides. "Such a row I never heard, not even at a Tourist Debating Class." They all ended up at a Buddhist temple, where the walls were covered with paintings of "the different kinds of hell".

"You can make your choice of sins and go to the hell of your choice. The paintings explain themselves nicely — much too nicely," Rusty wrote back.

The original plan was for the Australians to play a match in Colombo, but that had been called off at the last minute as the English Rugby Union had alerted them that several of the Ceylonese players had apparently dabbled in the professional Rugby League code. Even if Australia were unwitting partners in playing against a League team, the tour would still have been placed in jeopardy.

The Australians instead went back to the ship that night and headed for Port Said. As they approached, Moran produced his textbook, this time supplementing his lecture with uncomplimentary references to this open sewer on the Eastern highway. "Again we arrived at night, much to my alarm, but again, to our satisfaction there was no straying," Moran wrote.

Moran later boasted that during the tour, which lasted more than five months, not one player contracted syphilis, unlike many other touring teams "which have had to lament, in private, their venereal losses".

(Their only loss on the boat over was of Eastern Suburbs forward Cecil Murnin, who had developed an "internal chill", later identified as a kidney infection, shortly after the team left Melbourne, forcing him to return home when the tour reached Europe. He had also injured his spine, necessitating a painful voyage back to Sydney. According to the *Sydney Mail*, Murnin was "terribly run down, and quite a wreck of his former self".)

Moran's preview of Port Said was accurate. As Richards wrote home: "I think it will be impossible to find a place in the world more filthy or smelling more strongly. The streets are not drained, and the place is absolutely without sanitary arrangements. [The people] live close together in very narrow streets, into which the dirty water is thrown. Such a vile-smelling and fly-blown hole I don't wish to see again. Still, with all their dirty ways, they are the biggest and finest coloured race I have seen."

They continued to Naples, where the manager McMahon arranged for the players to visit the ruins of Pompeii before lunch at a nearby hotel, where Rusty and fellow Queenslander Parkinson discovered they were eating horseflesh. That didn't deter either, as "it tasted well, and we had a good lunch".

Rusty's analysis of Naples? Another stinking city. "Naples is built all of a heap, with very narrow side streets, which look rather picturesque; but the smell of them is pretty thick, and I don't wonder that when cholera was raging, 3,000 people died in one day."

Their last stop was at Gibraltar, where the team gorged themselves on grapes and peaches, returning to the ship armed with boxes of cigars and cigarettes, before making for Plymouth. To the amusement of the locals, they "cooeed" they way towards England.

Forty-two days after leaving Sydney, the *Omrah* arrived in Plymouth to be greeted by dignitaries, a large group of reporters, hundreds of well-wishers and a small fleet of boats that followed them into port. A number of them had bands onboard, which played lively marches. Members of the H.M.S *Davenport* ran up the wharf, waving hats and towels to the accompaniment of loud British cheers. In the throng, the Australian players were easily distinguished by their straw hats with a dark blue riband and the badge in green and scarlet. The only one wearing a normal felt hat was Moran, who stood to one side as the team performed their war-cry on the main deck for the officers of the *Omrah*.

They were now explaining that their war-cry had ancient associations, as it emanated from the once powerful Illawarra tribe that dominated the coast between Wollongong and Bulli. It had been taught them by the tribe's seventy-year-old elder Yung-ale, who now lived near Botany Bay. The war-cry excited the crowd, but their captain was not enthusiastic and did all he could to quash it. The Australians had been told by New Wouth Wales officials that they had to perform this war-cry before each game. Moran was aghast and in *Viewless Winds* wrote that "the gravest affliction we carried was an alleged Aboriginal war-cry which the parent Union in Australia had imposed on us".

"The memory of that war-cry provokes anger in me even after all these years," Moran explained in 1939.

"Now we were being asked to remind British people of the miserable remnants of a race which they had dispossessed and we had maltreated or neglected. We were officially expected to leap up in the air and make foolish gestures which somebody thought Australian natives might have used in similar circumstances, and we were also given meaningless words which we were to utter savagely during this pantomime.

"I refused to lead the wretched caricature of a native corroboree, and regularly hid myself among the team, a conscientious objector. None of the men liked it." The local press wasn't impressed either, with one Welsh newspaper remarking: "Was there ever anything more like tomfoolery on the football field than these Colonial war songs?"

The team eventually disembarked, with Richards looking noticeably bulky around his stomach. This had nothing to do with the bandaging around his ribs; around his waist he had tied Bertie the carpet snake, the team mascot brought along by the comedian of the team, Bob Craig. That morning, Rusty and Craig had met in the latter's room to work out the best way of getting Bertie into the country. They knew that if the snake was sighted it would be confiscated by English officials, as live animals and reptiles were checked for quarantine purposes. They originally considered placing Bertie in a cardboard box, and have him brought in with the team's luggage. But what if the box fell into the wrong hands?

Rusty was agreed to sling Bertie inside his singlet, tied it loosely around his stomach, stuck its head inside a sock, and its tail down the front of his pants. A large overcoat hid any bulge. The plan worked, even though Rusty grew exceedingly uncomfortable when Bertie started to wriggle during the official speeches. He later found a wooden box to hide the snake in. It wasn't alone in that box, as it sat curled next to a bunch of waratahs, which had earlier been sent by the NSW Rugby Union, packed in ice.

Moran was in full flight, using the opportunity to criticise the Scottish and Irish Unions for refusing to play them because they were supposedly grubby professionals. "Every trade and profession is, I suppose, represented in our Union, but we are very particular over our amateur status," Moran said that day. "We have more college and professionally trained men in our ranks than the other Union [Rugby League]. Three of our men are from Aloysius College, and one, Hammond, is a student of medicine, but in the main we are what you would call a working-class team."

But what to call themselves?

In his autobiography Moran tried to put a spin on how the term 'Wallabies' was evolved, by placing the blame on the English press in trying to force them to be called something else, the 'Rabbits.' "When we arrived at Plymouth a pack of journalists fell upon us," Moran wrote. "They were very anxious to give us some distinctive name, but their first suggestion of 'Rabbits' we indignantly rejected. It really was going a little too far to palm off on us the name of a pest their ancestors had foisted on our country! Ultimately we became the 'Wallabies', although we wore for emblem on our jerseys not the figure of this marsupial but the floral design of a waratah."

Moran's story is not entirely correct. The 'Rabbits' tag was not foisted upon them by the English press. Instead it had been suggested at the Sydney Town Hall function before the Australians left for Britain, with the name receiving favour from a small minority of players. The *Manchester Weekly Times* even went as far as announcing that at that dinner the Australians were officially christened the 'Rabbits.' On the ship, informal discussions on the name were conducted, and suddenly 'Waratahs' was the most popular.

On the day of the team's arrival, F.B. Wilson in the *Daily Mirror* wrote that the Australians "have been already called the Rabbits, but that won't do. They do not like it, and naturally so, for a rabbit in Australia is not only vermin, it's a curse, and no death is too bad for it."

The *Glasgow Daily Record* also explained that the main objection to the name 'Rabbits' was its uncomplimentary tone. "You might call a man who drops an easy catch in the cricket field a rabbit, but one prefers to call men who can drop difficult goals on the football field wallabies." Nonetheless this did not prevent postcards being issued in England, showing off the Australian team, above the name; "The Rabbits". One of these can be found in the official scrapbook kept by E.S. Marks, now housed in Sydney's Mitchell Library.

The *Express* believed that the team would be called the Waratahs, the NSWRU emblem emblazoned on the light blue jersey; the 1907 Australian team, of which Rusty's elder brother had been a member, featured a jersey with the kangaroo embroidered on the left breast. They could not adopt the name 'kangaroo', which had already been taken by the Australian Rugby League team, also at the time touring the Home Unions.

The *Express,* underneath a headline of "Colonial Rugby players to be called 'Waratahs'" quoted Moran: "We certainly draw the line at being called the Rabbits, for the only thing I can imagine worse would be to christen us the 'Convicts' - both, by the way, came out from England; but whereas one has died out, the other has become a pest. Therefore let us fix on something as distinctive as 'All Blacks' and 'Springbokken' were. Captain McMahon, as well as the team, think that Waratahs could not be beaten; this is not a speculative tip to other playing ambitions."

Eventually Moran gave a full explanation to the *Sydney News*: "With regards to our name, we dropped considerable cold water on 'Rabbits.' Modest though we be, we could not labour under an appellation borrowed from an English imported pest. There was considerable discussion in the English papers. Letters flocked in from all sides. Wallabies, Kangaroos, Kookaburras and Wallaroos were suggested. The position demanded a conference. For a brief day we, who for six weeks had been 'Rabbits', were 'Waratahs', but that was emblematic of New South Wales. All were agreed that any name would be preferable to 'Rabbits.' Wallabies won by a couple of votes.

"I was stopped by an English yokel, who, begging my pardon, seeing how it was a matter of drinks between him and his mate, did I mind telling him weren't Wallabies birds, with a funny laugh."

Some sections of the New South Wales press objected to the Wallaby tag, preferring Waratah. But as Bluemantle in the *Daily Mail* explained: "A team chosen from Yorkshire and Lancashire could hardly be called 'The White Roses.' The Australian players do not come from New South Wales alone; there are representatives from Queensland also in the side. Hence at a special meeting the players themselves chose the title 'Wallabies.'"

The *South Wales Post*, who attended their early training sessions and matches, suggested another name.

"The Australians could well be renamed the 'Yellers.' They are fond of kicking high, and when this is done the forwards bunch together, and swoop down the field, shrieking at the top of their voices, like a bunch of Zulus on the war path. This sort of thing gets on the nerves of the unfortunate man who is waiting for the ball."

It still took some time for the Rabbits tag to disappear. The *Western Independent* headlined its match report of the Australia-Devon match with "Rattling game by the Rabbits," and then on numerous occasions in the article referred to them as Rabbits.

The team originally settled in Newton Abbot, Devon, where McMahon and Moran organised a tough training schedule which began with a pre-dawn walk and, according to Rusty, caused endless complaints to the manager about the logic of such an early-morning exercise. On the walk, the players took with them "greased-up" footballs so players became accustomed to handling a wet ball. Their first training session involved a two-hour "kickaround".

For the opening match against Devon, Rusty did not make the starting XV, overlooked in the back row by Moran, Syd Middleton and Norm Row. However, Rusty still took the field, replacing the luckless Peter Burge who broke his leg just above the ankle when tackling the Devon forward E. Vivyan. The snap of bone echoed around the ground as Vivyan was hurled across Burge's leg, forcing four of his Australian teammates to carry him from the field. This came just minutes after a cameraman had been cleaned up by one forward rush which went over the sideline, seeing himself and his machine both completing double somersaults, with the players falling among the wreckage. Although replacements were not strictly allowed, requiring the opposition captain to issue his consent, Rusty was permitted to take Burge's spot, and according to the *Western Daily Mercury* the newcomer: "showed himself a speedy, capable forward, and he almost scored a try by a burst, kick and follow up from midfield".

The English newspapers, who targeted the Wallabies all-tour, were soon onto them, criticising the Devon captain for giving his opponents an unfair leg-up by allowing Richards onto the field. The *Athletic News* thundered: "Now this was sportsmanlike and all that sort of thing, but the question arises: Was it football? It is of course the custom of the Australians, but it is not the mode of, we believe, New Zealand or South Africa, and it is not assuredly that of this country. For one reason, it is undesirable, because if there are two well-balanced sides the substitution of a fresh forward well on in the second half would obviously materially assist the team who lost a jaded scrummager. There should be no giving or taking of any advantage in football." The newspaper argued that "Richards's appearance was not to be commended. After all, the Game, the Rule of the Game, is the thing."

The newspapers were also unimpressed with Australia's play in their 24-3 victory, believing it was "nothing out of the common", they played an "ordinary game" and that three of the tourists' tries were gifts. They were irritated because, each time the visitors scored, the non-playing Australians in the grandstand would rise and sing: "Advance Australia Fair". This was annoying behaviour from unruly colonials.

There was even a suggestion in the days leading up to the match the Australian players had been on the drink. The *Western Herald* wrote that "colleagues and football friends who saw the Australians at Newton races on Wednesday before their departure somewhat prepared me for a display below that of Saturday. They seemed to be the worse for too much feting and feasting, and did not impress the Plymouth brethren with their physical fitness. They certainly have been having a rare good time in Devon."

The press bleating at the Australians would continue all tour.

There were other distractions. As the ever-diplomatic E.E. Booth put it, apart from bulking up on fresh eggs, bacon, fish, meat and Devonshire cream: "Tonight a dance has been instituted for the team, and the ladies of Newton Abbott seem quite partial to the wearers of the waratah."

Burge was not the only casualty from the first match; Bertie the carpet snake died on the eve of the game. Peter Flanagan told Moran that the snake had caught cold from an Irish breeze. Craig, regularly photographed with Bertie slung around his neck, blamed the snake's demise on the local fare. Craig wrote in a newspaper article later in the tour that he thought England was "an exceedingly poor country, considering that my esteemed snake Bertie died after taking the risk of eating an English mouse for his first meal here. He had survived such ordeals as bushfires, droughts and starvation. To a great extent no doubt, if it had been his good fortune to survive until the advent of the Llanelly v Australia match, it would have benefited him greatly, as the wild and cannibalistic conditions that prevail there [in a football match] would no doubt have revived him." The *Western Daily Mercury* even ran a photograph of a limp Bertie, alongside Burge being helped from the field.

The press also decided to hit the team from another quarter. The *Athletic News* had been fascinated by a paragraph in the Sydney sporting newspaper the *Referee* stating that the two players from Orange, Charles

McMurtrie and Ted McIntyre, had been presented with a purse of sovereigns from local residents.

The *Athletic News* queried whether this made the pair professionals, arguing that in 1888 before the first Rugby tour to Australia and New Zealand, the Halifax player J.P. Clowes received a purse of fifteen sovereigns. "The authorities, keen as mustard in those days, got to know of this, and promptly declared the Yorkshireman a professional." Clowes did not play in any of the tour matches, because it would have automatically made his colleagues professional, simply because they had appeared alongside one.

Rusty played his first full match in the second game of the tour against his old county of Gloucestershire, a 16-0 whitewash, but a victory again pooh-poohed by the local scribes, who described the game as not up to international standard. Australia were rated as poor.

The mishaps continued against Cornwall, when in a freak incident, another Australian player had his leg broken. This time Flanagan was not on the field, but on the sideline acting as a touch judge when winger 'Boxer' Russell, in a counterattack, made enormous ground before being hurled into touch. Russell crashed into Flanagan, to the amusement of the crowd, which went eerily quiet when they discovered the accident was far more serious than first thought and another Wallaby was on his way to hospital.

But the incident, according to Moran, had its picturesque side. "The idle players stood around in groups on the Redruth ground while the injured man was being placed on a stretcher. Peter Flanagan was a fervent Catholic, and he could be heard mumbling his prayers, while Russell, also of the same faith, followed behind the bearers weeping a little. It was rather like a funeral procession. The amazed Cornishmen wondered what all the fuss was about."

If this was not emotional enough, the tour went into overdrive, involving endless dramas, when it crossed the border into Wales, and headed for the grim, dim town of Neath. There was a brief stop in Tonypandy to play Penycraig where there was twenty stoppages for supposed injuries to the miners before they were revived with a swig from a mysterious black bottle, and then they continued to Neath.

Situated just north of Swansea, Neath is the ultimate ugly Welsh town, a tough hamlet of miners, steelworkers and wild men, most of whom appeared in the black jersey of Neath with the white Maltese cross on the front. Their home ground, the Gnoll, is the most inhospitable of places, with the changing rooms more akin to pithead baths than a first-class football arena.

For decades, Neath had been renowned for their underhand, mischievous play, being known throughout Wales as the hillbillies of the local club scene. Even countless decades after the first Wallaby tour, Neath were upsetting Australian teams. In 1992 Wallaby coach Bob Dwyer described the town as 'the bag-snatching capital of Wales', after his players were grabbed by the testicles, spat on, had their eyes gouged and were stomped on during a midweek game. If Dwyer had perused the match report of the first Australia-Neath game of 1908, he would have expected nothing less.

It was one neverending stink. After the time of the game had been put back an hour to 4pm to allow the local miners to get to the ground on time, they had plenty to jeer and cheer about after one of their players was knocked unconscious in the opening minutes, after which their fullback Dick Hughes was winded.

The 8000-strong crowd immediately called on the referee, Edgar Johns from Swansea, to send Australia's Normie Row off, as he was the man closest to hand each time a Neath player collapsed. Johns ignored their pleas. By the second half, they were virtually baying for blood when their skipper D.H. Davies could not resume because of broken ribs, but went silent when Dix complained to the referee that he had been bitten, showing the teeth-marks on his hand. Not surprisingly when Johns whistled full-time in darkness he required a police escort to leave the field, while the Australian team returned to their hotel with "a mounted policeman in front and another behind, and an ordinary policeman on the conductor's step".

Rusty described the match as "a most unpleasant one. The crowd were out to see that their football heroes were right, and come what may, the Wallabies were wrong.

"This crowd was an extraordinarily cantankerous one, especially after Davies, their vigorous leader of a wild forward game, was led injured from the field. Then there was hooting, booing and shouting. There was some reckless kicking, and many stray punches going round which reflected badly on both sides."

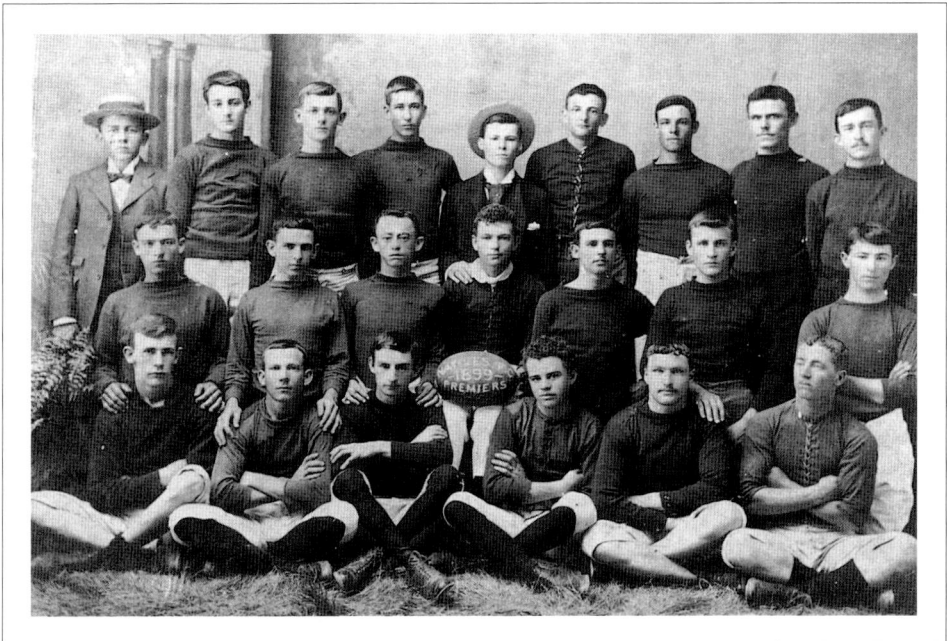

Tom Richards (top row, second from left) as a young footballer in the unbeaten 1899 Charters Towers Natives team.

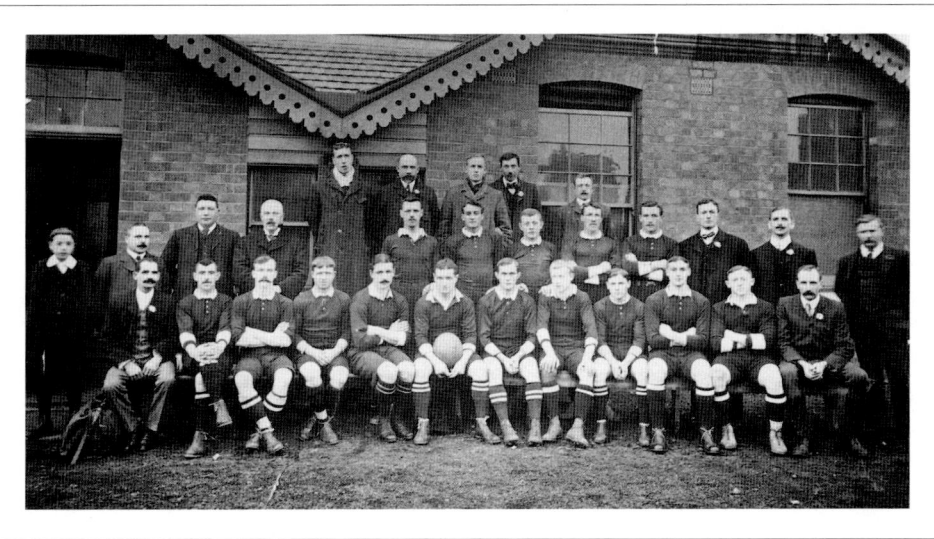

The Gloucester representative side. Rusty is sixth from the left in the centre row.

Tom Richards (fourth from left, third row) with the British Lions team in South Africa.

Tom Richards (third from left) on the boat from South Africa to England, in pursuit of the first Springbok team.

The young Queensland representative.

The 1908 Australian team arrives in England for the start of the first Wallaby tour. The ever-shy Tom Richards hides in the back row (eleventh from left) behind team manager James McMahon and to the right of captain Paddy Moran. From the E.S. Marks Sporting Collection, State Library of New South Wales.

The 1908 Wallabies arrive at Plymouth.

The R.M.S. Omrah which took the 1908 Wallabies to England.

An official postcard produced at the start of the 1908 Wallaby tour, showing that for some time the team were known as the Rabbits. From E.S. Marks Sporting Collection, State Library of New South Wales.

The 1908 Wallaby team that played against Wales in the first Test of the tour.

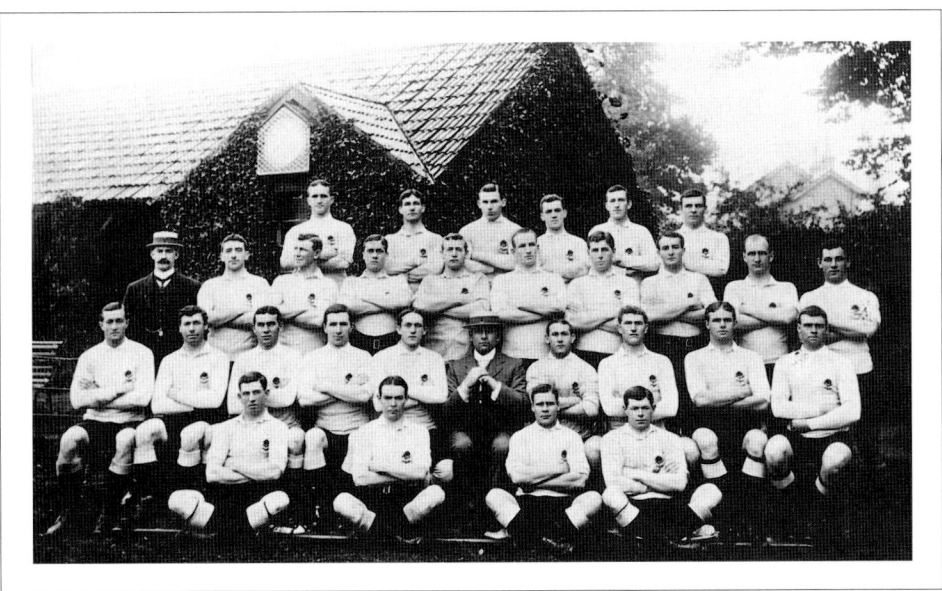

One of the many official photographs taken of the 1908 Wallabies.

The proud Australian representative.

The 1908 Wallabies revelling in the Cardiff snow. Tom Richards is at far right.

Australia, despite its 15-0 win, were roundly castigated, with halfback Fred Wood, who would cause problems on tour with his skill in convincing fellow selector Moran to continually pick him despite below-average form, described as "poor". Their star half Chris McKivat was lampooned for a lack of enterprise, while centre Dix was "very moderate".

One of the few to stand out was Rusty. He was described in the *South Wales Daily News* as a "resourceful player, and worthy of inclusion in the best side that ever was". But a few days later, even he, already being lauded as one of the best back row forwards in the world, had to suffer humiliation. Llanelly, an average Welsh club side, ended Australia's high hopes of going through the tour unbeaten, defeating them 8-3.

It was another nasty game, full of high emotion and refereeing dramas.

Moran had predicted trouble. "When we arrived we found feeling running high in this dingy tin-mining town over the appointment of the referee for our match. He had been warned solemnly that morning by a local newspaper as to possible consequences if he officiated. A very nervous man had charge of the whistle."

The *South Wales Daily News* explained that while the Australian manager Captain McMahon had agreed to Cardiff's H.J. Taylor being the referee, the Llanelly officials immediately objected, stating that they "would not be responsible for any scene which might take place should Mr Taylor be given the duties". Consequently an edgy referee made many edgy decisions, especially around the scrum, where the Llanelly pack put four players in their front row, obliterating any chance of Australia getting any ball from this set-piece. As well the referee refused Australia the right to knock their ball back from their own lineout wins, forcing them to keep the ball out wide.

Rusty's memories of the day were vivid, and not all positive. "It was a well behaved crowd, but a more frenzied, hysterical people could not have existed anywhere in the world … The saucepan had been adopted as the town's treasured emblem. At the door of every house we passed en route to the ground there were men and women standing in the doorways shaking a large-size saucepan and shouting in the Welsh language at us. At street and lane corners groups of people were singing 'Sospan Bach', or shouting and still waving saucepans at us.

"On arrival at the playing field there was a saucepan on top of each goalpost, and a mighty crowd, delirious with expectancy, singing and working up enthusiasm to a great pitch, filling the heads and hearts of their players with a primitive impulse to tear in and fight with deadly earnest, showing no quarter, giving no respite. The scene had an atmosphere about it which reminded myself of the heat and tension associated with the preparation of a Zulu ceremonial war dance, or the ominous uproar and straining before a festive dance or corroboree which I have seen Australian Aborigines."

Not surprisingly, with the referee having no control, the game turned nasty.

Rusty continued: "It was frightfully bad tactics on our part to attempt to play Llanelly at their own game when we were ever so much faster in the open than they were; but fight and wrangle with them as we did. I never imagined that men could stand up and kick so viciously at each other. I saw one of our men give a Welshman an unmerciful kick. The referee blew his whistle and asked him why he had kicked the man, to which he replied: 'He kicked one of our fellows just now.'

"That was exactly the position, everybody was kicking each other. One men, perhaps, kicked straight ahead more successfully than the opponents, but the Welshmen were superior at kicking from angles. I got kicked by back kicks from three different feet at the same time while going round a scrum."

As irritating was the after-match celebrations, and that song.

Everywhere the Australians went, they heard the Welsh refrain.

> Mary Ann's sore finger is cured
> And David the servant lies dead
> The baby in its cradle is quiet
> And the cat is now sleeping in her bed
> Sospan bach a boiling on the fire
> Sospan bach a boiling on the fire
> And the cat is scratching Johnny just like mad.

In the chaos, someone rifled Moran's bag, stealing his football boots.

Australia's memories of Wales were hardly helped two days later when they were to meet Monmouthshire in Pontypool. Due to torrential rain, the game was abandoned just before the scheduled kickoff. However no one told the Australian team, who had travelled from Cardiff. Like thousands of others, they were kept waiting outside the ground in the heavy rain, slipping and sliding in a steep, muddy lane. Eventually the Australian players and Welsh officials had to climb a fence bordering the lane, to escape the rush of angry fans who had just been told the game had been called off.

Aware that it was too dangerous to hang around these parts, the Wallabies left for London in search of rare gold.

SIX

OLYMPIC GOLD

THE GAME WAS A SHAM, a virtual afterthought. A lopsided non-event played alongside a bathing pool. But it saw Australia win its one and only Olympic gold medal for Rugby.

The 1908 Olympic Games in London, where Frank Beaurepaire excelled in the swimming pool and Snowy Baker won a silver medal in boxing with the Wallabies bellowing their support at ringside, was the most drawn-out affair. Olympic competition had begun in July, and was still going on three months later in October when a foggy afternoon was set aside to determine the Olympic Rugby champions.

Rugby had been introduced to the Olympics in Paris in 1900 where France defeated England, but it wasn't exactly the most popular event. Only three teams — France, England and Germany — competed. Rugby didn't make an appearance at the 1904 games in St Louis, and the 1908 event struggled to get off the ground, despite being held on supposedly strong Rugby territory.

The official report of the fourth Olympiad described the tournament as "lacking in interest". That was an understatement, considering that in the end the organisers struggled to get a quorum for a final and had to scramble to find even two teams — Australia, and Cornwall, who were chosen by the English Rugby Union to represent the United Kingdom.

Scotland and Ireland, at loggerheads with England, ignored their Olympic invitations. The Welsh argued they had better things to do, wanting to concentrate on their domestic competition, while South Africa and New Zealand filed the Olympics in the 'too hard' category. When the Olympic entries originally closed, only France had entered. At the request of France the invitation list was reopened, and the closing date extended for six weeks, prompting England and Australia to put in entries.

Then in the last week, France withdrew, citing "an inability to raise a representative team- so the Olympic Rugby tournament resolved itself into one match".

England were also offhanded about it all, prompting Moran to complain: "The Rugby Union has failed to see that a XV playing under the high-sounding title of the United Kingdom was not worthy to live up to the traditions of the Olympic Games."

The final, between Australia and the United Kingdom, was played at Shepherds Bush where, according to E.E. Booth, on one side of the ground, bordcering the touchline, was a 100-metre-long cement swimming bath with a long line of netting to catch flying balls and stray players. Huge mattresses were spread along the rim of the bath to prevent injury to any player who accidentally fell into the pool. To add to the bizarre scene, men with long poles and small nets fished successfully for the ball when it went over the top of the netting, into touch and into the swimming pool.

Before kickoff the Olympic finalists were photographed on the cycling track, which weaved its way around the football field and swimming pool.

The game itself was, in the words of one English newspaper, virtually a farce, as the tournament had degenerated to a "single match of no great interest between teams which had recently tried conclusions with a very decisive result". Three weeks earlier Australia had thrashed Cornwall 18-5.

The *Daily Graphic* described the final as a "practice match", while the *Leeds Mercury* complained that "never did a team in a representative match cut such an inglorious figure as did the Cornwall XV".

In an one-sided romp, only interrupted by balls flying into the swimming pool, Australia scored seven tries to win 32-3 over a second-rate opposition. Rusty said the day was forgettable, as it was a dull, foggy afternoon, not helped by a slushy game being played with a ball, "often kicked into the large swimming-pool along the touchline, and coming out sodden and waterlogged".

There was one highlight. As F.B. Wilson of the *Daily Mirror* reported: "Richards's try was a beauty. Coming along at full speed he jumped some four feet high, took the ball high above Jackett's head, and raced on between the posts, with no one, except three of his own side, within twenty yards of him. That was the plumb bit of work of the day ..."

Booth was as impressed. "Richards's try was positively brilliant, and in it he showed his aptitude and speed. McCabe, being blocked in running, punted to midfield over the opposing line of backs and the fiery Queenslander, racing up at top pace, took the ball on the full, and distancing all and sundry, scored under the cross-bar. It was rare football, and brought the house down. Cooees echoed across through the fog as the Blue score totted up."

While the Wallabies won Australia's only gold medal at the 1908 Games, their victory did not greatly excite the team. Rusty didn't even attend the Olympic medal and certificate presentation, which was made after the final, at a function held at the Waldorf Hotel in Aldwych. His whereabouts that night remain a mystery.

Moran, who did not play in the Olympic final because of a dislocated shoulder, also downplayed its importance by explaining in his Waldorf Hotel speech that the team "deeply regretted that they had not in the Olympic Games met a side thoroughly representative of the United Kingdom". He added that when Australia entered they hoped to be conquered, or conquer the best team in the world.

Moran still had his hands full on the day of the game, acting as a crucial figure in dousing down yet another controversy. Moran recounts in *Viewless Winds* that in the second half, a self-important Cornish official approached him, complaining that the Wallabies were using running spikes. Apparently during the break, the official found scratches on the bodies of some of his players. A seething Moran insisted at once on an examination of the boots of all the players as they came off the field at full time, "and I nominated an English doctor to carry out the tasks.

"In due course he reported that some of the sprigs on both sides were worn down, but that on the whole the boots of the Cornish players were in the worse condition. There was not the trace of a spike. In such circumstances I expected at least a graceful withdrawal of the accusation. Nothing of the kind happened. We heard no more from the disappointed Cornish official. He just faded out of the picture."

This was just one of many times Moran had to openly defend his players against accusations of unfair tactics, which was regularly thrown at them from the British Rugby establishment and the press in a concerted attempt to undermine the visitors. Around that time, the British media had dubbed the Wallabies "the foulest set of players imaginable". One persistently vocal critic, Hamish Stuart, said the Australian players "suffer alike from the lack of a conscientious education and the debasing effect of an unconscionable system of tuition … [they] are clumsy imitators of the New Zealanders."

Australia then travelled through Durham, Northumberland, Cheshire, London, and onto Cambridge University, with Richards remaining the outstanding player.

While the Wallabies explained in one newspaper advertisement that the secret of their success was "smoking Capstans", (with E.E. Booth describing the players as "inveterate devotees of the weed") Rusty put it all down to good, honest hard work and strong lungs.

His press writeups were invariably positive. 'Bluemantle' in the *Daily Mail* waxed lyrical in one lengthy column, explaining how Rusty was "winning golden opinions, and indeed, he deserves them. Bar, perhaps, Captain Moran, he is the most brilliant forward in the team. He shows up more than his skipper, but the latter equalises that by doing a tremendous bit of tackling and 'rush-stopping' which frequently passes unnoticed. Richards is tremendously fast, and the pace at which he follows up is phenomenal. I do not remember a forward who has ever 'got there; so quickly as Richards. He handles beautifully too, and thanks to his pace is often a fifth three-quarter in attack."

A few days later the headline in the *Mail* exclaimed, "Richards in great form" when Australia won in Newcastle. He was described as 'remarkable' and 'ubiquitous.' "Wherever the ball was, Richards was sure to be." There was even a cartoon of Rusty kicking the ball over his head to upset his opponents, with the explanation that " Richards is still an education in what a modern forward should be like". Against Cambridge University, Rusty was the best player on the field, instigating "two or three tries". It was a "brilliant display given by Richards, the greatest forward of the season".

F.B. Wilson commented that day: "If there is a better forward playing he must be something a bit extra."

Rusty also had great staying power, playing four matches in a row, including the drama-charged affair against Oxford University, forever remembered as the occasion for the first Australian representative player being sent from the field.

Syd Middleton, renowned rower, swimmer and Glebe back row forward, had been intimidated all game by his front row opponent G.D. Roberts. All afternoon they had been pushing and shoving each other, until at one lineout the blueblooded Roberts, after lashing out at his Wallaby opponent with his boot, called Middleton "a convict". Middleton let fly with a right uppercut which hit Roberts flush on the nose.

Roberts crashed to the turf, Middleton was pointed towards the pavilion by referee A.O. Jones, an old Notts cricketer.

The London press went ballistic. Their patience had been rewarded. It was now time to put the boots in, and give it to the "convicts". The *Daily Chronicle* described the incident as part of the "unfair and unsportsmanlike methods of the Colonials". Another recorded that Roberts was "struck such a severe blow in the face that he staggered around the field in a dazed condition, while the 10,000 spectators groaned their hearty disapproval. Had this happened in a match between professionals it might not have met with such wholesale condemnation, and I am glad that paid players were not concerned in such a disgraceful offence."

Rusty had anticipated trouble. Before the game, Oxford were being hailed as "the team of the century", and from some of the referee's early decisions, no local wanted that reputation tarnished.

Rusty said Jones "gave a lot of free kicks against us, mainly for obstruction, and it did seem to me that amongst the backs there was more holding and blocking than usual".

Then came the incident that "reflected badly against our reputation as sportsmen".

"It happened when one of our forwards was incensed by the mauling and the continually nasty remarks of a certain big Oxford forward (this forward had also made himself most objectionable in a county game). A lineout was formed, and without the player having the ball he was grasped around the head. To clear himself he pulled back into the open, with the Oxford man still holding on. Then I saw a vicious right-hand uppercut just glance off the opponent's face. He staggered further into the open. The referee had a good view of the affair and was probably justified in ordering our player off the field.

"I have but little sympathy with any man who uses his hands to punch while he is on a football field, yet I wonder if Mr A.O. Jones would have taken this extreme action if he had known as much of the affair as I did and could have seen the trouble working up from the beginning of the game."

Moran was sitting in the grandstand next to Sydney-born Rhodes Scholar, England representative and future Australian selector G.V. Portus when Middleton let fly.

"The man who committed this offence was a magnificent athlete, rower, boxer and footballer, and actually a very good sportsman, but irritable and hot-headed," Moran wrote. "I followed him into the dressing room with murder in my heart for one who was and is still a firm friend. But when I saw his bowed head I said nothing and walked out. He is still paying for that indiscretion. It has pursued him for thirty years. It followed him to the war and it still pops up ..."

Middleton's grief lasted for some time, as the English Rugby Union suspended him for five matches, ruining any chance he had of playing in the first Test against Wales. It took some time for England to cite Middleton, so he played two more tour matches before being suspended. He then fled to Scotland.

Moran was as depressed at the after-match dinner, especially when he "became horribly conscious that one of our players opposite me was using his knife in an entirely unorthodox way, while his Oxford neighbour was courteously trying to create conversation."

But what most upset Moran was the "convict" slur. The captain who had taken it upon himself to be one of Australia's first proper ambassadors and a father figure to his players was deeply angered that "there were many in England who believed that our misconduct was due to the old original sin breaking out like some hereditary disease".

"It is the curse of modern conditions that good fellows earning their living as journalists should think it necessary to make of their readers addicts perpetually craving for a new sensation. This is the gravest drug habit of our times."

To right the balance, Moran wrote to the *Daily Mirror*, shortly after the Oxford match, to defend the Australian tactics. Under the heading of "Wallabies and their Critics", Moran explained that the English law interpretations, especially around the scrums, were bamboozling the Australian players. English referees were finding fault in areas Australia thought were legal and were part of their natural game, including picking the ball up from loose rucks, and putting a foot up in a scrum. (Several referees were also not up to it, with Richards recalling that when they played at Taunton the whistleblower was "an elderly man, who turned out wearing a heavy tweed cap, golf suit, and big boots, who couldn't keep up to the game and several times blew his whistle so that he could catch up".)

Moran was also unimpressed that Australia were castigated for over-vigorous tackling. "Our tackling has been always hard — it won the match at Oxford — and has no doubt earned the disapproval of men who have never played. The player, however, who objects to a robust tackle should lay aside his jersey and leave it to become moth-eaten in disuse. For him there are other games, and, I believe, the newest is diabolo."

The complaints prompted an odd character who called himself Dingo Bill to write to the *Daily Mirror*, and remind all of the words of American novelist Richard Harding Davis: "The Englishman is the finest sportsman in the world — when he is winning."

The press worked in other areas to destabilise the Wallabies. The suggestion that the team were not blueblood amateurs but actual professionals was repeatedly raised in the English newspapers. Scotland, a Rugby Union renowned for its penny-pinching attitude as shown by its persistence in forcing its players to pay for their own national jerseys, especially when they lost them, kept up the attack. Apart from refusing to play Australia, Scotland would now not compete against England. Their complaint was that England had already competed against professionals because the New Zealand team, which had played a Test against them in 1905 had, like the Australians, received an allowed of one guinea weekly, on top of full expenses.

E.E. Booth was aghast, complaining that "Scotland had influenced Ireland and the discourtesy of both in refusing our Colonial visitors fixtures is really an affront to the English Rugby Union, who are responsible for the arrangement of the tour". McMahon said that when the Australian players were told of Scotland's stand "there were many remarks on Scottish characteristics that would make a rhinoceros blush". McMahon said the expenses complaint was a farce, citing the example of two Australian players who were suffering from severe bruising after one match. They were told by McMahon one way to alleviate the pain was to have leeches applied. "They paid a shilling each for the leeches, and the money was not paid until the receipts were produced."

The baitings increased in intensity with the suggestion in several newspapers that at least one of the Wallabies, centre Darb Hickey, had already signed up with the breakaway Rugby League organisation and would cross over as soon as the tour finished. It was claimed that Hickey had secretly played Rugby League in Sydney before leaving on the tour.

J.B. Cooke, the president of the Northern County Union, speaking at the Yorkshire-Lancashire match said that he had seen a photograph of a Wallaby surrounded by professional players, and he had also sighted the contract the player had signed with the Australian Rugby League. A week later Cooke came clean and said Hickey was the player he was referring to, and that J.J Giltinan, the manager and promoter of the Kangaroos, also making their first English tour at the time, had in his possession a League contract signed by Hickey.

There were immediate denials from the Wallabies, with the assistant manager Stan Wickham saying: "Had he [Hickey] done so he would have been sent back by the next boat," while McMahon described it all as a beat-up. Hickey stayed on the tour, but on returning to Sydney, accepted 100 pounds to switch to League. There was no doubt that Cooke's allegations were true. And there is also no doubt several other Wallabies had already signed, considering the mass exodus to League after the tour, to play in a special series against the Kangaroos. Before the Welsh Test, several Wallabies privately met with Giltinan, who sounded them out over whether they were interested in defecting. With the big money being thrown about, most were willing. They just had to keep their mouths shut until the Wallabies returned to Sydney.

Some attacks were even more personal. Wallaby fullback Phil Carmichael's appearance was sneered at. Rusty explained that: "He always wore a small tweed cap when playing, the outcome of playing on sunny days in Brisbane. It no doubt became a habit, and the cap was probably looked upon as a mascot by Phil. The papers remarked several times upon the peculiarity and the novelty of a player wearing a cap, and, being rather sensitive, he discarded his cap with great reluctance."

The players also discovered that the tour was not exactly bright lights and partying all night long. As Rusty wrote to his Charters Towers mates: "I suppose you hear about the grand time we are having over here: the dinners, theatre parties, receptions etc.

"Well, it's all rot. I am surprised at the entertaining. I expected more of it; in fact, I thought we would have to refuse entertainments, but such is not the case. I believe we could do with a little more of it."

Rusty added that the players were "amazed at the poverty that exists throughout this country", while on the playing side the team was not being helped by the backs playing " a puzzling game". The back line were missing "some of the easiest tries imaginable".

According to Rusty, overwork and heavy training had taken their toll, "so that when the big Welsh clubs had to be faced the team was practically as slow as mud, visibly stale and run down".

This was hardly an endorsement for the Wallaby management.

Despite all the external sniping and the big money lures from the Northern Union, the Wallabies were able to retain their focus, especially Rusty, who had absolutely no interest in League, believing it a game of the lowest form. He had taken great delight in following the bungled Kangaroo tour, which began on the worst note possible, with their captain Dinny Lutge telling reporters that he didn't even know how long the team would be in England, because nothing had really been organised.

E.E Booth, in an article revealing that John Buttery of the London *Daily Mail* had been the first to call New Zealand the All Blacks, said he didn't expect "Rugby League to survive long after this English tour." In another article for the Sydney Referee, Booth reported that "Northern Union agents" had approached several Wallabies "with a view to going over". "However, up to the present, all these overtures have been declined."

Undoubtedly Booth, who had heard of the 100 pound-plus approaches, was protecting his Wallaby contacts. Moran, obviously aware of the approaches, believed professionalism was among the causes of "national decadence".

Rusty still agreed to attend the Kangaroos match against Wigan. It disgusted him. "The crowd grew heated at the very sight of the despised colonials, whom they termed 'lags' and 'convicts' in no uncertain terms. I sat the game out and saw the Australians win. I left the ground sick at heart to think that the world could contain a concourse of people so utterly devoid of any kind of sporting sense and without any understanding of fair play or moral decency. I was also offended to think that any Australia would ever play before such a crowd. I couldn't imagine that so much humiliation could be heaped upon players."

There was only one thing to do — return to the safer confines of the Wallabies, where everything was now pointed towards the major test of the tour- the International match against Wales at Cardiff Arms Park.

Australia were feeling relatively buoyant, having lost just two of their twenty-three leadup games, while Rusty, on the morning of the game, could not have been more relaxed, having been described in the local press by the Welsh representative Percy Bush as "the best forward in Australasia; just about as good as any we can put on in the 'Old Country' now". His back row partners were Moran and Bob Craig- both also making their Test debut.

On the morning of the match, the Australians did not stray from their Queen's Hotel headquarters onto the Cardiff streets because of fears they would be engulfed by the swarming Rugby crowd that had taken over the city centre.

All morning, trains from every part of England, brought thousands of Rugby followers into Cardiff. One, Mr Leopold Hirsch, chartered a special train from Swindon to Cardiff. He travelled alone.

Blocking the entrances were former Internationals, officials and supporters, all wanting to know the latest gossip on the Australians, and why they were not favourites to roll the famous locals. There was a smattering of Australians, including two nieces of Australian Test cricketer and England Rugby representative Sammy Woods, who had caught the early train from London to join the swarm, but they were well in the minority.

Through the narrow streets echoed Welsh tunes, played by the Tongwynlais Silver Brass Band, which had set itself up on the Cardiff Arms pitch to entertain the early arrivals with an assortment of polkas, waltzes, marches and traditional Welsh songs. So concerned were they by the large crowd that Cardiff shopowners barricaded their front windows for fear of riots if Wales were beaten by those horrid colonials. Around the terraces the locals 'with immense volume' sang 'Land of My Fathers', 'Men of Harlech', 'Sospan Bach' and 'Molony's Bells.'

Within seconds of kickoff the ground was full, with an enormous cheer announcing the arrival of Paddy Moran and the Australians onto the turf. As Rusty walked in the middle of a queue of players, the moment hit him. The pins and needles were right in the core of his stomach, playing havoc. He calmed himself by looking around. All his teammates were in the same unsteady state.

"The Australians were slightly pale with anxiety; their faces were drawn, but set with determination and a desire to triumph in the first really great International game ever played by Australians in a distant land, on strange soil, and before such a vast crowd," Rusty later wrote.

"The weight of national representation was a heavy responsibility; the football honour of our homeland was at stak. This realisation brought the 'grit' of each man to the top. It was night-time back home in Australia, and we knew the morning papers would carry the result to our people immediately that play ceased. There was a prayer deep in every heart for strength to outplay those almost fanatically worked up Welshmen. It was our hour of trial — a test of mettle, nerve, character and spirit.

"The playing field was like a cockpit. Walled round on all sides were masses of densely packed people. Looking up at them from the arena they appeared to reach high into the sky; whichever side one looked there were people right close up. The closeness of the crowd was strikingly strange and unfamiliar."

A quick rendition of 'Our Colonials', a reluctant war-cry with Moran and Rusty again both hiding in the back row, and the Test began, coinciding with an almighty roar from the 40,000 plus crowd.

Wales kicked off, and within minutes Rusty was on the charge, heading towards the Welsh try line with ball safely tucked under his right arm, until the referee Gil Evans, who hailed from Leeds, called him back for an alleged knock-on. Then it was all Wales, scoring first when winger Philip Hopkins found space out wide before offloading inside to his thirty-two-year-old veteran forward George Travers, who with Wallaby tacklers all over him trying to push him into touch, found the try line.

Or had he? Many in the crowd thought the Australians had been duped, believing that Travers had knocked the ball forward, and it had instead been forced down by the Wallaby fullback Phil Carmichael. Several, who were near the spot, later wrote to local newspapers, explaining that the ball was lost in the tackle, and Travers came nowhere near to properly grounding the ball. Carmichael soon found himself involved in another hot discussion point. Australia immediately rallied from their 3-0 deficit, gaining easy possession when Wales lost the ball in midfield.

The upshot was an overlap with the Australian back line using it to full advantage, with McKivat, Ward Prentice and Bob Craig taking the ball up before Craig offloaded his pass perfectly to put Rusty away.

Craig's ability to draw his opponent into the tackle gave Rusty all the room he needed and to enjoy the accolade of being the first Wallaby to score a try in an International.

There was no disputing Rusty's try, but there was neverending debate over whether Carmichael's conversion attempt had been successful or not. Evans, who had already defrauded Australia with the Travers try decision, thought not. Virtually everyone else in the ground, including Australia, believed it was another dodgy ruling and that the ball had indeed finished between the goalposts.

A formidable breeze was whipping across the ground, prompting Rusty to hold the ball for Carmichael as he lined up for the conversion. The kick was smooth and perfectly directed. As Rusty recalled: "The kick at goal was surely the most remarkable thing that could happen. The ball, which was going right between the posts, got up into the wind, over the top of the galleries, it caught the ball and blew it away at an acute angle, but not before the ball had actually passed between the posts. Carmichael and I ran back to take the 'kick out' from halfway, but, to our amazement the Welshmen kicked off from the 25, which meant that the goal was disallowed."

Carmichael was so distressed by the decision that with the permission of the Australian team management, he wrote to the editor of the *South Wales Daily News*. He wrote: "With reference to the question of whether I converted Richards' try, I would crave leave to unhesitatingly state that the ball passed within the post fully a foot. It was as fair a goal as ever I kicked, and I remarked to Richards immediately afterwards, 'That makes my fiftieth, Tom.' He replied, 'Yes Phil, and a good one, too.' I do this in fairness to the team and myself."

Instead of Australia taking a lead, they instead restarted at 3-all. The frustration obviously got to one Australian forward, who then disgracefully kicked the Welsh captain and centre W.J. (Bill) Trew in the head after he had dived onto the loose ball.

The incident was recorded in the day's press, but the identity of the phantom kicker was not revealed. The *South Wales Daily News* reporter 'The Prophet' was astounded by the incident, believing it below "any man fit to be included in a football team". Percy Bush wrote that the Australian selection committee would "not be the sportsmen I think them if they pick the culprit again". Again, no name was given. However the identity is revealed in Rusty's scrapbook of the tour. At this point of the article, Rusty wrote in pencil: "Burge did kick Trew."

Rusty was referring to Albert 'Son' Burge, a flighty forward who had joined the tour as a replacement after his brother Peter had been sidelined with a broken leg. The players were unimpressed with the callup of 'Son', as he was a reckless and often dirty player. Several, who had been victims of his unpleasant manouvres, had even privately approached the team management, warning them of the dangers of bringing Burge from Sydney. Moran conceded that Burge was 'reckless.' The Swansea centre had to be helped from the field, was sighted looking exceedingly groggy in the pavilion, and admitted to feeling "rotten".

Wales dominated the second half, with a try and a critical penalty goal giving them a 9-3 lead. Moran later explained that the decision that cost them the game came when his forward Craig was penalised for offside, after he had rushed around the scrum to upset the Welsh halfback Dicky Owen.

Moran added this chilling note in *Viewless Winds*. "These two players who played hide-and-seek round a scrum, on the Cardiff Arms Park, both later on took up hotel-keeping. Both, too, committed suicide, using the same method; they hanged themselves by the neck, and were found swinging like trinkets from a Christmas tree."

Back at ground level Australia rallied in the final moments, with 'Boxer' Russell scoring, after being set up by McKivat and Prentice. Shortly after Russell again found himself in the clear, but made the fatal error of not sizing up his defensive opponent. As Moran wrote: "In the last moments one of our wings got clean away with only Winfield to beat. We all knew Winfield could not tackle. Our man could have dodged him easily or fended him off. Instead he ran hard right into him, and they both rolled over on the ground together. The match was over, with the Welsh winners." However Australia were hardly disgraced, and received overwhelming praise in the local press. Once more Rusty was singled out.

A few days later, Laurence Woodhouse in the *Daily Mail* put Rusty in the World's Greatest XV, selected from those whom he had seen play between 1868 and 1908.

On the same day, the Wallabies were challenged by the cash-strapped Kangaroos. In a small newspaper brief, the Kangaroos manager J.J. Giltinan challenged to play the Wallabies 'under Rugby Union or Northern Union rules on any ground in the United Kingdom.' The gate receipts would go to charity, and be controlled by a Rugby Union referee.

The Wallabies ignored the challenge, and pressed on through Wales. Again there was more drama, with hooker Tom Griffin sent off against Swansea, for slapping his opponent with an open hand, in a game where Rusty was again the hero. The *South Wales Daily News* said that Rusty was "ubiquitous alike in attack and in defence, and if one man could have turned the tide of battle it was this wonderful Australian forward".

J.R. Stephens, who wrote under the name 'Old Stager', said that Rusty "the great forward was the brains of the whole side ... even he has never played a better game".

The *Daily Telegraph* wrote that "individually, Richards, the Australian, was once again quite the cleverest forward on the field. He is generally at his best when his comrades are in difficulties, and yesterday he played better and better in proportion as the Welsh pack established their superiority".

There were no surprises when the infamous 'Son' Burge was sent off against Cardiff after kicking opposing forward J.P Westacott when he was on the ground and well away from the ball. Burge was booed all the way off the ground, and did not receive a consoling word from any of his Australian teammates as he left.

The Welsh press seized on Burge. 'Old Stager' went for the jugular. "This is the third man among the Australians to have disgraced the Commonwealth by failing to control his temper in the heat of the play. The other two, Middleton and Griffin, may be excused for having so far forgotten themselves as to punch at opponents if it be true that they were irritated or, it has been put, intimidated to retaliate, but there is absolutely no excuse for Burge, who after his glaring foul of Trew in the Welsh match, ought to have been sent home."

'Old Stager' argued that the Westacott incident "might easily not only have maimed, but have killed the man.' Westacott could have been 'crippled for life".

"Burge brought with him a bad reputation from Australia, and I am giving away no secret when I say that more than a few of his colleagues would have preferred him to have remained there, and that the Wallabies officials over here had no voice in his selection as most certainly they should have had."

Of the incident, the Wallabies' most vehement supporter E.E. Booth said: "The least said the soonest mended."

"Burge's affair completely spoilt the pleasure of the grandstand spectators, many of whom signified their disgust in leaving the ground." Booth said that Burge's boot flew "promiscuously into a melee", and Westacott "dropped like a bullock, holding his hands on a vital part".

"No excuse can be offered. The real persons to blame are, first, the selectors in Sydney; and, secondly, the selection committee of the Wallabies team themselves. This discreditable incident seemed to affect the whole team, many holding their heads low in consequence." Adding to the pain, Australia were thoroughly defeated 24-8.

Apart from the players, many of Australia's supporters were anticipating trouble with Burge. G.V. Portus wrote a letter to Rusty three days after the Swansea match, which read in part: "What has happened to the team? Two defeats in two matches, and two men off. The *Daily Mail* hints at a lack of esprit de corps. Who is responsible? Thought it would only be a matter of time for young Burge to be outed."

Portus was referring to a paragraph in the *Daily Mail* which read: "It is no secret that lack of esprit de corps is one of the chief factors contributing to the collapse of the Wallabies."

(In an article around the same time, Portus wrote that Burge "kicks too much and far too blindly, and I knew that it was only a question of time before he would attract the referee's notice".)

As the International against France in Paris was cancelled because of a treacherous blizzard that killed hundreds and restricted the Wallabies to sightseeing around Napoleon's tomb, the Arc de Triomphe, the Louvre, Eiffel Tower, Maxim's cafe and the Trocadero nightclub, the only major Test left on the tour was the International against England at Blackheath.

Again the key attraction was Rusty. According to the *Daily Mirror*, Rusty was "the star forward of the team, and is probably at the present day the best forward in the world- at any rate, there are none better. He is certainly the handsomest man in the team." Rusty was the first forward to be picked for the Test. Surprisingly this time around, his captain Paddy Moran wasn't beside him in the back row. The official story is that Moran had slipped on a piece of ice on New Year's Eve, spraining his Achilles tendon, and forcing him to withdraw from the team on the day of the match. The unofficial claim is that Moran was overlooked in a revamped back row, which now included Norm Row and Ken Gavin, the forward from the New South Wales bush town of Cudal who boasted the middle name of Australia.

The dropping of the Australian captain was inferred to at the time, with at least one newspaper suggesting internal squabbling, forcing McMahon to deny that there was dissension within the ranks. The truth was otherwise, with several of the players disgruntled by their lack of opportunities on tour, and that they had been unfairly forgotten by the selectors McMahon, Moran, Wood, McKivat and McCue.

After the tour, Gavin and McMurtrie, at a function in Orange, openly expressed disapproval of the treatment of one of their colleagues, Ed 'Daisy' McIntyre, by the selection committee. They were surprised that the selectors had ignored McIntyre who, before proceeding to England, had been selected in all major matches.

Even E.E. Booth publicly queried team selections, pondering the omission of Craig and Arthur McCabe until the ninth game, while he thought that Daly only playing in one of the first ten matches was "inexplicable". He also thought Dix, Prentice and Stevenson were strangely underused.

There were dictators on the selection board, especially the authoritarian manager McMahon.

McMahon liked to push his ample weight around, as one would expect from someone who had been an officer with the NSW Lancers. He showed off his rigid conservative views during numerous speeches on tour, including one where he announced that having spent eighteen years in the Australian army, it was his duty to maintain the supremacy of Britain. He told a Devon audience that they should never fear Australia becoming a republic, because it was not the best form of government.

McMahon was not liked by the players, especially because of his persistent demand to be the boss. He was forever an imposing, unbending figure. After the tour Rusty wrote of spending "a very pleasant evening with Paddy Moran. He is a splendid fellow- what a contrast to McMahon."

Wood, the team vice-captain, also caused problems at the selection meetings. For some time the stability of the team was affected by his persistence in picking himself at halfback, even though he was way off form, and McKivat was easily outperforming him.

Moran admitted that although Wood was a "great little player" he "never found his form in England.". "It used to be unpleasant for us when, in the face of this, he insisted for a long time on his own selection. We did not want unfriendliness, but for nine matches in succession he kept McKivat out of his proper position."

When the back row was selected for each match, Moran would leave the room after stating his preferences.

For the England Test, it was believed that several of the selectors were keen to try to find an alternative for Moran who, while consistent on the tour, had failed to be as dynamic as Rusty. Some thought that the forward balance would be better with Row and Gavin involved.

Moran's sore leg was a convenient way out, and an opportunity for the captain to avoid embarrassment. When Moran withdrew on the morning of the match, the English press took it as a sign that there were internal dramas. As Moran wrote: "A sensational press saw in the withdrawal further evidence of internal dissensions. Never once did I have any trouble with the team. Everyone remained a friend until death removed some, and distance took others away."

Moran said that some 'highly imaginative sporting writers' had referred to 'dissensions within the team.' "Except for some differences with the manager these never existed," Moran wrote.

Again Moran tried to blame the English press, but there was more to the story than he let on. Moran's football career was over, with him set to leave after the Test for Edinburgh and his post-graduate medical research scholarship. McKivat took over the Australian captaincy, up against England's lieutenant G.D.D. O'Lyon, who earlier in the tour had been brought from a ship by a torpedo boat and then put onto a special train so that he could play for London against the Colonials.

O'Lyon was admired throughout England, but the Australian team thought he was the weakest link. On the morning of the game, following a team dinner the previous night where pride of place on the menu was wallaby tail soup, Rusty talked to his teammates about targeting the English fullback.

When asked if it was risky business regularly punting the ball high to O'Lyon, Rusty replied: "No, our greatest chance of victory is in beating 'Torpedo' O'Lyon off his game today. We can't afford to give him any liberty or room to work in."

Rusty had noticed in the three encounters they had faced O'Lyon on tour, he stood a long way back in counter defence, and appeared hesitant. The best way to test him was under the high ball, with the Wallaby forwards charging upfield at him.

It worked. Early in the Test at the Rectory field in Blackheath, Australia kicked the ball high, and just short of O'Lyon. According to Rusty: "he hesitated, then set off after it; but as he got to the ball two Australian forwards were there also. The ball bounced, and Norman Row by fast and heady following-up scored Australia's first try."

"Our second try also came from a high punt, which confused O'Lyon again. We caught O'Lyon in possession several times that afternoon. English critics after the game proclaimed O'Lyon a failure."

England also failed, losing 9-3 in an unremarkable International. Unlike the Welsh Test, all the drama was before kickoff, with the Wallabies almost forced to forfeit the game, as their team bus broke down twice on the way, and the team arrived at the ground only minutes before kickoff. Moran was farewelled; the team presenting him with a large writing pad and inkstand, with pens and pencils in silver mounting, before they played several minor matches in Bristol and Plymouth.

The team was farewelled from England in less glowing terms, with the press giving them another unpleasant send-off. In his Test report, E.H.D. Sewell could not resist the barb of: "Before another team from Australia is asked to tour in this country it is to be hoped that the Rugby Union will have satisfied itself that the objectionable features, which all coinnoisseurs know to exist, have been completely expunged from the Australian moral code of the Rugby game." The persistent slaggings prompted Ward Prentice to go public, and complain that "practically all the newspapers were dead set against the Wallabies ... we got no praise."

They headed to California and Canada, via New York and San Francisco, for matches against Stanford University, California University, All California on a newly ploughed paddock with its fair share of boulders, and Vancouver, in front of a far more appealing press contingent. But most importantly there was endless partying with anxious-to-please American beauties. It was the ultimate end-of-tour mind blowout for a team that had won thirty-two of its thirty-eight matches.

Eventually seven-and-a-half months after farewelling Sydney, the Wallabies, fat and jolly because of the cuisine on board the R.M.S *Moana* (an average dinner involved sandwiches, ripe olives, fresh haddock with oyster sauce, calves heads, filet mignon, filet sardines, spring lamb, cold york ham, Spanish brisket of beef, roast capon, plum pudding, iced pears, vanilla ice cream, muscatels and almonds plus assorted nuts), returned through the Heads- with Rusty probably the proudest. Under his arm was a bundle of congratulatory articles by the British press, praising him as one of the greatest footballers of all time.

Some of the more spectacular, from writers who had also recently witnessed the 1905 All Blacks and 1906 Springboks, were:

The *Daily Mail*: "The greatest player seen during the season was Richards, whose pace, tackling, cross-kicking and resourcefulness stamps him as one of the finest forwards who ever put on football boots. Throughout the tour he was the best man on the field in every match, and how many tries he gained for his side indirectly it would be difficult to say. He is a brainy player of the best type and, to my mind, would take his place in a 'World XV' of this or any other year."

The *Yorkshire Evening Post*: "In almost every match he stands out like Saul among the prophets; and 'Richards has it' is becoming quite a common expression at the Wallabies matches. One wonders how many Northern Union clubs will angle for this talented player?"

The *London Evening News*: "Richards is the star forward of the team and is probably at the present day the best forward in the world- at any rate there are none better. He is certainly (now girls!) the handsomest man in the team."

The *Daily Telegraph*: "Richards, I believe, is the cleverest forward in the world today. He not only plays scrupulously fairly, but chivalrously as well ... It is almost superfluous to write that Richards played a good game forward. Richards plays forward, half, three-quarter, or fullback just as it suits him."

The *London Times*: "If ever the Earth had to select a Rugby Football team to play against Mars, Tom Richards would be the first player chosen."

Earth and Mars had to wait. Somewhere else beckoned.

SEVEN

WALLABY WANDERLUST

AS THE WALLABIES sighted the Australian coast in the distance, Rusty muttered: "In a few days, boys, you will have to clean your own boots, and ice cream at eleven and afternoon tea at four will be things of the past."

The honeymoon was over. After a few days of civic receptions, luncheons, and calls for them to do that hideous war-cry just one more time, the heroes filtered out into the general public, and were almost forgotten. Once more they were mere minnows with the same problems as everyone else in the workplace: how to earn a quid?

Many in the first Wallaby team found a comfortable way. Shortly after returning home, they succumbed to the easy dollar being offered by the Rugby League entrepreneurs, with fourteen of the Wallaby touring party crossing codes and becoming professionals. The lure was irresistible, with League officials offering enormous sums to entice Wallabies into playing a three-Test series against the Kangaroos.

McKivat was the critical signing, being paid 200 pound, the equivalent of two years' ordinary salary. The rest, who included McCabe, McCue, Craig and the Burge brothers, received between 100 and 150 pounds.

Although every Wallaby was approached by League scouts, Richards immediately knocked them back. He held no interest in League. He knew that Rugby Union was the proper passport to seeing the world, and was going to use it to the hilt. Besides he didn't think that those big-talking League officials had the money to back up their huge statements.

He was also unimpressed with the manner of the League players. In his large personal scrapbook, Rusty had stuck in and circled an article describing an Australian League team on tour in Manchester, who at one function had carried on like pigs. The article said the Australians had not waited for their opponents to arrive, and had instead "attacked the delicacies already on the table — jellies, blancmange and fruit — in the most revolting fashion. When dinner concluded, they left the table without a word."

Rugby officials gradually learnt of the defections, which made them hastily try to keep hold of their most valued players. In May 1909, the NSWRU management committee agreed to pay Rusty's return home expenses which totalled more than nine pounds, while the secretary, W.W. Hill, was requested to interview the star forward to see "if he could stay in Sydney until the proposed Wallabies match [against NSW] was played".

Instead Rusty headed back to Charters Towers on the steamer *Wodonga* to one of the largest civic receptions held in the mining town. It was the return of the prodigal son. Rusty was first welcomed back at a dinner staged by the North Queensland Rugby Union, where there were endless speeches, toasts and cheers, before their hero gave them a brief run-down on the tour. There were more tears the following weekend when his club mates organised a smoke concert at the ANA Hall.

Rusty's speech, which culminated in discussing Parisian women's fashions, prompted a wave of songs, with 'If those lips could only speak', being followed by 'Dear old Pals', 'Home Sweet Home', 'Knick Knock', 'Mary's Little Lamb', 'She's Only Seventeen' and finally a recitation of Adam Lindsay Gordon's poem 'How We Beat the Favourite'. But it appears no one at that function could be trusted. At the bottom of the invitation were the words: "Please keep your seats till the end of the programme. Leave them there, they belong to the ANA."

Rusty made occasional appearances, but was eager to rest up. He opted against chasing a Queensland jersey in 1909, instead restricting himself to representative games for Charters Towers. He even decided to try out the captain-coach role, in charge of the Towers team that met the Newtown club side from Sydney and that included Rusty's Wallaby mates Paddy McCue and Peter Burge. The Towers players never had a chance, especially as several took the field wearing canvas shoes, and were lucky to lose by only 23 points. Rusty proved the ideal host for the Newtown visitors, organising a billygoat race and another smoke concert at the Town Hall.

Rusty's disenchantment with the Wallabies who had left for the big dollar did not affect his friendship with numerous players. Several months after returning, he and McCue opted to go on a big adventure.

Taking the train to Katoomba in the Blue Mountains of New South Wales, they walked to the Jenolan Caves and back, a distance of more than 100 kilometres, along winding, dusty tracks and rough terrain. Armed with "clumsy-looking swags", and wearing their old football boots with the heels cut off because it improved traction, their week-long jaunt was punctuated by nights spent sleeping against fallen trees, with branches and leaves used as blankets and pillows.

So ruddy-cheeked were Rusty and McCue that when they began their journey walking down the main street of Katoomba, the local constabulary became suspicious and stopped them, wanting to know "where such motley persons had come from, and where they were heading".

Rusty was again looking well beyond the Towers. He was restless and wanted greater challenges.

The big escape route was provided through his family connections in Johannesburg. A mining supervisor was required for one of the main Johannesburg gold mines, and Rusty was again on his way. Elsewhere, he was anxious to branch out. Although frustrated by his lack of education, his prime passion was writing, and he harboured a private ambition to be a journalist. He had made his name on the Wallaby tour, and he felt that it was now time to sell it, writing a series of football-related articles for the *Referee*. The first appeared in early 1910, under the heading: "Scientific side of Rugby Football. Training the mind, the eyes, the limbs and the body."

In it he elaborated on some of his more unusual theories. They included how to overcome a parched and dry mouth on the football field. "This can be easily remedied by discontinuing drinking or sipping liquids with your meals — you must learn and practise to keep your mouth moist by natural circulation, not by frequent sipping or artificial means."

As important was for a player to learn how to deceive and mislead an opponent, by looking one way and going the other or by improving one's peripheral vision. At training, one of the most crucial tasks was to learn how to fall, dive or throw oneself heavily on the ground, so "that a severe fall in a match will not sicken you and interfere with your game".

And the best place to think about the game? "The most opportune time to reflect over the day's game is in bed that night. You must lie awake, think, and find out how and why you were so badly beaten, or where you were when the winning try was scored against you, and think how you came to be bumped so heavily in attempting to tackle a man. You must also consider how you came to fall so awkwardly when you were tackled. While lying in bed is where many a class player finds out his mistakes, also where he discovers how to remedy these mistakes." Still the most crucial element was being in the right place at the right time. Richards's International career was about to go on a bizarre tangent, primarily through a touch of luck. Shortly after he had been reunited with his parents, the fourth British team to tour South Africa had arrived for a nightmarish twenty-four-match trip, including three Tests against the Springboks in Johannesburg, Port Elizabeth and Cape Town.

The combination of a fragile touring party, formidable opposition, unforgiving playing conditions, never-ending train journeys across the country and the most demanding of schedules saw the British Lions squad soon decimated by injuries. One player was even feared to have typhoid, another blood poisoning from gravel rash. So hard were the grounds they played on that elbow-guards and reinforced kneecaps were ripped to shreds.

Most players were sidelined though through the fearless tackling of the South African provincial players, forcing forwards to deputise in endless unusual positions, simply to fill gaps. It wasn't long before they were looking for anyone who could help out. It also didn't take long for the Lions management to realise a perfect candidate was hovering nearby. They had heard from South African officials that the great Rusty Richards was in the country, supervising a mine in Johannesburg, and due to his Bristol club links, could help out.

The officials knew Rusty was not just a stopgap, he was good enough to skipper this rag-tag mob. Considering the dire nature of their situation they didn't even mind a colonial in their midst. Then again, he was almost one of theirs: a Bristol, Gloucester, a sturdy West Country man. The call was immediate. Get Rusty to the rescue.

By invoking his Bristol club membership, Rusty became the first and only Australian-born national player to also boast British Lions representation. The Melbourne-born Dr A.B. (Alec) Timms toured Australia with the 1899 Great Britain side, but never appeared in his home country colours – nor did the Victorian-born Ian Smith, who represented Scotland and went to South Africa with the 1924 Lions. In mid July Rusty received a letter from the British Lions manager William Cail, who said that permission had been received from the South African Rugby Board for him to join the tour and that he must meet them in Bloemfontein within a week. "You will easily find out where we are staying, as we arrive there early that day," the somewhat stern letter said.

Rusty was in Bloemfontein well in time for the rendezvous, tracked down the team hotel for the start of two of the strangest months of his life with a colourful crew of players, led by the Irish doctor Tommy Smyth and England's adventurous five-eighth-cum-No 8 'Cherry' Pillman.

Rusty immediately discovered that the freedom he enjoyed as a Wallaby would not be duplicated as a Lion. He received a notice that any player who missed the team bus for training would not have his cab fares paid; and in no other circumstance would cab fares be paid; an allowance of 1s3d per day would be made; each player would sign his own afternoon tea card, and no cards would be accepted in the grill room or lounges.

And while the Wallabies had time to sightsee, the Lions were cleverly sent by the South African Rugby authorities on every railway trip imaginable, endlessly crisscrossing the country to each corner of the harsh, parched veldt. As countless Rugby tourists in South Africa have discovered, they are unwitting victims to every ambush imaginable.

Most of the tour, the players found themselves cooped up and trying to get comfortable on overnight trains, as fifteen train trips had been set-down in the itinerary. Then they were dumped in frontier towns to play on the most dangerous of surfaces.

At Kimberley against Griqualand West, players dug out from the ground stones as big as their fists, and were "astonished to see the field bare of grass". They were later criticised in the *Cape Argus* for using rude language during the game. "Several of the visitors frequently overstepp[ed] the bounds, and were clearly audible by spectators, which included a large proportion of ladies," the *Argus* said.

They also hit the booze in Kimberley. Rusty explained that six of the player, after a "heavy night" on the drink at a local club decided in their drunken state to form an organisation called the "Sudden Deaths" .When they arrived back at the team hotel, they wanted to initiate the hotel proprietor into the club. The proprietor, who was beckoned out of bed, "strongly objected and went outside to call a policeman, and when he returned with two policemen he found the door was locked against them, and that the footballers had charge of the hotel". The footballers could not be pacified until the proprietor and policemen were "initiated into their order, when all reigned peacefully for the rest of the night".

The locals were disgusted. One Kimberleyite wrote to the *Athletic News* to complain: "One member of the side played a disgracefully foul game, and would have been ordered off the field if he had been a local player. Then the language indulged in during the scrummages was deplorable, and was heard quite distinctly all over the field. Off the field a good many of the team seem to think they are out on a glorious 'beanfeast', judging from their behaviour here in Kimberley, either in the hotel, on the streets at night, or at the station after the game. Frankly I can tell you that we home-growns are disgusted with the team."

Elsewhere they only had a few hours to acclimatise for a game after yet another overnight train trip.

And the press were onto them. When the Cape Colony thrashed them by 19-0, a week before the first Test, the *Cape Times* was in a state of apoplexy. "No-one could be more amazed than I was in witnessing the peurile, clumsy schoolboyish way in which the British XV strove today," their scribe wrote. "It is hardly an exaggeration to say that in the whole course of the game a decent pass was not given among the British backs.

It was pitiable to see the way in which time after time the ball was tossed high and tamely in the air on the chance that a colleague would be there. More oftener than not it was an opponent who simply walked in and took it."

One who was blameless was Rusty, who again received glowing press. Against Transvaal, Richards excelled "scoring a fine try, after a combination which completely nonplussed the Transvaal defence". As expected, he was one of the few to hold up under the pressure, and was an automatic back row selection for the first Test against the Boks at the Wanderers ground, alongside Welshmen Phil Waller and Jimmy Webb.

The Brits were given no hope against the Boks, especially as the home team included such luminaries as the prodigious placekicker Duggie Morkel and the unpredictable attacking player Bob Loubser. However, the Lions surprised everyone by stretching the Boks, losing by just four points- 14-10. With their result came rare praise. The *Cape Times* said that in many matches, the British had appeared indifferent. "Today all indifference was cast aside; they played as if they had a task before them, a rich prize to win; they meant to win if they could. In general play, Jarman, Stevenson, Smith and Waller were best. Piper was great in the loose, whilst Richards, at the lineout and in giving assistance to the backs, rendered yeoman service."

Then came an almighty shock. The Lions won the second Test in Port Elizabeth 8-3, with Richards "conspicuous the whole time for consistent work in the scrum and the loose". Pillman was the main star, according to one report "playing a game invented by himself". Although listed as the team's half, Pillman instead wandered all over the field, playing centre, wing, fullback, and even leading one forward charge. He initiated both the British Isles tries, while his tackling was in the relentless Springbok class.

According to the Cape Town newspapers, the British vigour "completely took the South Africans by surprise. The forwards booted with judgment, and never gave their opponents time to think." They added:

"The forwards played magnificently, and it is somewhat invidious to individualise, but the best all-round men were Stevenson, Smith, Webb and Jarman. Richards did fine work on the line, and on the defence."

The series decider was set down for Cape Town, but it came close to not being played at all. By this time, the British Isles management were fed up with the onerous itinerary, and that they had been forced to play midweek games in Test week. The South Africans laughed this off, but the tourists called their bluff by announcing that after the Border match, they were heading for "tomorrow afternoon's train to Cape Town homeward bound".

Suddenly midweek matches were cancelled to appease the British. But the locals were unimpressed, as shown by the moan of the Springbok team manager J.C. Carden. "I am full of amazement and an intense feeling of humiliation. It must be remembered that these gentlemen are our guests in every possible sense of the word. Without going into the pros and cons of the case, how can we possibly justify a message from our guests which says in effect: 'Accept our view of the argument or go home?' Surely no more colossal blunder was ever perpetrated, or a more extraordinary message sent."

So the mood was edgy in the Cape. But the British players were having a good time, as hinted in this aside in the local paper. "The gathering of fashion and beauty showed that Cape Town girls can more than hold their own with the fair dames of other better financially favoured centres." And: "The hold which rugger has on the fair sex in this country is one of the strongest proofs of the manly, honest way in which the game is played."

Rusty assumed that he would be playing, as after all he was part of a historic winning Test team. On the morning of the Test he was publicly announced in the team. However less than an hour before kickoff, the British selectors changed their minds. They decided on the radical move of rearranging their back formation and moving Pillman into the forwards, thus omitting Rusty. Pillman was originally selected at halfback.

The *Cape Times* reporter, writing copy on deadline for the afternoon edition, was excited. He realised the Brits had messed up. "Writing before the teams took the field, I have no hesitation in saying that this is a bad tactical blunder." His words were prophetic. Two hours later, the Boks were revelling in celebration, the Brits reeling from a 21-5 thrashing.

Rusty watched helplessly from the sideline, still astounded that he had been in the team until the last few minutes. He never publicly

The 1908 Wallabies, led by captain Paddy Moran, take the field for the opening match of the tour.

The 1908 Wallabies performing the dreaded war-cry.

In his official 1908 Australian team blazer.

Action from the Olympic Gold medal final, with Tom Richards at far right, deliberately shielding the Cornwall halfback.

A rare photo of the Australian Olympic Gold medal team.

Tom Richards's Olympic gold medal certificate.

The 1912 Wallaby team that toured the United States.

The 1912 Wallabies in the United States on their day off. Rusty, with large hat askew in the background, is once again the serious onlooker.

About to hit the training paddock during the 1912 Australian tour of the United States.

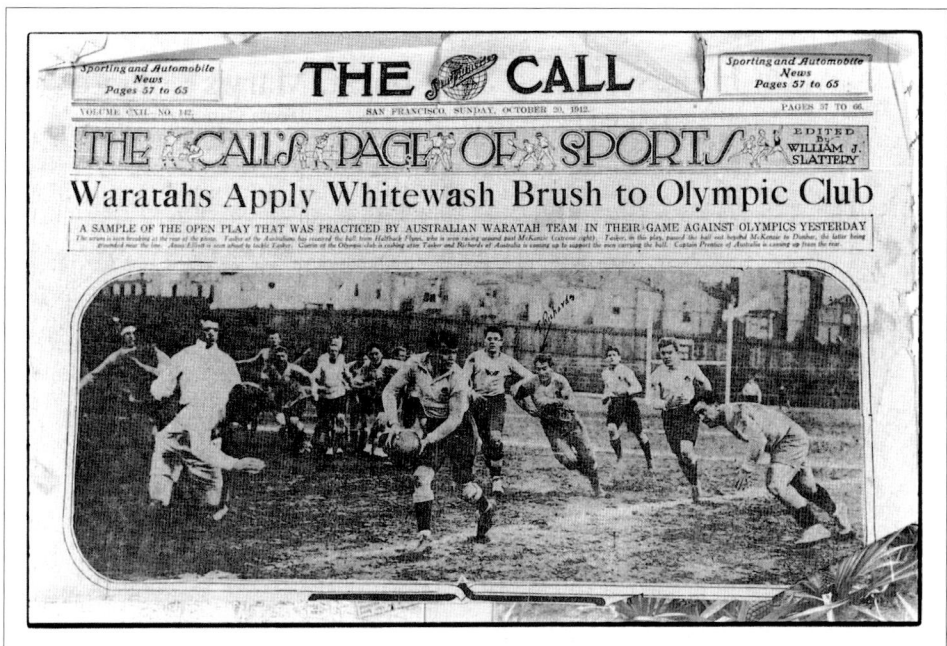

The front page of the San Francisco Call, showing Tom Richards racing after the ball during the 1912 Australian tour of the USA.

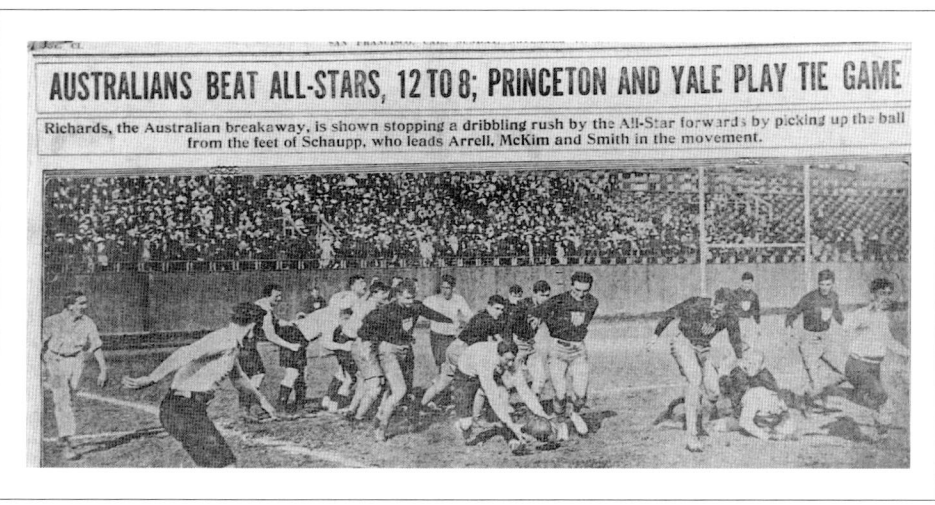

Tom Richards breaks through and is away against the American All Stars.

The 1908 Wallaby player reunion, held in Sydney, 12 years after the tour. Opposite Tom Richards is the great Chris McKivat.

discussed the moment, but considering his later disparaging remarks about the calibre of the British male, he obviously regarded his omission as a major slight.

While not embarrassed to be a British Isles representative, eventually playing in eleven games, for Rusty being a Lion paled against being a Wallaby, especially when the tourists were sent home with the *Athletic News* calling them a "poor lot".

For the rest of his life, Rusty hardly mentioned that he had been a Lion. In a letter to a Charters Tower friend, he revealed: "The Britishers did not leave an enviable reputation behind them, either on or off the field. They were very loosely managed, but still, they deserved, or were entitled to a good deal more consideration from the principal football centres visited.

"The team was much too weak for the undertaking, some of the players knew very little about the game at all, and it surprised me how they were even brought on tour. The Britishers have returned home, rather disappointed with the social side of the trip, much greater hospitality was expected than received.

"I never did much good with them, trouble seemed to follow me everywhere, and between weak ankles and gravel rash, I had no opportunity to do myself justice. But I was glad to have been playing when Britain won the second Test game in good style. I had a most interesting and enjoyable time, and learned much of South Africa, which does not cause it to loom any higher in my estimation."

In the end, the tour highlights for the British, who only won thirteen of their twenty-four games, was visiting diamond mines in Kimberley and famous Boer War battle sites, including the long rows of graves. "On several occasions we stood reading the various headstones, time and again the boys had to turn away to wipe their eyes, our hearts were so full of sorrow that none dared to speak."

Rusty also didn't stay in South Africa for too long either, finding mining work exasperating. While agreeing to his father's wishes and pursuing a mining career, he hated it, especially when in charge of a black mining group."A miner's occupation is at all times, and in any country, a dangerous calling; but when applied to Witwatersrand in South Africa, it becomes distinctly hazardous," Rusty wrote. "Not only does the African miner have to guard himself against falls of rocks and the ordinary risks that go with mining, but he has to face the death-dealing veil of 'dust' that hangs and floats through the working places like murky vapour. No man employed below the surface can escape this poisonous atmosphere. "

Rusty estimated the mortality among mining machinemen at about thirty per cent. "Those who do survive suffered the miner's disease, phthisis, or are treated terribly by the managers.

"It is not a hard matter to raise a miner's anger, and then the niggers come in for some tall cursing, probably a good thumping, and even a kicking.

"Several of the miners sitting around are plainly affected by the dread disease. Their eyes are sunken and glassy; holes are burrowed out behind the ears, and they cough long and painfully. When a miner is so badly stricken down that he has insufficient breath to climb up the slope, another man will take his place, and use the same big boxes in which to keep his coat and lunch, and to sit and sleep on. No one thinks of cleaning the boxes, or removing them." To overcome their pain, the natives resort to drink, which "in time becomes a necessity, a habit, and a curse". Not surprisingly there were countless shootings and riots around the Johannesburg mines.

Rusty was as disenchanted with the mentality of the South Africa. In a letter to his old Wallaby teammate Paddy McCue, who asked him of the possibility of a South African Rugby League team touring Australia, Rusty, when explaining that the professional game did not exist in that part of the world, said South Africans suffered from the "dreaded disease known as swelled head … and they have it in a most chronic form."

Rusty had to get out. The future looked far brighter in Australia — but this time not in Queensland. Instead the seaside village of Manly was his destination.

EIGHT

STARS AND BARS

MANLY, A TUCKED-AWAY HAVEN near the Sydney Heads, had the motto: "On the wings of pleasure-seven miles from Sydney, and a thousand miles from care". Rusty revelled in the seaside holiday atmosphere, parading along the boulevard, loved being a Manly Corso cowboy and a local identity. Manly was the perfect locale for the established sportsman. It was a village that centred on outdoor adventure, with the sea, surf, football and golf clubs close by. The big metropolis was a leisurely ferry trip away; all inhabitants thought themselves a member of a private club, and indulged in all local pursuits. As Rusty put it, Manly was the ultimate "Idler's Paradise."

Rusty moved into the area in 1911, and was soon involved in all its main sporting pursuits. He became a foundation member of the Manly surf lifesaving club, and took to the sea every morning and evening, battling the waves in front of the Corso and the breakers near Fairy Bower. He was surrounded by numerous sporting luminaries along the Manly coastline, including champion swimmer and boxer Harold Hardwick, and was the first Wallaby member of the surf club; later members included Bob Loudon, Aub Hodgson, Rex Mossop, Brian Cox and Tony 'Slaggy' Miller. Rusty's handsome, rugged features had every eligible and not so eligible Manly female chasing him, too.

He linked up with the Hill brothers, Ralph and William, who apart from strong links to Rugby administration were, among numerous other ventures, involved in the garment-knitting industry. Rusty worked for them as a travelling salesman throughout New South Wales, offering the latest line in singlets and sporting undergarments.

It was only to be expected that the local football club would take advantage of his talents. The links between the Manly surf and football clubs have for many decades been very strong, and a member of one invariably joined the other. This partnership has provided endless triumphs and trials for one of the more incestuous Rugby clubs in Australia. At the top level, it has not been one of the most successful in Sydney, with friendsship often getting in the way of pure, proper team selection, but it is still one of the most closely bonded of football clubs.

The club gave Rusty the base to pursue his next goal, a spot on another exotic Wallaby tour. The following year, Australia would embark on their first and only full-scale tour of the United States. Wallaby wanderlust had again struck Rusty. While Queensland were eager for him to play for them again, with him excelling on the side of the scrum in their 12-11 victory over a star-studded 1911 Sydney side, he decided that would be his farewell match for his old state.

He was now devoted to the Manly club, but his work on the road restricted his footballing appearances to just three games at the end of the 1911 season, against Newtown, Sydney University and Western Suburbs. He still enjoyed every minute on the field.

As he wrote in a letter to English journalist Laurence Woodhouse: "Football is much more pleasant to play in Sydney at the present time, the Northern Game [Rugby League] has weeded the players out.

"A few years ago, kicking and punching were freely and openly indulged in by the players. Now I am pleased to say the Union is hard and vigorous, but perfectly clean and fair. I feel sure our game will be bright and flowing when the Northern Game is dead and gone."

He was more committed the following season, again missing May and June because of his business travels, but playing in the final five matches for Manly at a variety of venues, including the Epping racecourse against Glebe. His versatility was again to the fore, playing in the centres against Central Southern, Easts and Glebe, and then five-eighth against Norths.

The Australian selectors still weren't convinced that Rusty was up to it. He was approaching thirty, and his flitting all over the field had not aroused the enthusiasm of the Sydney-based officials for a US tour.

The original invitation had come from the Californian Rugby Union, who had suggested a combined Australian and New Zealand team to tour. New Zealand knocked the invitation back, but Queensland accepted in their place, very much as a minor partner to New South Wales.

The team would be termed the Waratahs rather than the Wallabies, playing in the light blue NSW garb including the Waratah motif on the left breast, but with the word 'Australia' underneath. Rusty might havebecome a Manly resident, but the NSW selectors could not think of him as anything other than a Queenslander.

According to the *Sydney Mail*, Rusty was not selected in the original touring party. But his performance against University, when he returned to his rightful back row position for Manly, changed all that.

Rusty later said that at the time he was terribly out of form, and unfit. But he knew if he put his mind to it, he knew he could make the Australian team. He arrived at University Oval just before kickoff, with no football jersey in his kitbag. As there were no Manly jerseys left, he played in borrowed garb. As he later wrote: "In the different colours, they couldn't miss me."

Rusty also wouldn't have any problem getting time off work, as his employer, W.W Hill, was one of the main officials on the tour, in his other role as the secretary of the NSW Rugby Union, while brother Ralph, who had played for New South Wales against Queensland that year, was a member of the Australian forward contingent. W.W Hill, who eventually refereed several matches on tour, naturally gave his close mate and employee time off to accompany them on the most invigorating of adventures.

It was nowhere near as long as the Wallaby tour, but as fascinating, involving thirteen matches in the United States, including two against Stanford University, three against California University, and finally a Test against an American All Star team. Three games in Canada followed.

There was a core of 1908 tourists and some new names. Ward Prentice, who had played in both Tests on the first Wallaby tour and now boasted of being a Sydney cattle salesman, was skipper and led the back contingent, while Rusty was in charge of the forwards. Other team members were lawyers, teachers, postmen, draughtsmen, wharfies, labourers, builders, tram drivers, policemen, accountants, clerks, carpenters, and at least one "gentleman of leisure", as forward Ted Fahey was described by his teammates.

They also had an outgoing and sometimes controversial manager in Dr Otto Bohrsmann, who was prepared to talk publicly about any subject.

The team went via New Zealand on the *Moana*, with Bohrsmann immediately hitting the headlines in Wellington by saying that Rugby was not missing those who had taken the dirty Rugby League dollar.

Bohrsmann said that although Rugby had suffered a setback by losing players, "the cleavage had acted on Rugby like a spring cleaning, and the game had emerged cleaner and better in every respect". He added:

"Any man who had the slightest trait in his character towards playing the League game was absolutely worthless to the Rugby Union. Afterwards he would become worthless to himself. Professionals became wastrels on the sea of society forever."

The good doctor was as scathing when the Australian team arrived in San Francisco, after a rocky trip which saw most of the players suffer from seasickness and a small group not sighted on deck for the first week of the voyage. As the *San Francisco Chronicle* explained: "Even at so recent a date as Wednesday several members of the team were feeding the fishes and declining to accept any nourishment."

The *Evening Post* headlined its report: "Bohrman [sic] talks of Rugby paid coaches a disgrace". Then followed some fairly wild quotes for the times. Bohrsmann argued that the US training system was "mainly bosh", the paid coach system "a disgrace", and the Americans "haven't the right idea of their Rugby."

Stretching into full stride, Bohrsmann elaborated: "The minute you tell a man what he can and can't eat you make that man a prisoner. We never tell our men what they shall eat. They eat what they want to and they are always in bloomin' good condition. And smoking – it's a shame to deny a man his pipe just because he is playing football. Moderate smoking cannot hurt any athlete who is in good condition. Every one of our twenty-three men smokes right along. We find it does not impair their condition.

"For the paid coaching system I have no use. In Australia we know of no such system in our sports except among professionals. Paid coaches are a disgrace. They commercialise the game and degenerate the spirit of it. The game becomes a fight to win, not to play the game for the game's sake. 'Pon my word, it's a nasty abomination.

"And the chief difference, I think, between your American Rugby and the way we play it is that you play the man while we play the ball. Your ruggers play a closed game while we make it open."

With such an extroverted manager, the players knew they were about to have a good time. But not even they realised how outrageous it would become.

As five-eighth Bob Adamson later explained: "We were never in bed. That was the trouble. I never had such a time in all my life." W.W. Hill at one stage described the tour as being "very much of a holiday for these players." Often they were billeted on campus, and revelled in the wild student life.

They were soon notorious for playing up. Douglas Erskine began his report in the *Examiner* with the paragraph: "'Late to bed and early to rise' was the motto of the Australian Rugby players yesterday. The naughty boys stayed up until after midnight with their hosts at the British residents' smoker on Thursday evening, and they jumped out from under the covers at the stroke of seven."

One newspaper cartoon summed up everything. It showed a dashing American beauty pulling the petals off a Waratah bloom, while gazing longingly at an Australian player who bore an uncanny resemblance to Rusty. She was saying: "He loves me, he loves me not, he loves …" At the bottom of the cartoon was the caption: "All our girls are doin' it, doin' it, doin' it." No wonder the nights were long and arduous.

Even Rusty, the itinerant tourist, struggled with the pace, writing in the University of Nevada newspaper that "We have not had a dull moment since we first set foot in California. So much entertainment has been crowded into so small a space of time that it seems like so many months instead of weeks since our arrival."

Somehow they kept their minds together to perform up to par on the tour, even if there were the regular dramas. Rusty was soon the team mainstay, excelling in the first game against the Barbarians, played on a dirt ground that had been sprinkled with dust. According to Rusty "the dust was so thick that at times they were unable to locate the ball in the scrum or in the loose".

Australia won easily 29-8, and according to one reporter, William Unmack, Rusty "upheld his reputation as the greatest forward the world has ever seen". He added: "Richards was in the game all the time. In a lineout he pulled off one of the most remarkable kicks ever seen on a local field. He was falling, and had no one to pass to. Quick as a flash, the ball and his toes met with a single action, and it went flying for a back screw kick overhead, landing safely in the arms of one of his teammates."

Not so appealing was the sending off of five-eighth William 'Twit' Tasker for a late tackle when the Australians lost to the University of California in Berkeley. As Tasker left the field, he was involved in another altercation, later explaining that he "saw a Californian man make a pass at me, and I admit I took precautions to defend myself. That blue and gold man should also have gone off."

As Tasker headed for the dressing sheds, there was fun and games on the sideline. The Californian coach, James Schaeffer, approached Bohrsmann and gave the Australians permission to bring on a replacement for Tasker. But Bohrsmann refused, wanting nothing to do with Schaeffer, especially after his captain, Prentice, had complained that the Californian coach was the crux of the whole problem.

Prentice said that Schaeffer had run onto the field and instructed the referee to send Tasker off after the Australian had wrestled the University fullback to the ground. Tasker complained that he had not heard the referee"s whistle, and believed his actions were innocent.

Tasker was not the only send-off for the tour, with the youngest party member, Jimmy Flynn, who had just turned eighteen, ordered off for abusing a referee in the match against Combined Vancouver—Victoria.

The highlight of the tour was the Test against America, and it almost ended in a total disaster for the Waratahs.

Australia were expected to win easily, as, after all, they were up against part-time players who were relatively new to the game.

However, after an hour the Americans were leading 8-nil, with the Australians totally outplayed. The score could have been even more embarrassing, especially as two early American tries were disallowed, during a period where according to one report the Waratahs were "hopelessly outclassed". A forward pack which had never played together "made the Waratah celebrities look like novices in contrast".

So disgusted were the Australian supporters in the 10,000 crowd that the call of "throw your cigarettes away" rang around the St Ignatius Ground in Berkeley, in an obvious complaint about the team's apparent lack of conditioning, from a month of long days and late nights. Eventually Australia awoke from its slumber, scoring 12 points in as many minutes. The bald Toowoomba winger Ludwig Meibusch scored twice in as many minutes, but Prentice's inability to convert saw Australia still trailing at 8-6.

Eventually one of Australia's most versatile sportsman, Dan Carroll, who later coached the United States to Olympic gold success in 1920 and 1924, saved the tourists when he finished off an excellent backline move, started by Arthur "Wakka" Walker, a halfback renowned for drinking a glass of sherry at halftime to steady his Test nerves. Walker's early work and Carroll"s completion of the try secured an edgy 12-8 Australian victory.

The Australian players staggered off the field in near-disbelief, their manager explaining their feelings with: "My word you had me badly frightened." Bohrsmann then told the press: "It was a relief to see our boys come from behind. I thought we were in for a drubbing."

While Rusty was instrumental in saving Australia's skin, he also used the tour wisely, taking the opportunity to make some money on the side and fine-tune his journalistic skills by writing a series of articles for the *San Francisco Call*. Each article was highlighted by a photograph of Rusty in his training garb, with a football in his right hand.

The series was relatively staid, offering analysis of recent games, tips for coaches and players of training and match strategies. Rusty also gave advice on fitness, including further information on how to overcome a parched mouth. He offered the gems that one should never have supper in bed, and must always avoid pastries and "sluggish" foods. There was even the occasional barb directed at the local referees, who "seemed altogether too self important."

The Waratah management was also targeted. Rusty was unimpressed that in one game against the University of California, Bohrsmann had not allowed the home team to bring on replacements, and were restricted to thirteen men. "This is a most regrettable matter. One side or the other (or perhaps it was mutual) most certainly showed obstinacy, or lack of discretion. Nobody was more surprised and grieved than the Australian players when, at the conclusion of the match, they discovered that only thirteen men had opposed them."

But wherever possible he was positive, theorising that "Rugby is a game that develops the manly and unselfish qualities in a man. Players are taught self-preservation, adaptability and determination; to be courageous; brave in doing brave actions, resourceful and chivalrous."

It also was imperative to speak one's mind, as another Waratah players attempt in print showed.

Bob Adamson, the Waratah five-eighth, wrote a piece on Australia for the University of Nevada newspaper. It showed that back home racial equality was a long way off. "At present the population numbers about 4,750,000, made up almost entirely of white people. The comparatively few aboriginees [sic] that now remain represents, perhaps, the lowest type of man in the world today," Adamson wrote. "They are treacherous, wild and unintellectual. The advance of civilisation has driven them farther and farther into the back country where they are gradually dying out. It is now but a matter of a few years when the Australian aboriginee will be no more."

A few weeks later, the tour was over, after losing every game in Canada, where they struggled against oppositions, bolstered by British imports, including several Internationals. The bulk of the team immediately headed home, but Rusty had other plans. He had further adventures in mind, deciding to return via England and Europe.

The Bristol club soon heard of Rusty's inevitable arrival in their part of the country and immediately sent off letters in all directions in a bid to find him. He was sighted at Twickenham in the company of a number of old friends in the South African team, which was touring Britain and France that winter. He was soon coerced into playing for Bristol. Rusty was not exactly thrilled by this. He believed that his Rugby days were coming to an end, especially as he was struggling with a chronic ankle injury. But the lure of a trip through France with the

Midland and East Midlands counties team, who were about to play Toulouse and Perpignan, was enough incentive for him to get intensive treatment on his ankle and prepare for another adventure.

France was the ideal release, as he was soon depressed by the wettest of English winters. Again Rugby was the ideal passport for him to see sights no other Australian had enjoyed.

Rusty received an invitation from the East Midlands Rugby Union to meet the team at Charing Cross Station in time to catch the 9pm continental train to Toulouse via Dover, Calais and Paris, and "a little gargle first to break the ice". It was a rough trip even though the team, which included four English Internationals, had reserved compartments on the train. At every stop, "each available seat in our compartment were snapped up by Frenchmen, and the pressure of our best linguist and the presence of several menacing faces glaring at them did not make them retire; they simply sat on contentedly."

Rusty immediately revelled in everything French. The most memorable moment of the Toulouse fixture was the banquet afterwards. "The speech-making failed miserably, because it mattered not which language was used, one half of the room could not understand it, and would not wait for the interpreter to repeat it," Rusty wrote. "French and Briton drank deeply to one another without any burdensome exchange of words."

The next day he told his new teammates he wouldn't be accompanying them back to London. He had had enough of England and wanted to see the Continent. By himself.

He had a swag, a few tour guides, several books, a trusty pair of shoes and two changes of clothes. And he was off on an extensive walking tour of the country. Most nights he slept under the stars, in barns, in hollows, anywhere he could avoid using his small savings.

As a *Sydney Rugby News* correspondent later related: "He had 50 pounds. His teammates were much concerned. He could not do it. He had no French, etc, but Richards stated it was too cold in England for him. He would be all right."

Rusty left the team in Marseilles and immediately headed for Spain. After several weeks south, he walked along the edge of the Mediterranean, back over the Pyrenees, then the coast of France, to Biarritz, Tuscany, through northern Italy and into Switzerland through the Alps. For a time he lived in Biarritz, earning the honour of introducing surfing to France. Showing off his bodysurfing skills honed at the Manly surf club, he hit the Biarritz waves and astounded all with his ability to catch one into shore. "The sea ran in there and it became a custom for people to congregate on the beaches, to see 'the mad Englishman' come in on a wave. They had never seen a surf swimmer in Biarritz," explained the *Rugby News*.

For the best part of a week he tramped through the Pyrenees, catching the train on Saturday so he could play for Biarritz. He was even seconded by Toulouse to manage their side when they went on tour, including one trip to Bayonne, where he was convinced to put on the boots and add to his long list of illustrious teams for which he had appeared. In the end, Rusty played a succession of matches for Toulouse, and could proudly claim that he had helped make them win the championship of France.

There were occasional sightings by fellow Australians. In a letter to the *Sydney Mail*, W.M. Early wrote: "With a party of tourists, I was sitting outside a small cafe in a Spanish village on the Pyrenees Mountains when a lanky individual covered with dust and carrying a swag, strolled up and called for food and wine in a strange mixture of Australian and French.

"Richards had been playing rugger with an English team against France. He left the team at Marseilles and went for a stroll into Spain. He was then making his way back along the South Coast of France through Northern Italy, over the Simplon Pass in Switzerland, to Paris and back to Englan — all alone on foot, and carrying a swag in real Australian fashion."

At the start of his walking tour, sitting in the Cafe Lafayette in Toulouse, where he had dined on fowl cream soup, hare Saint Hubert and beef rumpsteak Renaissance, world Rugby's first true globetrotter wrote back to his Charters Towers mates. The letter was run verbatim in the local newspaper.

He explained why he was travelling alone. "The weather in England since my arrival there from America on Christmas Eve has been most wicked, nothing but rain and fog, impossible weather for a lover of a bright sky and fresh air. And as the south of France offers soft sunshine, I could on no account return with the team to England.

"I have yearned for foreign experiences, and now I have that opportunity in all its fullness, and return to Australia only when my purse is too light to remain any longer in Europe."

He even ended up in Paris, where his sporting career took another unexpected tangent when the French authorities asked him to join their coaching staff for a week to prepare for their International match against Wales. For several days, he attended the French training sessions, offering them advice and tactics to counter a team he had tussled with five years previously. He almost masterminded an unexpected 8-all draw, until the home side lost when the game unexpectedly went into extra time because of a refereeing error, enabling Wales to tally three points for victory.

As far as Rusty was concerned, it was still a moral victory for his newfound friends. "My Frenchmen won, but they played a minute over time and Wales, kicking a goal, had the victory, but by jove, my Frenchmen really won." It took France another fifteen years before they eventually defeated Wales.

Eventually the money ran out, and Rusty had to return home via South Africa. Such was his fame that the *Sydney Morning Herald* was there to greet him when the *Ballarat* came into Sydney Harbour. The *Herald* said Rusty boasted "the distinction of having played the game in more countries that any other living player". He waxed lyrical about his moments in France, stating that the locals "seemed more inclined to trust me than their own countrymen". "I did not know a word of their language, but I always managed to make myself understood. It was a fine experience, and I saw some magnificent country that one could not reach other than by touring in this way. The Pyrenees were absolutely glorious, and the sights there alone repaid me for any hardships or trouble I had to go through."

Rusty, who believed that his weak ankle prevented him from playing any more serious football, then officially announced his retirement. However his links with football, or the *Herald*, would not cease. Realising that journalism was easier than being a travelling salesman, he contributed a series of articles on international football for the *Herald*, including one of the attitude of different crowds. The English were noble sports as long as they winning, leaving an "atmosphere of superiority and haughtiness" which was obnoxious. The Welsh, in the smaller towns, were "one-sided and unfair." The Americans delighted in making a terrific noise, "devoid of sporting sentimentality, and, unlike the English, have no time for a beaten man". The French are a "shifty, impulsive and unreliable crowd", while the South Africans were probably the most level-headed where "the best sporting traditions of the British race are splendidly maintained".

Rusty even covered several matches of the 1914 English Rugby League tour of Australia for the *Herald*- including the third Test at the Sydney Cricket Ground, where in the home side were several of his old teammates, including Robert Craig (former owner of Bertie the carpet snake). Rusty picked a good Test to cover as this was the famous Rorke's Drift match where, in the tradition of British soldiers repelling waves of Zulu natives, an undermanned British team defeated a full-strength Australia XIII to win the Test and series. In the second half the visitors lost three players — one damaging his leg, the second a shoulder, while the third was concussed. Rusty led his report with: "Never was a more heroic exhibition of pluck and determination seen on a football field than that displayed by the Northern Rugby team in winning the third Test match and rubber from Australia."

But Rusty's days in hitting a typewriter for Australia's most prominent broadsheet were relatively shortlived.

NINE

OUR COUNTRY'S FINEST

IT IS NO SURPRISE that when Britain declared war on Germany on 4 August 1914, Rusty was on the road.

In northern New South Wales he was mixing work with pleasure, travelling through the New England region selling underwear for the Hill brothers, while managing the Manly Rugby team against a succession of country sides. These included Inverell, and one of its wings was his younger brother Bert.

But the never-ending reports of unrest in Europe, and the near daily declaration of wars between different nations, distracted Rusty. While hardly a passionate enthusiast for everything British, with his view tainted by his close sporting ties with the Mother Country he, like thousands of his fellow Australians, believed there was no alternative but to enlist immediately. It was the right thing to do, an opportunity to show that the young, flourishing nation of Australia was willing to respond in time of need. As well, enlisting appealed to his broad adventurous streak.

Recruitment for the Australian Imperial Force began on 10 August and Rusty applied straight away. However because of an onrush of volunteers from all over the country, he found himself caught up in red tape, having to travel down from Brisbane to Sydney by boat, and after several days on a "rough, seasick passage" appear in person at Victoria Barracks to enlist. Rusty wanted to join the Light Horse Brigade, believing its sense of dash was more exciting that the supposedly more regimented military. But "after wasting four days I found they were full up."

Instead he joined the Army Medical Corps, enlisting in the First Field Ambulance, First Infantry Battalion, and going into camp at Queen's Park on 26 August. The first few days revolved around haphazard organisation and a general lack of leadership.

"The first day I drilled with an awkward crowd of fellows and was also an awkward man myself. The officers did not know their drill either. Most of them are doctors and without much in the way of military knowledge," Rusty wrote in his diary that night.

Camp facilities were rudimentary. His bed was "hard and cold", his neck stiff, hips and shoulders aching. He was surrounded by painful low-lifes, stupid enlistees, while his demeanour was not helped by endless drills. Thankfully relief came with the occasional sighting of old footballing friends. Harald Baker, who almost matched his elder brother 'Snowy' Baker in all-round sporting achievements, arrived at Queen's Park one night to provide an escape route. Harald, who had just played in the three Test series against New Zealand as a back rower, was adept in boxing, swimming, water polo, wrestling and swimming. He was an Eastern Suburbs hero, especially after he and fellow Wallaby Jimmy Clarken saved eight lives and brought in four bodies in a mass surf rescue after bathers were carried out in a rip at Coogee.

That night, Harald showed off his horse-riding prowess, and revealed a family secret to Rusty. As Rusty wrote in his diary: "Harald Baker came down to the camp on a lovely horse and took me away to his home in Randwick for dinner."His wife is nice and very young. They were married when she was only seventeen years of age. It appears that Harald, as well as the girl's mother thought she was seventeen, but when her mother's lawyers in England started to fix up her estate they discovered their mistake. They have one child. We wandered around Coogee in the moonlight and I admired it immensely. I got into camp at 10.45pm, after taking off my leggings, boots and socks, and leaving them in a tree to return for them, as I had to beat the guard."

Beating the guard was not Rusty's only problem in his early weeks as a soldier. Due to delays in the departure for Europe the drillwork soon became tedious, the food, dominated by bully beef, roast mutton, bread and jam, was hardly appetising, those in command he considered lacked intelligence, direction or morals, and his fellow soldiers generally appalled him. He found those in the Light Horse Ambulance "conceited", the camp dominated by "loafers", with all of Australian manhood's worst attributes coming to the surface when free clothing arrived at the barracks.

"It seems to me that the average man has, with all his years of civilisation, raised himself but little above an animal, as when these clothes were given out their eyes were as those of a begging and anxious dog."

Adding to his overall irritable state was that the level of conversation among the recruits was gutter stuff, and he believed he was being wasted in doing ambulance work rather than undergoing proper military training.

"The language one hears in our camp and all around the place is vile and noticeable amongst the empty-headed young fellows mostly. I regret more and more the fact that I am not in the real fighting line instead of buggering about with ambulance work, or "linseed lancers." There is always that doubt that a fellow is likely to be termed a 'quitter'. I feel ashamed to be with a non-combatant side; ambulance work is pung and unfit for an able-bodied man. I should be with the Light Horse and got right into the fighting line."

Overall camp life was "perhaps not so hard as it is depressing.". Marathon marches to the beach at Maroubra didn't help, even though there was light relief when Rusty was allowed to ride the camp horses to Coogee for a swim in the surf. These were moments of sunlight in an otherwise gloomy world.

"The average soldier, as far as my experience goes with the A.M.C., is an arrogant, conceited and boastful person, 'superb grandstand players'. Always judging their standard of manhood by the worst man in the squad. The Englishmen mostly are a loud-voiced, empty, inconsiderate lot, and can be easily picked out by their stiff and bound up movements." His seniors were as unimpressive, including a Sergeant Coleman, who "does not know decent English ... His commands savour of Woolloomooloo. He is a disgrace."

Rusty, like thousands of other restless recruits, could not leave Australia quickly enough. However there were endless false alarms and delays before the first contingent sailed towards the European battlefields because of concerns at government level over the lack of escort or cover for the convoy of ships containing Australian and New Zealand soldiers, and the fear of German naval attacks. Eventually the concerns subsided and the transports headed for Western Australia. Among them in the convoy on 20 October was the *Euripides*, with Rusty, the 1st Infantry Brigade, the 3rd and 4th Battalions and the 1st Field Ambulance, all on the ship.

"The eventful day has at last arrived," Rusty wrote in his diary. "The camp was astir at 5.30 with kits packed and handed in by 7am. A damned poor breakfast and we were on the road by 7.45." Tram cars were used to transport the soldiers to Fort Macquarie, where the *Euripides* was docked. "There were but few people out this morning as we passed along Oxford Street, yet there were some stirring little incidents as we drove by. One aged man holding a stout stick for support tried with as brave a heart as ever a soldier possessed to stand at attention. Another old warrior straightened himself by the aid of a verandah and saluted. Lots of men and women waved a pleasant good-bye, but it was only skin deep; nobody but ignorant people could treat such a mission as we are about to undertake so lightly and almost with frivolity."

As the 3000-plus soldiers boarded the *Euripides*, the Coast Artillery, with their brass band aboard the S.S *Miner*, floated around the boat, "playing cheerful tunes, but just before leaving they struck up 'Auld Lang Syne'". They finally played 'God Save the King' and I was fighting again to keep back the tears as we stood lined up at attention on the top deck. Many of our well-wishers waved flags and shouted frantically. They were in earnest too, but it was a couple of people on the *Burra Bra* making for Manly that made water come to my eyes.

"They stood still and held a blue Australian flag outstretched. It was plain to me what was meant. They were cold, level-headed persons and seemed to say 'Keep your end up, boys, wherever you're going to, just for the honour and for the glory of your dear Australia, and your love for the mother country.'

"It fairly thrilled me through and through. It was one of those silent signals 'full of meaning and respect'."

Eventually the *Euripides* steamed down the Harbour at 5.30pm, but to everyone's astonishment anchored in Mosman Bay for the night. Ten minutes later there was a mad scramble for any available bunks or hammocks.

"They were hung very close together, so much so that when one man turned over he woke up the man next to him and set a whole line of them swinging. Yet the fellows seemed to favour sleeping on hammocks to the ground at Queen's Park."

The next interruption was at 5.30am when the ship eventually headed towards the Heads, and "steamed down past Watson's Bay with a high wind and blinding rain".

"We were running fairly steady yet before breakfast the decks were covered with prostrated forms. The 'fall in' was sounded at 10am, and it was sorrowful to see the fellows dragging themselves and one another up for the parade. No more forlorn spectacle could be witnessed than a crowded troopship on the first day at sea."

Adding to the discomfort was the lack of hammocks for the soldiers, leading "to a terrible congestion of men both underneath and on decks". As well, the announcement of their meagre ship rations failed to raise their spirits. Their weekly ration consisted of 1 pound of bread per man, ? of a pound of meat, 8 ounces of jam per week, 2 ounces of salt, 6 ounces of pickle, 1 pound tin of condensed milk per week, along with 14 ounces of sugar, $10\frac{1}{2}$ ounces of butter and $4\frac{1}{2}$ pound of potatoes. Hardly a feast, especially as the soup was "as thin as water and salty" and the corned beef was as "tough and hard as possible". And there appeared to be a lack of upright young men on the ship as well. "There are some really terrible-looking fellows amongst the troops and reports that the Germans have been looting and murdering will not be any worse than what these wretches are capable of."

Rusty, who all his life had been a wandering loner, soon distanced himself from the other troops, hiding away whenever he could to read and write. Before leaving, he had approached several newspapers and magazines, including the *Sydney Morning Herald* and *Sydney Mail*, with the intention of writing first-hand reports from the war.

He had bought a camera from the *Sydney Mail* in the hope of providing graphic shots from wherever he ended up. Always with him was a small leather-bound notebook in which each night, no matter where he was, he would record his thoughts of the day. It soon became his release, where he graphically outlined his emotions, fears, loves, and failings, a chance for him to attempt to explain the mysteries of life, especially the futility of war. Each day there would be a revelation, or an unexpected elaboration. He never shirked any issue.

He could be harsh, but also soft, especially when talking about lost loves back home. On the *Euripides*, he had a lot of time to think about one passionate lover he had left behind, a Manly girl named Zelda. As the ship approached Albany Rusty admitted writing a six-page love letter to her, where he "confessed much of my longing for her, and at the same time giving her liberty to get another man".

"If he is a man I won't grumble. I would not say this, but how is it possible for me to offer anything in the way of comfort and convenience. Yet it will come hard to part with her, and I cannot keep her waiting for what may be a forlorn hope."

Five days later Rusty wrote: "I am very worried over Zelda today. I try to talk and keep from her, but alas I cannot! Yet I don't quite know whether it's real affection or longing, but it's got me down."

The following day, Rusty admitted to being "very lovesick indeed." "My mind floats back to it, and its many problems as soon as I take it off my reading. In fact I am so badly hit that I compare every female character I read of with her."

Several weeks later … "She occupies a lot of my mind. Sometimes I feel sorry that I ever left Manly, then it dawns upon me that it would be better for both of us if I never went back there at all!"

Not even the incessant gambling on the ship could distract him. Although all gambling games were barred, with one man sentenced to ninety hours in the cells when caught playing crown and anchor, there were numerous betting schools, with large sums of money changing hands every day. The most popular games were two up, under and over seven, top of the house, poker, and naturally crown and anchor. The gambling became even more popular during the week the *Euripides* was berthed with the rest of the Australian convoy in Albany, after making the grand entrance in the harbour with her decks, according to the peerless war historian C.E.W. Bean, "lined with troops standing rigidly to attention, her band playing …"

While the British Cabinet deliberated over whether the Australian and New Zealand convoy should head to Europe via the Cape instead of by Egypt, Rusty had to deal with a family tragedy. At Albany he discovered that his brother Charlie had been killed in a mining accident in Johannesburg, crushed by a groundfall. After reading the report of how Charles and a "native" had been killed by a "fall of hanging ground in the Glencairn Mine", Rusty wrote: "I have read hundreds of similar paragraphs in the years that I was mining, and every one of them only helped to tell me that my own name would appear there if I did not get away from the damnable mining gamble. Charlie got away from it too for some time and seemed to be settling down to a business life, but the lure of big cheques without any financial responsibility was too great. I wrote to both Ruth [Charlie's wife] and Mother tonight and tears streamed down my face. It all seems so hard, cruel and unwarranted. Poor Ruth, and fancy little John, asking anxiously for his daddy.

"A father's pride and joy left without a guardian, friend and father. Lilly is only a few months old, but a girl should have the guiding hand and advice of a friend and father also. Mother must be in a terrible state, with Father so bad too, and I playing soldiers, with our lives in danger.

"The first tears that have rolled from my eyes for many, many years did so when writing to Ruth and thinking of little John asking so plaintively for his daddy. It's a harder and a more cruel, unaccountable world than ever I have previously accused it of being and I have been very bitter from time to time. I went to bed very despondent this night …

"Yet death is always on the list in mining occupations and more particularly in Africa where I have found lives are cheaply held. Father is surely close to his end, judging by his own letters — even mining has cost him his life too. I recognised the danger a long time ago and fought hard to influence the family against the miserable slave-like work, and now that the extreme penalty is paid I feel it very much. The misery of my last five months' stay [in Africa] there in the mines still haunts me. Mining is unquestionably a horrible occupation."

Rusty needed no reminding that his father's two brothers had also both been killed in mining accidents in America. Another cause of anxiety was that whatever he sent back to his family was now being censored severely, to the point where "we get printed cards with sentences on, and you have to cross out, leaving something to the effect that 'I am quite well and hope you are the same'. Damned nonsense, we all seem to think."

He remained in a state of depression for some time, complaining one night: "My age is troubling me considerably of late. I am too old in years and in mind to be travelling with a crowd of fellows like this."

And as the ship left Albany on November 1 for Egypt, he began to think more and more of the horrors ahead. A few light craft followed the *Euripides* out to sea, where "in one a woman continued to wave her handkerchief enthusiastically to give us encouragement on our voyage of legalised murder.

"The whole business seems almost unbelievable. Thirty-five ships laden with men and weapons, some 30,000 in number, including some of the country's very best men and most valuable assets. There is something wrong with the world. This is how we sailed out from Albany, in mournful procession, for a destination unknown, enshrouded in mystery, making a course westerly."

Not even a church service a few hours later could settle Rusty. "The Chaplain tried to justify the Allies' position and asked God for protection and deliverance. The irony of it all! What hypocrisy! Surely this great God, if he had the power to influence victory in any particular form, would also have the power to prevent it at the very first and before lives were sacrificed." His father's religious fervour had not rubbed off onto Rusty.

Adding to his humiliation was that he had to stand guard over the isolation area, "or in other words the pox patients, of whom there are still 40. My duty was to keep men away from the isolation area which contained venereal patients, with three already discharged. This seems terrible on one ship only and gives an idea of the prevalence of this disease even in Sydney where prostitution is prohibited."

This was far from the only serious illness. On November 8, Rusty wrote: "We learnt that a private named Kendall, a policeman from Bathurst, had died of pneumonia. Our ship pulled out of the line a little and buried the body off the well deck. It was a silent and impressive ceremony."

Another soldier died of pneumonia the following day, while a third was on his deathbed downstairs. The only news that could brighten the troops was that the *Sydney* had successfully veered off from the convoy and had bombed the German cruiser, the *Emden*, which had already sunk or captured twenty-five Allied steamers, two warships, and effectively paralysed Britain's far Eastern sea-trade.

At 11.10am on 9 November came the signal from the *Sydney*: "Emden beached and done for." This message prompted scenes of jubilation on all of the other Australian ships. "Great excitement prevails," Rusty wrote that night. "Men are cheering wildly at the news of the *Sydney*'s defeat of the *Emden*. We have had three different messages during an hour telling us of the *Sydney*'s victory. The men and singing and cheering still. The band play 'God save the King', with all standing at attention and midst perfect silence." Adding to the joy was that the troops were given a half-day holiday.

After a brief stop in Colombo, where the troops were not allowed on shore, much to Rusty's relief as there would have been "much stealing at the native stores and generally bad and childish behaviour", the ships were again directed west. Still hardly any knew where they were going. Some thought they were headed for India to act as garrison troops, to release British regulars to fight in France.

Most hoped they were heading closer to the action, with the bulk eager not to be mere observers, but actual participants in the biggest adventure of their life. Virtually all wanted to be at the Western front. Rusty simply wanted to get out of it alive. The voyage gave him time to evaluate himself and be brutal about his strengths and weaknesses.

He wrote on 19 November: "I should get down and study figures so that I may be able to follow a commercial life on my return to Sydney and hold my own at it. If a decent position came along I would, I feel sure, marry and force myself to settle down to a domestic life, which I now believe I was more cut out for than aimless wandering, but should I fail in a commercial life I, being used to solitude, would go into one of the hard fighting mining countries and try my fortune at prospecting.

"A city life on less than 4 pounds a week would be no good at all, then someone may have to look after Mother when Father is gone. This is indeed an uncertain and precarious world, and although I have come through it fairly well still I have a long way to go yet to reach a desired standard.

"I sometimes wish I was like the other fellows around about me so that I could take part in their cheap, but often humorous conversations. I seem to have set all social matters to a certain standard of refinement and honesty which I believe is really too high for even myself to live up to properly. Then again I am purely a practical, and perhaps a methodical kind of person with a sense of taste that is easily jarred and thrown out of gear. Then again I am irritable and almost offensive.

"This trouble – impatience — leaves many of the fellows wondering what sort of a case I really can be. Perhaps I should not regret it as very little hard can come of it but I would like to be brighter and freer in my light chatter."

Eventually everyone on board realised that somewhere near Europe was their destination, and on 29 November a "hell of a chatter was going on" when they found they were bound for Egypt. The Gulf of Aden "a dreary, desolate place" was negotiated, and the *Euripides* steamed into the Red Sea, with what seemed to be "the whole of our fleet with us and the British cruiser *Yarmouth* at the head.

"This morning I sat down midship on a large pile of potatoes which have been there for six weeks, so you might well imagine the stink of diseased potatoes that arose, and to make it 50 times worse the sun beat terribly hot from the awning." Apart from the stench, the lack of accommodation was also getting everyone down. "There is quite a lot of ill-feeling in the ranks as to the kingly way the officers are living compared with the roughness of ourselves. There is a two-roomed cabin at the isolation area half of which is used to treat 44 venereals with two hospital attendants to care for them. In the other half is a young officer, who is also a venereal patient and, mark you, he has the same room as the 44 men and three orderlies to wait on him alone. The men sleep all over the deck and get a very rough time when it rains. This it frequently did before reaching Colombo."

And it became even more cramped when 120 men were placed in the hospital confines suffering with ptomaine poisoning which had emanated from the cookhouse. The meal that brought everyone down was boiled rabbit with beans."The fellows are lying everywhere and 'bunny' is the accused one, though many of the troops solemnly argue that no blame can be attached to our great and natural production."The next day Rusty, too, succumbed to food poisoning. "I was one of the 900 men to suffer last night. While I was writing at 8pm with troops groaning round about I felt the symptoms coming on and at 11pm I got the axe right through. My tummy twisted about like a spring mattress and felt as though a violent thunderstorm was raging therein.

"Boiled rabbit is being blamed for all of the bother, but surely poor bunny could not have caused all this commotion. When I came downstairs men were lying in heaps. Some had fallen out of their hammocks, others hadn't sufficient strength to get into theirs, so they just lay there. Some had slipped under the mess tables vomiting and groaning — never have I seen or experienced anything of the kind."

Not surprisingly few were up on deck while the *Euripides* negotiated the 160 kilometres of the Suez Canal through the Sinai Desert, to Port Said, where "gangs of niggers on each side were running baskets of coal weighing, perhaps 45 lbs, up planks ... All around the ship are boats of traders and musicians, but they have to pass us and go on the other transports as our sentry are told to keep them off and in doing so several shots have been fire, blanks I think."

The following day the first of the Australian convoy reached Alexandria, the final stop. This was Rusty's first chance in seven weeks to get off that godforsaken boat and feel solid earth beneath his feet.

TEN

SCALING THE SPHINX

HE TIMED HIS ESCAPE PERFECTLY. The troops weren't supposed to leave the *Euripides* but Rusty, who had been cooped up on a ship without leave for so long, had other ideas. A new city beckoned, and not even the presence of military police on the dock was going to stop him.

And he was desperate to get off that horrible ship. As he later wrote: "The starvation and misery endured on the voyage over in the *Euripides* will never be forgotten, much as I would love to overlook it." Realising that the MPs were stationed on the most direct route to Alexandria, Rusty and a mate, Bob Marrott, "bribed a nigger boatman to run us across to Marine Street for a shilling … Once safely on the streets our hearts beat much lighter."

They went through the native quarters and onto the Hotel Majestic, where Rusty celebrated the journey with a shot of whisky before enjoying their first proper meal in weeks. A French cafe was found and three eggs, a little finely chopped bacon with bread, toast, butter and delicious coffee and milk were "served cleanly". Then it was time for some old-fashioned haggling, and a view of Pompey's Pillar and the Catacombs.

"We had a terrible row with the cabman over his payment question as usual. The official to show us over the ruins and Catacombs which run underground for 100 or more metres had a very poor grip of English, so that we only discovered that this huge pillar was made of five stones of red granite. The cabman was still waiting for his fare when we came out, after going through the tunnel with a lamp and seeing the niches into which the mummies were once placed. I gave the cabman the same fare that he previously refused and muttering to himself he drove away." Another clandestine trip with a boatman, and "we got aboard safely, passing the guard on the wharf and gangway in such a business-like way that we were unchallenged."

At 8.30 the next morning, with a tin of bully beef and some bread under their arms, everyone was herded off the *Euripides* and onto a train headed for a special railway siding built especially for the Australasian troops in the heart of Cairo.

Rusty was again restless. After unloading some waggons, sneaking off with some tinned fruit and a bottle of whisky, Rusty waited with the rest for a tramcar to take them to their training camp.

"The journey was full of Egyptian wonderment, more so with the Pyramids standing out representative of 5000 years ago. The distance was about eight miles, then we had to unload and look after baggage. Murphy then came along and we decided to 'bolt off' and do the Pyramids and Sphinx.

"It meant walking ¾ mile only. There we were assailed by several guides and as usual in black tourist countries they would not take 'no', emphasised with a flourish of adjectives, for an answer. I despised the thought of having a guide at all, but as we were laden with the whole of our tin can equipment, and there was no place to put it away safely, with Murphy a little doubtful as to his athletic ability, I consented to taking guide No 25 chiefly to carry our equipment.

"The moon was showing signs of an awakening as we started up the uneven rock steps, mostly between 2ft 3in and 3 foot high. Therefore it was awkward, being a high stretch from one to the other.

"Murphy's legs suffered before reaching the first half. The nigger gave him a hand. This worried me to see a black man lending aid, so I got in and assisted him to the top where we remained for perhaps 40 minutes, deeply inspired by the whole scene, a scene altogether too huge to form any first impression other than the easy ascent and the stocky shape compared with the needle-like appearance at a distance.

"The point that bothered me most was the fact that all these huge boulders were brought from miles away taking thousands of labourers and years of work just to satisfy the vanity of a king.

"On one side, looking to the east and in the direction of Cairo, there was little but flooded land; on the other two sides was little but sandy desert.

"The mystic haze was particularly noticeable. We discharged the guard and went off to the Sphinx which was perhaps a mile back over a rough sandy track. It was disappointing as we approached it from the north-western side. It seemed so small and different to what we expected, but when we moved around to the east it pleased us and was three times as high.

"Fancy a poor miner from northern Queensland seeing and glorifying in the world's great sights as I have done. It makes me feel sometimes as though there is a screw short somewhere." The pair, dazzled by what they had seen, returned to camp, and in the shadows of the Pyramids, with numerous other battalions, "dossed down in the moonlight".

Strangely Rusty almost felt at home. Between Alexandria and Cairo, he had sighted Australian gum trees, mulberries, bananas, cotton, tomatoes, maize, date palms, castor oil, thorn trees, weeping willows, sugar-cane, even bougainvillea. And within a few days, an Australian flag was fluttering from the top of the Second Pyramid. His first impressions were "very good".

Soon Rusty, with thousands of other AIF soldiers stationed in Cairo because of a delay in constructing the required camp accommodation in England as well as the entry of Turkey into the war placing Egypt under threat, found himself working to a rhythm. They endured at least eight hours of hard, intensive training, and then at night enjoyed the delights of Cairo and nearby villages.

The ratbaggery of the Australian soldier was never far from the surface. They were all innocents wanting to see the world, refusing to waste any opportunity. After a five-course meal at the Continental Hotel, they would wander down to the European quarter, "where low-down cabarets were going big guns, brothels of the most horrid type with soldiers walking in and out, or laughing and holding the foul slatternly bitches. The lanes and alleyways were as putrid and ugly".

Despite the warnings of syphilis and signs in the camp explaining that every prostitute in Egypt was re "more or less infected with disease", and through sex soldiers would be infected with venereal disease, smallpox, enteric and dysentery, each night the brothels were overflowing with Australian troops.

Eventually this led to wild scenes, especially one night where Australian and New Zealand soldiers rioted in the Wasser, the brothel district of Cairo. When told of an unconfirmed rumour that one of theirs had been stabbed in a brothel the soldiers, already disenchanted by the bad alcohol in that area as well as the diseases received from the prostitutes, took revenge, throwing prostitutes, their pimps, even pianos from the brothels into the alleyways, and setting fire to beds, furniture and clothing. A Greek tavern was burnt down, while the military police, attempting to bring order, were bombarded with stones and bottles.

The locals were as keen to have the Anzacs on, especially as they were upset that so many of them had frequented brothels without paying, or were simply wandering through the area causing trouble.

When it was time to go home, the soldiers would coax the cabdrivers to race each other.

"After six miles we came upon a number of cabs with Australians getting back to camp. Our driver got warmed up and racing started. We beat several at the trot, then we took them on at a gallop. The race was terrific for so narrow a road, lined on both sides with large acacia trees closely together. The wheels came together and grated. It looked a certainty on a smash-up but with our horses tiring fast the other cab drew away and won an honourable and exciting race. I never had such dare-devil excitement for years."

Another diversion was camel rides for afternoon tea at Mena House, the historic hotel located in the shadows of the Pyramids which had become a hospital staffed by Anzac nurses. Or one could explore the tombs of the Sphinx and the Pyramids, which by now had been graffitied by Australian solders, who had written the initials all over it. Rusty's were among them. Rusty found the Temple of the Sphinx "very much in ruins", but decided that the tombs of the King and Queen tomb were far more impressive.

Within weeks, the Pyramids had been placed out of bounds, but that did not stop Rusty. "I waited some time for officers to pass by, then I started up, not so much with a view to reaching the top, as to having a good look so that I could return at another time. The view was glorious and so was the satisfied spirit of conquest. I took several photos, and prepared to descend as dinner time was approaching. I found coming down rather difficult and many times I had to rest a minute to collect myself, as looking down 450 feet between one's legs to find a foothold just beneath one is not conducive to steadiness." Another time Rusty attempted to throw a rope over the Sphinx, so he could climb up its side and onto its head, but soon gave up as he couldn't get the right trajectory.

But Rusty could never succumb to the distraction of the brothels, or the street prostitutes. "The prevailing price seemed to be two shillings, but, ah God! I don't even get an idea, much less an understanding, of your way of working when such women exist to ruin and kill by their foul diseases, the young, ignorant and unfortunate, inexperienced men as they do. It's just awful."

On the night of the Wasser riot Rusty was at camp, trying to avoid the officers who were conducting a gambling raid outside the mess room. He kept his head down. Instead he remained lovesick for those back at home, especially Zelda, and another woman named Win. His diary repeatedly mentions them both, explaining in one sentence that he is depressed about being a guard because it is a "farce and waste of time"; the next that he "cannot help my thoughts running back to Sydney with a decent job in town travelling and settled down with Zelda. At the same time I know full well that we could not blend."

Over the weeks his entries included: "Wrote a letter to my dear W.T.B. Oh this woman does make me think of my duties in life. I feel as though I must get her, but then how are we going to live in peace and at ease; though I am willing enough to work surely and like a man amongst men. ... A letter from Manly today was something to make me think very deeply about, as we is waiting and God knows I do not think I would actually keep a girl waiting. A girl's life is so different to a man's and it is a shame to keep one waiting with a chance of nothing ever happening ...Win wrote a nice kindly letter. By jove, it's up to me to marry this girl if the fortunes of living favour at all ... W.T.B. is troubling me frightfully. I feel in my heart I must win her, but then she does not seem my type and marriage needs money to make it successful. ... It's strange that I should be so hopelessly overcome by this girl, when all hard reasoning sums against having anything to do with her, moreso when it means a poverty-stricken existence such as mine seems to hold out. It all seems so hard that a person has ofttimes to remain single owing to the abnormal cost of living."

However his thoughts were also diverted towards local women. Throughout the weeks, Rusty took hundreds of photographs of the local area and scene, sending them back to the *Sydney Morning Herald* and *Sydney Mail*. In Cairo, he found a convenient photo developing shop, and an attractive woman behind the counter.

"The little Italian girl behind the cash register has a pretty voice and her English is so entertaining that I gave her a note requesting her name and address so that I might send her a postcard. It's a treat to hear a woman's voice after the men, men, men around the camp. Things are so bad that it even sounds pleasant when in conversation a fellow is referred to as 'miss'. It might look stupid in cold ink, but it is a relief to hear it nonetheless."

Her name was Victorine Warshafsky, but Rusty was unable to get past first base with her. When he next went to the developing shop, she said shyly that it was against the custom of the country to meet or go out with young men. Then he received a letter from her, explaining that her brother-in-law had sighted the letter, "and would not let her see it even". "A woman's lot in this country is the very devil right enough," was his comment.

The festive season arrived, with Christmas Eve spent exploring the interior of the three Pyramids, as Rusty "had no desire to go amongst the noise and drunkards of Cairo". The main task was avoiding the native guides, with Rusty having "a happy knack of shaking these fellows off but there are so many of them and they just 'come out of the ground', interrupting one's conversation with a nasty jar, especially when one is living and puzzling with 5000-year-old problems, which are so common in this weird part of the world."

Christmas Day was spent in Cairo, fighting the hordes. "At a cafe we fought hard for a light meal and a glass of beer, and were pestered by peddlers who wanted to sell razors, cigarettes, silks, sticks, small boxes, and any number of bootblacks. Even a juggler came and added to this cadging, robbing herd of niggers. It is this kind of bother and interference that makes Cairo a bore for me.

"Xmas in camp was only recognised by the extra rations allowed for dinner and the inspection of the messes by the whole outfit of officers was more cheered by the fellows. The extras consisted of a 1lb tin of plum pudding to three men; one tin of fruit to four men; two ginger nuts and two soda biscuits per man and four bottles of wine to the mess of 24 men. Everybody was remarkably happy and the scene mindful of a Sunday picnic. The usual portion of stew, however, formed the basis of the dinner."

It was hardly surprising that most days the soldiers complained about the standard of food, and lack of. The officers were repeatedly cursed, as shown in one of the most popular songs in camp.

> The officers get turkey
> The sergeants they get ham
> But all the poor old privates get
> Is bread and bloody jam.

Rusty was relatively restrained compared to the bulk of Anzac troops over the New Year period. On 26 December he wrote: "The New Zealanders are having much fun about town with cars and bagpipes, or other music. They race around the town and very often parade, with hordes of niggers in their wake. Tonight I am told three of them on donkeys went into a cafe and caused quite a good-natured uproar. The Australians are more given to getting drunk than lighter frivolities. Anyway, Xmas had started the fellows going in for practical joking, and I kind of think they will continue it, and Cairo will wish the Colonials were never in Egypt, though at present we are in great demands and considered big fry for all kinds of dealers, particularly in the brothel quarter.

"The women in Cairo have been making enormous sums of money, even at as low a figure as five piastres. I have not been inside one of these places, but I am told from six to a dozen soldiers are often waiting in the one room for their turn. It also shows up a terrible weakness in our educational affairs when young men must run this awful risk to get their knowledge of the world, and thereby learn to curb his carnal appetite."

On New Year's Eve the camp was dominated by booze, with the "fellows beastly drunk and making an awfully foul and hideous night of it", while during that period there were 300 cases of desertion, prompting the dire penalty of any guilty party being sent home and discharged from the army.

Rusty didn't have time for such wayward behaviour. On New Year's Day, he was given the onerous task of cleaning out "a stuffed up incinerator … a dirty stinking job."

This on top of endless guard duty, and uncertainty over what exactly he and all the other soldiers would be doing in the war, prompted a general sense of exasperation. It even turned him into a liar. As he needed to transfer money to his family in South Africa, "I went before the damned nuisance of a Colonel this morning and asked for leave. He granted it after asking questions as to the genuineness of the story. I lied and beat him, and for once in my life, I am glad of having told a lie. This soldier game has no conscience at all. It's just a matter of get what you want in the easiest way, but get it. I am tired of this monotonous nothing-to-do military life, and am getting as big a dodger of work as any of our party. I often think, when the jam tin is empty and I sit chewing at dry bread and washing it down with crude, black tea, that it is a miserable life."

Diversions were required, with Rusty whenever possible disappearing to swim across the Nile and back. He also showed off his vast athletic skills, winning on one day in the garrison sports meeting, held on a track overgrown with grass and weeds, the 100-yard race, the 440 yards, as well as the long jump and hop, step and jump.

Football became another important diversion, with him organising a match against the Fourth Battalion. "Our side turned up in full strength, and ran out winners by 11-0. Our Colonel is a poor sport. Although he gave us leave to play, he did it very grudgingly indeed. I took matters very easy and still scored two tries."

In a letter to Harold Austin, the Manly Rugby club secretary, Rusty said that football was "a splendid break in the irksome routine of military life, which dulls one's wits and brings on a state of general carelessness."

Rusty later wrote in the *Sydney Mail* that most of the football matches before the soldiers travelled to Gallipoli were played under the shadows of the great pyramids- "games that meant as much to the players and the keen followers as ever did an international game on the Sydney Cricket Ground".

The playing area was marked out in the Nile Valley, with the ground crusted with "sun-baked mud that rashed and cut all unwary players, or several inches deep in heavy, black mud" depending on the rise and fall of the Nile. Some games, according to Rusty's close mate George Hill, were played on "beautiful flat grass land", and involved numerous Sydney and NSW Country representative players. The star performer still was Rusty.

"Games were fought out with the vim and earnestness of a rival inter-town match. Whether the surface was soft or hard, what mattered it as long as the prestige of the company or battalion was worthily upheld? Playing on the Delta country, with the mighty monument of Cheops towering to a height of nearly 560 feet above our playing level, stirred everyone with a feeling of awe. It was certainly a venerable spot to play on. On one end the old fortifications, high monumental tombs, and a mosque that stands out strongly in its architectural grandeur, with the finest of the splendid mosques built in many lands by Mohammedan worshippers, could be easily seen and appreciated from a spectacular standpoint.

"There was an atmosphere so full of Eastern mesmeris — the mystic veil of the East — that all young Australians conjured up wild imaginations of and played their manly game with the same vigour and dash as if they were in an amphitheatre, where any lack of determination meant 'thumbs down', which, in turn, meant death to the losers."

The highlight was the NSW-Queensland match, which was played under League rules. "I would have been playing but for my gravel-rashed knee, which is very slow at healing. I don't like the League game though. It's altogether too continuous, like a hurried-through film at the picture show. The Union game gives more scope for thinking and seeing ahead of movements, and also a chance to see them succeed or fail according to the understanding and ability of the players.

"Yes, the more I see of League brand the more I find in and think of Rugby Union. There was a time when I did give some little thought to playing League for the money there seemed to be in it, but I am now very thankful that I did not do so, as professional sport has not the same honour and enthusiastic achievement. It does not carry the 'hallmark' on it."

His anti-League view was not improved by a visit to a nearby camp to see the Member of Parliament, Ted Larkin, who before the war had been the NSW Rugby League's first full-time official. His reign as NSWRL secretary followed a short Rugby career where he played one Test for Australia against New Zealand.

Rusty described Larkin in his diary as "a peculiar type of person to be a Member of Parliament. His tales circled round can-can and the lewdness of Cairo in a light jocular manner. He played football the other day and boomed the miserable game in the Cairo press. I can't see how the Australian Government is going to be strengthened or even run on honest lines when this type of man can secure recognition and a seat in the House." The Australian Government never found out, as Larkin was killed at the Gallipoli landing.

As bewildering was a speech from the Dean of Sydney, the chaplain to the forces, during the first service held in the mess room. The Dean "spoke in very strong terms regarding the foul language and the cases of venereal diseases that are so prevalent amongst our troops. The Dean said it was a humiliating shame and an everlasting disgrace for any young man to visit the brothels of the large underworld that exists in Cairo and take the awful risk of contracting (such as some hundred of our troops have done) a disease that is not only filthy and degrading, or stops at the physical suffering to yourself, but it is carried in the system and transmitted to and breaks down the health of the innocent wife. A man who violates the law of chastity in those dens of infamy should have a harlot for his wife." Rusty said the lecture "carried tremendous weight and has given the fellows something to think about. Why this lecture did not take place eight weeks ago before there were so many young and inexperienced fellows dosed with dread venereal troubles, is difficult to understand."

By March, the distractions subsided as the soldiers began to hear whispers that their days of training in Egypt were about to end. A theatre of war somewhere in Europe was soon to engulf them. On 2 March Rusty wrote: "Our camp is all excitement, awaiting orders to move off at any moment, but where to is problematic, though to my way of reasoning, there is but little doubt but that Turkey will be our objective. I feel pleased with it as the type of fighting will be more suited to the undisciplined and impatient Australian than the trench-to-trench kind of work now going on in France."

Another hint was given that night when they were lectured by a doctor, who had spent the last thirty years in Turkey. He spoke of how corrupt the Turkish Government was. "Their small-mindedness, avariciousness and sensuality was certain to destroy them as a nation sooner or later, and the time seems to have arrived and you men will do it," the doctor told the troops.

A week later, there was "a lot of drunkenness and gambling going on about the camp just now. The fellows want to get busy. This desert camp and training is growing sickening, moreso as the men will never be any more fit than at present — in fact we seem to be wasting time more than anything else."

At last, action. Early on 3 April they were herded into a train heading for Alexandria, and several hours later stood in front of their troopship the *City of Benares*- which was set to carry 600 men and 300 horses.

"So we are in for a dirty, foul-smelling trip if they don't soon land us somewhere," wrote Rusty. "The decks are mostly iron too and the devil to stand on — so slippery."

On 5 April the *City of Benares* left Alexandria, heading for Lemnos Island, in the Mediterranean Sea just off Turkey. The atmosphere on board was relatively calm, with Rusty "loafing all day", reading and sleeping. It was almost like an afternoon cruise of Sydney Harbour, rather than a voyage to battle.

On what he presumed was his thirty-third birthday, Rusty was just off Lemnos Island, anchored in the harbour, with thousands of other Allied troops, not knowing "anything about our movements at all, though there are such a lot of rumours about". There was apparently very little if any water on the land they were about to approach, wherever that was, and any there was probably poisoned. They were told to drink as much water as possible before landing. With them when they eventually hopped ashore would be one blanket and two bags of iron rations. Most of all they had to rely on commonsense.

All around there was action. "New troopships arrive here all day long," Rusty recorded on 10 April. "There must be many thousands of troops waiting now. The Dardanelles are only two hours or so from here and it's really hard to realise that we are so close to the bombardment and danger. Whether we are to storm forts or land on Constantinople is hard to say."

On 22 April came the instructions; Major Croxton addressed the troops. "On no account do you turn and run. If you are walking along quietly with a pick on your shoulder and a shell should burst nearby, for your very life, don't dream of turning round and running, as fear may spread like wildfire, and utter confusion as well. A victory turned into defeat will probably result. Stick to your ground, men, no matter what befalls us. A large number are sure to fall, and you will have to take your chance. There's honour in dying while still fighting."

Rusty wrote: "Our officers have told us also that we are in for a very rough time, and there may be as many as 2,000 men to attend to, but damn the injured men, I wish to glory I was in the firing line somewhere. Anyhow I am in charge of a squad and must play my part right up to the hilt."

On 23 April the unit was gripped with "considerable anxiety", especially as the *City of Benares* started to make its way out of Lemnos Harbour, until "to our surprise and dismay, instead of going to the Dardanelles, we dropped anchor". At least Rusty enjoyed some form of ease, when at parade that day it was announced he had been promoted to lance-corporal.

By 24 April, everyone knew where they were headed. They may not have known the full circumstances or the reasons, just the basic understanding that they were helping the British cause by invading the Gallipoli Peninsula so the Navy could force the Dardanelles Straits. It was assumed that this would effectively end the deadlock on the Western Front through the capture of Constantinople, knocking Turkey out of the war, and guaranteeing a safe route to bring supplies and arms to their Russian allies from the Mediterranean into the Black Sea.

The argument, pushed by an obsessive young First Lord of the Admiralty, Winston Churchill, was that opening the way to Constantinople and being able to link up with Russia would bring British victory, as it would expose the German underbelly and end the painful slogging away in the trenches of Western Europe.

At Gallipoli, the Australian soldiers were to be used as a diversionary force, to distract the attention of the Turkish troops in readiness for another invasion further south by British regulars.

"Tomorrow is the all-eventful day," Rusty wrote on the evening of 24 April. "We have our bully beef and biscuits with a full water bottle for two days or more. There is no water on the Gallipoli landing place at all, so we have to take great care of our water and fill ourselves up to the neck before landing. I listened to Major Croxton speaking from the bridge deck this afternoon. He gave particulars of the numbers and the battalions landing and what was expected of them. His speech was full of fine humour, dealing chiefly with our funky condition and likely fear. It was hardly the kind of speech one would expect on the eve of big doings, as there was plenty of ridicule, nonsense, but no hard facts or detailed information. It seemed more as though we were preparing for a pantomime instead of grim warfare. I don't mean for one moment that he should have made us melancholy and miserable, but he would have given us something like an idea of what to expect."

Later that night, Rusty inspected a sketch plan of where they were going to invade the Peninsula. He soon realised it was "going to be a regular inferno. Anyway there is some satisfaction in knowing that we Australians have got a chance of distinguishing ourselves at last. It will be hard and thrilling work right enough, in fact a gigantic task for the first time in action, but I think they will make good right enough. My money, anyhow, is on our boys tomorrow."

Then he realised what could happen. "I have told Win much about my love for her, and my desires. But where it will end is beyond my solution just now. There is war to face. Goodness knows what it might mean or hold for me, yet for my part I don't much care what happens. I am going to do the best for my country regardless, yet I suppose it's my duty now not to be foolish and take unnecessary risks. I am not quite the free agent of past years now."

ELEVEN

GALLIPOLI

"**AFTER A BAPTISM OF BLOOD** on his first day on the inhospitable cliffs of Gallipoli, fetching bodies, dodging gunfire, trying to keep himself and all around him alive, Rusty could not sleep. The rifle fire, the shrapnel, the endless ping, ping, pinging kept him awake. By 3am he was clambering towards the Turkish line yet again, wanting to witness what exactly was going on. Eventually exhaustion hit, and he slept in a small dugout on the side of the hill.

All around him fellow illustrious Australian sportsmen, and a multitude of famous footballers, were working on instinct, some luckier than others. It wasn"t long before several were fatalities. The first was Blair Swannell, the ugly English-born knuckleman man of Australian Rugby. Swannell was hated because of his violent streak when on the football field. He was just as fearless on the battlefield. As C.E.W. Bean wrote in his official history of the war, Swannell "had felt sure that he would be killed, and had said so on the Minnewaska before he landed, for he realised that he would play this game as he had played Rugby football, with his whole heart".

Swannell, who had fought for England in the Boer War before

moving to Sydney, had been made a 1st Battalion major, in charge of one of the main companies that headed deep into Turkish territory towards Russell's Top and the Nek.

Swannell was the most courageous of leaders, leading the charge towards the Turks, forcing them to retreat higher up in the cliffs, and into a safer trench. Swannell's company soon found themselves being shot at from the front and the right flank. All Swannell could do was lie still, and try to keep up an effective fire. While kneeling to show his troops how to take proper aim at the Turks, Swannell was shot dead through the forehead. It was a heroic death, as Bean explained: "From the moment they saw his bearing under fire, he became the hero of his men."

In *Viewless Winds*, H.M. 'Paddy' Moran said there had been a rumour that Swannell's "own men had shot him down. But the story of his being shot from behind was just somebody's canard," Moran countered. "It was always expected of a Roman Emperor that he should die on his feet. Swannell, no doubt, thought a footballer should perish following on."

Rusty soon learnt of Swannell's death. "I am really grieved as 'Swanny' with all his faults, was quite all right, though he is a character seldom met."

But Rusty had little time to reminisce. There was too much going on. "Rifle fire is going on along our front to the right of where I am sitting, camera at my feet, and by reports of the terrific firing I should say our men are beating off an attack," he wrote on 26 April. "The warships are shelling hell for leather, while the Turks' shellfire is at rare intervals, although they just landed one amongst some engineers working about 200 yards from my present position.

"At 10am with three stretcher parties we were dodging shrapnel for $1\frac{1}{2}$ hours under the side of the gorge. The rain of lead poured down incessantly and as each whistler was heard overhead we ducked each time. I am beginning to pick up the sounds of the different guns and to know the bullet pellets. This is indeed a wonderful experience and seeing there is so much slaughter and lead flying about we all take it mighty coolly and joke all the time that we are dodging."

Four hours later, Rusty began to wonder how wonderful the experience was. Higher up the cliff, in ravines similar to the Blue Mountains, except "covered with low thick bush and a natural hiding place", while looking for casualties, Rusty encountered a "very despondent Third Brigade going back into the firing line.

The mistake made seems to have been in following the Turks $2\frac{1}{2}$ miles back from the beach, which in this country meant getting away from ammunition and all supports, so that when the Turks stopped, the Third Brigade got cut to ribbons and were too far away to be assisted. This happened on our left flank, and I am of the opinion that the same thing happened on the right flank yesterday as we got a lot of wounded from there, and the cry going along the communication lines was like a lost soul crying: 'For goodness sake, hurry along more men and ammunition as we are losing ground like hell.'

"Our fleet must have sent in 1,500 shells yesterday, which quietened down the Turks' shrapnel fire, but to my surprise they showered in shell after shell on to our battleships just before dark and continued into the darkness making almost a fireworks display. Our fellows are shooting mercilessly, showing no quarter to anybody they can see and, though, against orders, are taking no prisoners."

Australia stood up to the challenge on the opening day, but the battle was still a fiasco. Apart from some parties making enormous ground after the landing, the bulk of the Australian troops were pinned to the cliffs, and the front line appeared to be breaking. The charge had been thwarted by the Turks, prompting Major-General William Bridges, the commander of the AIF, to call that night for an immediate evacuation in a bid to save lives. Bridges was angered by the confusion of the landing, and did not believe his already overstrained troops could last another day. He was overruled. The invasion continued. Bridges was mortally wounded a few weeks later.

As early as 28 April Rusty was writing that the strain in the Anzac trenches was "terrible", especially as "the nights freeze you and the sun roasts you. I met a party of Third Brigade men last night and it was impossible to imagine how worn out they looked, a glassy stare in their eyes and quite a ghastly colour."

A Third Brigade officer told him that only four officers of the thirty-four who landed were still alive. "He states that deeds of marvellous daring and unheard-of determination took place all day Sunday. One fellow was shot through the heart at short range by a Turk some few yards away, but so determined was he that he first ran his bayonet through the Turk before falling over dead.

"When the Third Brigade made their gallant landing they threw off their packs on the beach in the rush. These kits belong to the killed and wounded and it did look painful to see them strewn about. Yet even worse was the letters, Xmas greetings and even birthday cards that now remain on the shingle beach. They all speak of sad hearts that the loss of their friend will bring when the news is made known. Reverend Green buried a few men yesterday, but away in the front they are buried in holes and no ceremony.

"The first patient I had this morning had his head terribly blown about. The doctor said we should leave him to die- nothing on earth could save him. Anyway we started out for the depot thinking that the operating table there may give him a chance but no, he died on the stretcher. Around his neck were charms of several kinds, one a religious charm, but alas, charms, beliefs or creeds play no part in man's preservation during war, bloody war.

"Some of the cases are terrible, This afternoon my squad brought in a fellow shot right through the body penetrating the lungs. He was in agony, and asked for something to send him to sleep, but like all Australian soldiers he was game and did not complain or grumble." One soldier was brought in complaining of nervous attacks. The doctor in charge took one look and called him a shirker. The next day the soldier, shattered by the accusation, blew his head off with his own rifle.

Rusty was impressed by the courage of the maimed soldiers he picked up in the battlelines and carried to safer areas for either treatment or burial. "Our fellows take their injuries with remarkable fortitude. The last patient I brought in was along the muddy gully, now known as 'Dead Man's Gully' on account of the men and animals that are killed there from shrapnel, as anything that bursts on or over the firing line falls along this deep gully.

"Well, this man was shot through the lungs and I fear had but little time to live, but on the way down he said several times: 'By God, that Turk could shoot well. He got me a beauty, didn't he? I thought I had him right enough but he beat me easily. Ah lads, how long is this job going to take to mend? I would like to get back on that damned Turk. I feel pretty bad and expect I'm done for. But, strike me dead, that Turk could shoot all right.'"

The next day Rusty went out to help five soldiers that had blown away in a trench. "Some were blinded by the dirt, peppered by the gravel and their clothes were badly shattered and torn away from them. When the smoke and dust had died away, Robertson of the 12th Battalion was the only man who could not rise from the debris, his body being partly buried.

"When we got him he was in the best of humour and seemed satisfied with the feeling that the Turks will get hell when the boys get fairly at them. He consoled himself with the fact that it might have been a lot worse. Our next case was shot through the body and died before we were 100 yards on our journey. We placed the remains on the hillside and went back for a fellow with a shrapnelled leg, an easy injury. One of the 8th Battery fellows with a shrapnel wound in the back came along too. He walked all bent and doubled up, but what a lovely long, lean, raw-boned Australian he was too."

The Australians first hated the Turks, but gradually respect grew for their opponent's fighting skills. On 4 May Rusty wrote that the Turks "seem to be damned good fighters. He later added "I've never heard an Australian who really fought against the Turk condemn him. In fact, we all just love him for his gameness and good sportsmanship. The Turks seem to be very cheeky, to say the least. One wounded infantry man told me that while the Turks were trench digging 300 yards distant he fired at one and missed. The Turk stood up and clapped his hands at them, 'but' said my patient,'"my next shot stopped the bugger and he won"t clap his hands any more'." Few Australian soldiers took seriously a note from the commander of the Allied Dardanelles Forces, General Sir Ian Hamilton, that was read out to them the same day, explaining that the Turks "are tired of fighting and prepared to throw in the towel at any moment".

At dusk, Rusty prepared himself for a stew made out of potatoes, onion, thyme, tinned beef, a little bacon and hard biscuits. "We had no sooner sat down to enjoy this stew to be followed up by cheese, jam and hard oatmeal biscuits, when shrapnel began to fly around. The very first one broke back 20 foot from us and directly overhead. The pellets passed by us and landed fair amongst a party of fellows having dinner 20 foot away. One was seriously shot through the abdomen, one had his hand badly damaged, and another his arm smashed about. I took two of them into our doctors, but the shells came along more thickly, so I got the Macconochie ration tin with my stew in it, three biscuits, some jam and a mug of tea and screwed myself into H. Miller"'s 'dug-out', and between eating, watching and ducking from fiercely-burstling shells I had about as exciting a time as ever I want to have."

The following day, shrapnel was bursting within inches of him, and the next, they were out in the open, dodging everything. "There is of course no reason to go through this hellfire, but there may be a bad case waiting and we fellows must not shirk our part in the struggle, particularly if there is a soldier's life dependent upon it. "

They soon found " a shrapnel-shattered patient in a semi-delirious and weak condition, his face and both eyes being damaged and a ghastly sight. He's matted and covered with blood. I thought that bleeding men, and worse, dead and dying men, would make me feel sick and dizzy, but no, I get amongst all kinds of frightful injuries without any effect. We brought the above case down in haste and through a field of raining lead.

"It is a terrible experience to walk slowly with a loaded stretcher across open country with shells bursting all around you. Any of the many reports might mean the end of both patient and four bearers. You have to walk slowly on and let the pellets fly where they will and keep as cool and collected as the circumstances will permit. It's a task that would rattle some of the bravest."

They even had to cope with those who wanted to inflict wounds on themselves."I have noticed several cases of lost nerves and strained minds, also a number of fellows accidentally shot through the foot or hand. There were 12 such cases in one battalion of the Third Brigade. Enquiries are held as some men shoot themselves to get away from it all. I did not think it possible that men would shoot themselves in the hand or foot, so as to get a spell, but it has happened several times here."

He then heard that another of his footballing comrades had died in the trenches. While encouraged that fellow Wallaby- William 'Twit' Tasker was nearby on the cliffs, and begging a visit, he discovered virtually the same day that his front-row teammate from the 1912 United States tour, Harold George, "got the axe after a very brave action. "It appears he was one of five to go at midday and attempt to locate a machine gun and Turkish trenches. The sergeant got a rough time and was finally shot. Harold, after a while,

found the corner too hot and taking the sergeant's body he made under a heavy fire back to the trenches.

When he was preparing to get into the trench himself a bullet passed through his body low down ."

Thus ended the life of one of New South Wales's most pugnacious forwards, who before leaving for war boasted of holding the record for the most first-grade appearances for the Eastern Suburbs club, alongside eight Tests for Australia and twenty matches for his state.

There were occasional pleasures. Rusty delighted in the bravery of the fellow Australian soldier, including a north Queensland kangaroo shooter who "wanders about with a small telescope and actually accounted for eleven snipers in one day." Once, when Rusty was walking towards White's Gully, he was surprised to see "a football floating through the air. I set off down into the blind valley, and joined in with a number of Victorians who had brought the ball from Egypt with them." For half an hour, until the threat of gunfire convinced them to find safer territory, they played forcie-backs, each group attempting to kick the ball over the heads of the other.

Sometimes Rusty was able to write his diary sitting in the nude, because the sun "is just perfect", and wander back to the main beach for a "lovely swim, though it is an uncanny business with shells screaming and bursting overhead". The colour of the water had also improved, after "the dead horses and mules had been dragged well out to sea".

He was on hand when several newly arrived Scotsmen were washing their clothes in the sea at Anzac Cove, even though bullets were whizzing past their ears. "An Australian water-carrier went by and forgetting entirely that he was in the narrow strip of firing area between the walls of the hills and the ocean, told the three Scotsmen that they would be shot through the guts if they did not get out.

"The lads said: 'What? Are the bastards shooting at us?'

"'My bloody oath,' said the Australian, at which all three scattered over the shingle beach in an exasperating hurry, and the Australian angrily said: 'Strike me dead! There's no need for such a bloody rush. You'll let the bastard see he's on the right spot.'"

In the water, rank meant nothing. The Australian and New Zealand Army Corps commander General Birdwood joined the troops for the swim, and usually was laughed at by the Australians, telling the "silly old cove" to take cover, and also cover up his naked body. One swimming Digger surveyed Birdwood's ample stomach and exclaimed: "My bloody oath mate, you 'ave been among the biscuits." Birdwood soon grew accustomed to the weird ways of the Australians, particularly after one of his cars was taken from his Cairo headquarters and later found abandoned on the sand in the middle of Mena Camp. He knew whom to blame.

Even church services weren't a safe haven from the horrors of war. After a lull in the shooting, Private Andrews opened the service, held near some dugout shelters, until Rusty wrote: "a wounded man came stumbling forward and pitched upon his face down the incline. Three medical men were on the spot almost immediately and as the five descended, a shell broke with a cruel harsh explosion a few feet over the heads of the party. The Church service was held spell-bound and silent for the few minutes that the above drama was being enacted, and when the prayers concluded, they all rose and sang: 'Abide with me'.

"But as the men continued to come over the brow of the hill, so the Turks sent out their death-dealing missiles. Another wounded man was followed by still another, carried in the arms of their trusty comrades. Private Andrews went on explaining the beauty of St Paul's letter to the misbelieving people of Corinth, punctuated here and there by the callous bursting of shrapnel shells.

"Before we rose for the final hymn 'Nearer My God to Thee', the casualties numbered five. Whether a testimony to Brother Andrews or not, he at least has conducted a service under circumstances seldom heard of, much less experienced by many wearers of the cloth."

Rusty was also on hand when a large barrel of claret washed up on the beach. He succeeded in getting a kerosene tin and a bully beef tin full of it before an officer, accompanied by an armed guard, smashed the barrel. "Some of the men got stupidly drunk and possibly the whole of Anzac would have along the right wing also as many casks came ashore but were emptied into the sand by an officer. At 9pm that night, a party of fellows saw another barrel floating in off Hell's Spit pontoon wharf. They went into the water and helped it along for perhaps a hundred yards and after a big struggle to get it ashore, aboard a barge, an officer came along and tipped the wine into the sea. Never was there such disappointment and swearing amongst a party of men. It was a great and glorious day.

"Beachy Bill (Turkish guns aimed at the beach) shot some of the fellows around a cask, but this did not interfere with them in their attempt to get the wine away."

Rusty in front of the Sphinx before heading for Gallipoli.

Rusty's photograph, taken from the beach at Gallipoli, shows the 1st Field Ambulance going ashore at 6.45 on the morning of 25 April 1915.

Rusty's photograph of the Australian soldiers on the beach at Anzac Cove, 25 April 1915.

Rusty when he first arrived in Egypt, 1914.

The serious military man.

Tom Richards, about to go underground on the Western front.

Flirting with a nurse after being wounded and sent to hospital behind the lines.

Tom Richards in London on R and R.

Tom Richards, a proud member of the Australian and New Zealand Army Corps.

Rusty's son Jim, aged nineteen, as a young World War II fighter pilot.

The war-weary soldier.

1st Anzac Corps, 27th June, 1917.

Dear Richards,

I write to congratulate you very heartily upon the award to you of the Military Cross, in recognition of your conspicuous bravery and good leadership during the operations near Bullecourt on the 4th May. I know what good work you did in charge of your bombing party, extending your line for 250 yards, and establishing and holding a strong post, notwithstanding the determined opposition of the enemy, among whom you inflicted many casualties in killed and prisoners. Your fine example inspired confidence in your men, and I thank you so much for it.

With good wishes.

Yours sincerely,

W. N. Birdwood

Yours faithfully,

Officer i/c Base Records.

On this date, 1915, I was serving as a "Stretcher bearer" with the 1st Field Ambulance. I received a Commission & joined 1st Battalion November 1916...

The official letter from the commander of the Australian forces, Field Marshall William Birdwood, telling Rusty he has won the Military Cross.

A studio portrait of Tom Richards, shortly after winning the Military Cross.

As intoxicating was being a witness for an unusual armistice between the Australians and the Turks on 24 May for nine hours, to "allow both sides to bury their dead". The thousands of stinking corpses had become a serious health problem, as explained in one ditty of the time, which went to the tune of 'Little Grey Home in the West':

> We've a little wet home in a trench
> Where the rain storms constantly drench
> There's a dead Turk close by
> With his heels toward the sky
> And he gives off a beautiful stench.

"At about 9am the sentries were posted halfway between the lines of trenches and each side had to keep on its own side of half way and bury their own dead, taking all the enemy's dead up to the halfway and leave them to be buried by their own comrades. The Australian dead had been lying there four weeks, since the first day, and in fair numbers. The Turks, who lay about in heaps, must have numbered 3,000 and had been lying there since last Wednesday, five days ago. It was so strange to see a Turk and an Australian standing together on guard every 70 yards. They tried hard to exchange a few words of conversation too, but it was impossible.

"The Australian upheld the most noticeable of his characteristics by sitting down with his white flag while the Turks stood up the whole time. The bodies were mostly pierced through and through by shot and shell. I helped to dig a few trenches, but the smell was awful … The bodies were buried in both narrow and shallow trenches. The burial service was read by Captain McKenzie. The Turks did not appear to read any service and buried their dead six and eight deep in large trenches."

As astounding was a Turkish officer Rusty sighted at the armistice. It was the same Egyptian whom Blair Swannell had befriended in Cairo. "Swannell took a great liking to an Egyptian fellow and he was allowed to wander anywhere at will. He often wandered alone for hours in the officers' rooms waiting their return. He was aboard the troop ship when the Battalion sailed from Alexandria and was made a big fuss over. Well, on the day of the armistice at Gallipoli, a Turkish officer came over and spoke to Major Stevens, congratulating him upon his promotion, and here sure enough was the Battalion and Blair Swannell's Cairo friend."

Unbenown to the Australians, a Turkish spy had been in their midst for many months. This member of the enemy wasn't as lucky as another, according to one story making the rounds of the dressing stations. The story, probably apocryphal, related to a Turkish prisoner who persisted in telling his Australian captor on the way down to Anzac beach about his wife and children, that according to the digger "he got on my nerves so much, I shot the bugger".

Rusty even found time to write a multitude of letters home, usually using either a "smellful slush lamp of bacon oil" or a home-made lamp from a tobacco tin with a lint bandage for a wick, to scribble away at night in different cramped dugouts. Many were written on scraps of toilet paper. Some were even reprinted in full in newspapers back home. These included one which appeared in the *North Queensland Register*, and gave a graphic description of what life was actually like on Gallipoli.

When explaining that the "very air" they breath was "whistling and screaming with missiles of destruction and death", the soldiers felt like rabbits in the trenches. "Oh, but how callous our gallant soldiers are to danger. Just two mornings ago, I was in swimming, and saw the bullets from a sharpshooter turning up dust around the soldiers passing along the beach going for water and on various duties. A few moments later there was only one man in the danger zone, and bullets whistled along towards him as he approached with a tin of water in each hand.

"I lay well down in the sea water, and as this gaunt devil-may-care fellow plodded on, he said, without hardly turning his head any more than to look ahead, and in the direction from which the shots were coming: 'That bastard will be shooting someone yet.' He was right too, although he got through alright, eight men were wounded there that day. It is hard to believe some of the things one actually witnesses.

"We've got the fighting material here right enough; their language and manners may sound horrible to a stranger, and maybe there is room for improvement, but they are born fighters and staunch comrades, possessor of the finest of manly qualities."

Particularly heartening was the bravery of the 15th Battalion, who were last sighted filing up a zig zag path.

"Here they were ready to the hour thinking not of home, nor of death; these men never knew what danger was, and as the cruel shrapnel cut gaps in their struggling, overburdened line, the next man stepped up and on over the path that leads to glory and daredevil achievements they marched.

"What a magnificent spectacle! The price they paid was very very high indeed. Oh! If the people of Australia could only be brought to feel and realise the valour of their boys on this particular day, and through the fifty or more hours of bloody warfare that followed, how proud and elated they could really afford.

"It was almost a practicable and physical impossibility to hold those ridges, with but scant protection against artillery and constantly attacking lines of Turkish infantry. Yet those magnificent young Australians did it despite suffering and pain. Victoria Crosses were won by the dozen, but alas, hardly any officer got out alive to report this bravery. Wounded men refused to leave the front, and if they could not fire themselves, they gave their rifles to a comrade and went on loading up for him to shoot. I was always a patriot Australian, but now love for the great fighting spirit of the nation is welded to my very soul."

Soon the Anzacs were following to the letter General Birdwood's instruction to "Dig in and fight it out". It was going to be a slow, long, drawn-out battle on those horrible cliffs and caverns. The war around Anzac Cove had turned into a stalemate. And already the landing had cost at least 2,300 Australian and New Zealand lives, alongside British, French, Indian, Senegalise and Gurkha casualties.

Not all were victims of the enemy, as Rusty explained on 26 May. "A terribly sad affair took place in front of the 12th Battalion trenches yesterday afternoon. Three of our scouts had gone out in front of our own trenches doing dangerous work and were returning to our lines when some of our damned fools opened fire on them killing one and wounding one through the jaw."

Others had no idea why they were injured. "Remarkable! George Hill woke up this morning with a bullet embedded in his shoulder and does not know how it occurred. It must have happened while he was asleep."

And everything had turned nasty, especially some members of the 15th Battalion, "a lot of bushwhackers, coppergougers from the Cloncurry district" who had resorted to "bayoneting and killing when mercy should be shown and prisoners taken". There is no doubt that our men are hard and even cruel. Then again what else can be expected when so many of our finest men and companions for eight months are shot down beside you and your turn may come at any moment. It makes men restless and revengeful.

"It seems to me that war such as we read about and glory in, such as honest open hand-to-hand or man-to-man conflicts where the bravest man gets the upper hand, where the strongest arm and the noble heart wins the honour and gratification of the country, is old-fashioned and out of date, like the flintlock rifles and the broadsword. Today is long-distance fighting with artillery and close fighting between the men with picks and shovels. In short, it is a pick and shovel war. It's not war- it's a display of uncanny mechanical contrivances in which the initiative and valour of men is taken away by the pick and shovel.

"The miles and miles of travelling ways, trenches and communications, cuttings and tunnels, to say nothing of the dug-outs for sleeping purposes, would make a railway contractor ashamed of his workmen and the poorness of their labours on Australian construction jobs.

"There is no word, or for that matter, series of words that can convey any realistic idea as to what war actually means. Dante's vivid description of the inferno or a Hindu idea of Hell are as nothing compared to it. The reality of war I have been through, it is relentlessly cruel and does not give a brave man a dog's chance."

Nor did the ridiculous messages from their superiors. "I read hurriedly a flattering message from Ian Hamilton to the Australians giving them much praise and prevailing upon them for another effort. Nevertheless I wish Ian Hamilton would give us bombs instead of bullshit."

As frustrating for Rusty was that he was not in the front line. By mid June, he had opted to sneak into the trenches himself, retrieving wounded including one who had his foot "blown clean away", and also help out in the shooting, "firing a clip of five into the Turks trenches myself". Whenever possible he was close to the front line, with camera in hand, shooting rolls of film. One day he was in the trench with the 5th Light Horse, helping to drag out their wounded.

"Two fellows threw one man out of a trench who had been struck by a shell and taken away the whole of his right leg. He was quite conscious and spoke to several of his mates. I have never seen anything like this fellow in my life, as calm as ever a man was, nor have I seen a more gruesome sight. We left on retiring a number of dead. I hit them with stones from the trenches to make sure they were not conscious.

"By God, I should be in the firing line instead of amongst a jealous, cringing lot of lazy devils that we are here in the 1st AMC from the officers down. Our officers were never able to get on one with another, and much jealousy exists even in such unexpected circles.

"I hate them more so because they allow the quartermaster to rob us and cheat us out of even our bit of tucker, to say nothing of the presentation goods. The Colonel of a Corps who allows this vile plundering state of affairs is no man in any sense of the word. The 6d allowance in Mena was truly a terrible piece of work.

"The fighting for one's King and Country is fine and spurs us all on to do deeds of noble daring, but it's the other side that troubles me at the moment, the buffeting and robbing of just rights and the mean overriding of unscrupulous officers and so-called superiors. I wonder that the big dogs at the head of affairs don't pay more personal attention to the wants of the men in the firing line.

"They have worked like slaves for three months now and by the weakened appearance of them and the long sick parades, I have come to the conclusion that the men are worked and starved almost to death. It is truly cruel. The rottenness and robbery that undermines this military business makes me very bitter …"

Officers hardly endeared themselves to the soldiers by permitting the canteen to exorbitantly overprice goods; offered a blind eye to the post office staff stealing their parcels, and then trying to sell them back their own gear. Rusty directed his biggest attack towards the colonel in command of the 1st Field Ambulance, Dr Newmarch, claiming that he was a "man of mean principle and a lover of a filthy story" . He added, "This man was in the DTs from drink when we landed at Anzac and when hundreds of wounded men were groaning and dying, he was in a cabin with a guard over him to prevent him from getting out on deck. So much for an Honourable Knight."

Rusty also had no faith in the second medical staff officer of the Australian Division, Major Stokes, describing him as "inconsiderate", "mean" and a man who "acted as though he were a demi-god" because he was now restricting letters to family to just one page.

Rusty's love life was as edgy. For some months, communication had dried up with Zelda. On 23 June he scribbled: "It is over 40 days since I heard from Manly. I suspect that I have gone right out of the betting to the extent of being forgotten." Then on 12 July came a letter from Zelda. The message was succinct, stating "her intention nicely of marrying Basil, which I cannot complain of and I do wish her luck". He revealed more two days later, angry that she "so coldly wrote declaring to be finished with me now. But it is yet a hell of a conundrum for me."

By August, with the horrendous Battles of Lone Pine, The Nek and Sari Bair leading to apparently endless deaths, Rusty found himself invariably surrounded by bodies. The day after the Nek massacre, where waves of Australian soldiers charged to a futile death, he wrote: "Yesterday morning the poor fellows were lying in hundreds around the beach- a truly terrible sight. The ghastly reality of war lies in front of me now as I sit writing at the Dressing Station at 4pm, and there are ten bodies lying in line. Yesterday these were fine specimens of Australian manhood. Men that any nation in the world would be proud to claim. It is a sickly sight if one is willing to permit the mind to dwell on the humane side of life, but this we must not allow as there is so much blood and slaughter about to face that one cannot be sentimental.

"The bodies of two Turks also lie nearby. These are the smallest I have yet seen and very puny specimens. Their boots were badly worn and crudely repaired in one case, while the other had on a pair of light open-topped shoes. All the Turks I have yet seen wear underclothes and about ten rolls of a long cloth around their middle, while as a comparison our men are wearing mostly shorts and only a thin singlet under their tunics. This garb though not picturesque keeps the troublesome lice down effectively.

"This morning early I went out through the tunnel under the original firing line to the advanced aid post where there were 21 seriously wounded lying about in all weird heart-breaking positions. We took a brick of a fellow with an arm practically blown off at the shoulder, and after scrambling over the bodies of some eight Turks, we reached the way out. It's uncanny walking on dead bodies!"

There was as much devastation down on the beach, after the Turks in early August had bombed the Australians out of their trenches. "The bombs knocked and shattered our men over the whole of their body.

Some cases were swaddled in cotton wool, gauze and bandages from the hips right down to the feet.

"Sad sights they were. Worse even was the congestion down on the beach where the poor fellows, with marvellous fortitude, lay about in dozens and were showered in shrapnel from Beachy Bill. Yesterday morning the poor fellows were lying in hundreds around the beach, a truly terrible sight. So many troops were landing this morning and overnight too that the small launches did not appear to be available to take the wounded aboard the hospital ship. The landing Indians (the 10th Gurkhas) looked very frightened as they scrambled one over the other out of the barge and raced along the beach for shelter, where they immediately regained their composure and wore a bright, harmless expression of a child. I am going to try and sleep, but those fine fellows being cut and battered to fragments (our men are walking over the bodies of their comrades) keeps me awake, more so as I know that the 16 weeks here of awfully hard digging and fatigue with an average daily sleep of six hours of the poorest class of food, has weakened the men to such an extent that I fear nature will not stand to them in a long stubborn engagement. I fear for our men very seriously. They should be fed better, or at least have the advantages of a canteen. Tired and languid they take unnecessary risks."

Later, Rusty admitted that not even gorging himself with a piece of his mother's cake, sent through the mail, could satisfy him. "I am kind of melancholy and full of feeling for the loss of so fine a lot of men, and the grief occasioned in their far away home when the wire ticks out the sad news to their dear friends. The fact that they died well is no answer to the question as to why they should die at all, but alas, it's hell. God what a relief it will be to get away from this truly bloody place."

Eventually on August 14 Rusty heard of an escape route. That night he sat at the clearing station waiting for a boat for Mudros on Lemnos Island, after being given a clearance because of damage to his spleen, suffered during weeks of dangerously clambering all over the cliffs searching for injured and dying.

At last a glorious night's sleep on board; the first mattress he has used in eleven months, and "lo, the soft loving voice of a woman ... the first feminine voice for four whole months — hard and nasty months too — but she vanished all too soon.

"I would have given the world if she would only have spoken to me and given me a chance to reply. Nothing could have sounded so pure and holy (though I know they're not) in my harsh ears, yet I did hear the voice and it did me a lot of good."

As encouraging was that he was told shortly before leaving for Lemnos that he had received a special mention in the Divisional Order for acts of gallantry or valuable service between 6 May 6 and 28 June. This included fearless work near Chatham's Post late in June when under heavy fire he attended to many wounded, including bringing one to safety on his back.

He eventually drifted to sleep, and imagined there was something hovering over him. "I tried to stir my thoughts. But yes, it was an angel right enough, moving about and talking in the soft voice of the blessed. I listened and watched, afraid almost to trust either my eyes or my ears. It was an angel alright! Where could I possibly be amongst angels?

"Angels don't come hovering amongst dirt-begrimed and blood-spattered soldiers. I closed my eyes a moment expecting my dream to vanish, but no. I was surprised to find my angel still there when I ventured another peep, and, behold, she was coming towards me. She spoke to each prostrate form as she came.

No it could not be; no angel would talk to a rough, primitive and unshaven men like me. Yet she came nearer and nearer. A tender hand was firmly laid on my shoulder, quickening my blood and stirring my soul; then the most gentle voice I've ever heard said clearly: 'You will have a cup of warm milk, my boy, come on now!' I tasted it, and sure enough, it was nectar. I tried to say 'Thank you Angel,' but I could not speak. Words could not come to address an angel, who, in the guise of a nurse, had given me nectar to drink, and had spoken in a voice almost forgotten or overgrown by associations with man and devil only."

For the next few days, Rusty was shunted between Imbros Island, just off Anzac Cove, and Lemnos, putting up with English medical officers who were all "so arrogant when placed in charge of anything". His antipathy toward the English constantly rose to the surface, especially when away from the war zone, when he was able to properly think and put everything into perspective. On 21 August he observed a troopship "crowded with Australians" leaving Mudros Harbour for Gallipoli.

"These lads must know the hell that they are going into and yet they went brightly and gleefully. I wonder if any country on earth possesses men so willing to make sacrifices. I am certain England does not possess the same spirit and not within 40% of the physique. It"s a shame to see some of the weakly, undersized, premature-looking Englishmen we have aboard.

"They are earnest and willing enough to fight, but they are not of the same material as the Australians. Their minds seem dull and their actions hobbled. They have neither initiative nor resource in comparison with Australians. The more I see and mix with these Englishmen the more I think of Australia and the independent, quick-witted fighting men they breed.

"Most of the Englishmen around me want to throw in the towel and are praying that they will go back to England. They are poor spirited and alas, have no inclination to even up their own score with John Turk, or to their everlasting discredit have they the honour to avenge the death of their own comrades killed by their sides when making for Hill 971 from the new landing at Suvla Bay. I am exceedingly disappointed with most of the Englishmen I have come in contact with. It was an English regiment that lost Quinn's Post in the early part of our campaign to the Turks, while relieving our men, and so we have no confidence in anything English at present."

Adding to the irritation was that Englishmen thought Australians "wickedly bad-mannered", and didn't say thank you. Maybe that had something to do with being away from civilisation "and living that awful dugout life at Gallipoli" where one could be killed any moment, "lie out unburied to rot like a drought-stricken sheep," or live "in the support trenches where in several places the maggots crawled away from their human prey and wriggled over the supports, blankets, and climbed over the sleeping form, over their bare legs and into the face.,If people could only understand the misery and the hell of a soldier"s life in Gallipoli week after week for months on end, they would overlook a few mannerisms and the failure of a man to say 'thank you'.

"None of the returned men will salute officers about the camp or the lines, although the Tommies make a habit of it. Our men have seen so much and worked so hard at Gallipoli that they care nothing for military law or anybody at all. Many of them are partly dismantled and would take many months to get back to their normal state. It is pathetic to hear and see them carrying on."

"Heart and soul these men are volunteers and are here to fight, not simply to obey fruitless orders issued only for the sake of enforcing authority."

Like so many other Australian soldiers, he knew whom to blame for the Dardanelles stalemate— the English. On several occasions, including at Lone Pine and the Nek, Australian soldiers had shown extraordinary initiative and courage to charge the Turkish line, only to be thwarted by poor direction and haphazard planning by their leaders, who were not always British. Numerous Australian officers were of similar poor quality, but the blame was usually redirected towards the British, primarily because they were in charge of the overall botched campaign.

"The Turks are easily defending the Dardanelles, while the British are fooling about, without sufficient men or big land guns. Their proud and boastful nature has led them to waste faith on the Navy. The Navy makes one sick, the way the poor self-deluded English brag about it and expect it to do the impossible. All this pomp and boast and swank of the British soldier, more especially the officers, makes one laugh at the imaginary victories and successes these swelled-headed officials are anticipating and have been anticipating for 14 months now and still make no progress."

Late in August Rusty was transferred back to Egypt, to the Gheziva Palace Hotel in Cairo, and onto Mena House, in the shadows of the Pyramids. He soon discovered the best way to recover was not to join the hordes in Cairo, where young soldiers were still admitting to him that despite all the warnings they "go down to the brothel, put in a couple of hours there, go to the picture show and take the 9pm tram home". Instead Rusty reunited with his old friends — the Sphinx and the Pyramids — making numerous visits, and exploring every centimetre of the area. He soon recuperated, but like so many around him, was not keen to go back to Anzac. "As a fellow gets time to read, he finds that the waste of life through bungling at Gallipoli has been terrific, so much so that I don't blame men for not wanting to go back there again," Rusty wrote on 24 September.

In the hospital, fellow patients were using more elaborate methods to ensure that they weren't sent back to the front. One was taking cordite to increase his temperature and inflame his eyes. Several others were making out they were deaf. All were disturbed by what they had witnessed.

"The dead and maimed while in action I take but little notice of and seldom fret about, but here in civilisation once again my memories fairly haunt me," wrote Rusty. Many around him simply didn't care. As he explained on 8 October: "On parade yesterday there was a brilliant incident in connection with the casualness of the men from the Dardanelles. The sergeant whilst calling the roll called a lad's name who was in the adjoining section. So he came slouching over to the Sergeant, saying: 'Strike me dead, I didn't know I was in your —— lines.' 'Your name is here,' was the abrupt reply of the sergeant. 'Well,' said the rough'un, 'I expect I"d better —— well fall in here, eh?'

In early November, with the authorities convinced that Rusty after several weeks of guard-duty was again fully fit, he found himself back on a ship, leaving Alexandria, heading to either Gallipoli or Greece. The latter, Rusty certainly hoped. "To go through the horrors of Gallipoli Peninsula is more adventure and novelty than I again want to see but alas I suppose I will be there again."

On 8 November Rusty realised that his wish had not been realised. In the distance he could see the flash and pop of Anzac Cove. On arrival, he went off in search of his unit, only to discover that they were all now on Lemnos Island. He instead signed up with the Second Light Horse Field Ambulance, and was put in charge of a dressing station, high up the cliff-face, in Brown's Dip leading into Lone Pine.

He did not time his move well. Apart from suffering the endless bombardment of Beachy Bill, which had "racked the beach from end to end", a dreadful winter had set in. Rainstorms were followed by blizzards of snow, and then two days and nights of near Arctic conditions, where the thermometer hardly rose about freezing point. If the trauma of the trenches wasn't hard enough, now soldiers were being frozen to death, and 3000 had to be evacuated with frostbite and exposure.

Adding to the eerie atmosphere was that for several days there had been virtual silence on the battlefront. With the British government contemplating a Gallipoli evacuation, the officers-in-charge decided to accustom the Turks to periods of silence, so that when the moment came they could bluff their opponents, who would not immediately realise something was amiss.

"Today has been remarkable indeed," Rusty wrote on 26 November. "Not one single shot has been fired from our line by artillery or rifle throughout and the silence is intense. The strangeness is appalling as we have grown so used to noise. This is the second day now."

The next day: "Today has been another day of weird quietness, not a shot being fired from our lines or from any of our guns, although the Light Horse found it necessary to destroy a bombing party of Turks who came up to the trenches at Chatham's Post."

Rusty went to the battle zone whenever possible to help out- even if just to provide water. "On this particular day I went along to see how the right flank was 'sticking it' and though they had been working at their narrow knee-deep trenches, with trenching tools and bayonets, and fighting like demons only can for about 60 incessant hours, they were as firm and as determined as only Australians could possibly be under such cruel circumstances. I had my water bottle filled, and a fair drop of brandy in it, and those hardy men looked at me with tears of gratitude in their hollow, staring eyes as they took a mouthful, the first moisture some had had for thirty hours. I don't remember any of them saying thank you; words expressed nothing at that time, though several of them clasped my arm, and went silently on with their work."

Then came the snow. "The roadside and hills were completely covered by three inches of snow, and you can well imagine how the water-carriers, dismal and cold, swore some as they slithered along up and down the greasy track with a frozen grip on their water-cans. None of our men as yet have their winter clothing and naturally there were complaints to be heard all along the line from the fatigue parties. It is the fellows in the sunken dug-outs that will suffer terribly."

To keep warm, Rusty was soon wearing all of his clothes, three blankets, two overcoats, all his spare shirts and clothing "worked amongst them" as well as a copy of the *New York Sun* newspaper. As all the water in the tanks were frozen, for some time the trench men had nothing to drink, there was no bread for six days, and everyone was complaining of agonisingly cold feet.

Rusty found himself forever being jolted. One day he found a group of soldiers, oblivious to all the danger, playing two-up for big money with the common call of "A quid I head 'em". The next a wounded man from Lone Pine, covered in dirt and dust, was transported to the dressing station. "He saw that I did not know him and he said after several attempts: 'It's Griff, Richy. Don"t you know me … Griff. And they've got me damned badly. I'm done Richy. I'm done this time." It was a colleague from one of the fatigue parties- Snowy Griffiths. "I got such a shock and saw the great weakness of my strength. I could not help him. Words failed me. I could only say: 'Stick it, Griff, my boy. You"ll be all right again. Good luck!'"

That night Snowy died.

"From the wounded I find that our trenches were blown to pieces. On Lone Pine all the parapets were knocked in and the communication trenches battered. This I quite believe by the number of men that came by suffering from shock and suffocation through being buried, and I am told there are a number still buried, some probably never to be got out. It is murder for our boys to have to stay in the front line of trenches while a terrible bombardment is in progress. One of the wounded was much annoyed to think that he and so many others had been broken up and never even saw a Turk to have a go at. Lots of men were blown out of their dugout behind the lines, and quite near to my dressing station."

A week later a wounded 1st Battalion private was brought in. "He was out in front laying down barbed wire when a bullet passed through his body. The night was dark and the road rough, so naturally the stretchers bounced a little. God knows we were steady and careful enough, but with each movement he groaned. He asked 'Whereabouts are we now?' I told him we were passing the water tanks in the gully and that we would not be long in getting him to the ship. 'Oh I'm not complaining for myself. It's you fellows I'm thinking of.' Later he asked: 'Will they put me on board tonight? My feet are terrible.' He died 30 minutes later. The bullet had cut into his spine."

Another soldier arrived with frozen feet, even though it hadn"t snowed for well over a week. The next two men were buried in front of the station.

On 11 December Rusty was told to pack up. Evacuation was now a reality. The Dardanelles campaign had been a fruitless disaster. They had failed in toppling the Turks, and it was now time to get out before there were any more unnecessary deaths. At last the commanders realised enough was enough.

For the Australians, apart from the dread of failure following eight months of hell, was the deep despair that they would now be separated from their dead comrades who would be left in enemy hands. Rusty wrote: "We got away loaded up like mules back to the camp, where nobody had the slightest idea as to where we were bound for. The feeling was in favour of a new landing. But where on this weird burdened earth could we be going? To make another landing on the Peninsula was unreasonable. When we got aboard ship last night and I saw the scraggy appearance of the troops I was quite satisfied that Lemnos was to be our destination."

In the ultimate irony, the evacuation of the Anzacs was the most successful operation of the whole Gallipoli campaign, with the Turks unaware of the mass withdrawal. The Australians went to great pains to camouflage the moment, with virtually no sound made by the Anzacs' muffled boots and conjuring tricks organised, including delayed action rifles going off and those soldiers who could be sighted by the enemy making out they weren't leaving when they were. As importantly, on the way out — unlike the way in — there was virtually no loss of life.

Two days later. Rusty was on the football field in Lemnos, padding himself up, helping his Corp team win 23-0, and afterwards watched the hive of action on the wharves. "The Australian troops are still pouring in and the idea that a general evacuation of Anzac is about to commence. If this is so, I reckon there will be a terrible feeling of depression and some hard words from Australia. It is hard to do, but being messed up and insufficiently equipped as the all-too-few troops have been on the Peninsula, nothing else can now be done but leave it, or give us some hundreds of Howitzers and thousands of tons of ammunition. If this latter cannot be done, we will be better at Mudros doing nothing than remaining on the Peninsula mere practice for the Turks to train and feast upon. It's just scandalous the weak manner in which Britain, or rather the Allies, are handling this Balkan problem and the relief of Russia from her miserable plight."

The mood on the island was all gloom. Rusty admitted that he seldom saw an Australian soldier smile, and feared that they may never will because ANZAC was "back again in the hands of the Turks". "What an awful bungling mess these short-sighted damned fool Englishmen have made of this business. I doubt if our good Australian soldiers will ever sing again after this terrible Peninsular setback through no fault of their own."

The only plus was the success of the evacuation, which according to Rusty, "was a splendidly planned move and wonderfully well carried out". "If we (or those English devils of Generals) could only plan and carry out an attack as thoroughly as this evacuation, Turkey would have long since been at our mercy. Instead of that, each succeeding month of this war has brought defeat and devastation. Having to retire from Anzac Cove has robbed us of all the glories of achievement."

Surely it could not get any worse.

TWELVE

THE FRONT

FOR SOME TIME RUSTY THOUGHT that his life as a soldier, together with that of thousands of other idle Anzacs, would be confined to dodging the incessant sandstorms around Cairo and Tel el Kebir, on the edge of the desert, defending Egypt against an anticipated attack from Turkey. Like most other Australians, Rusty was not exactly overwhelmed to be back in Egypt. The Anzacs, although relieved to be having a rest, still thought it was "a land of sin, sand, shit and syphilis".

A general address from their commander General Birdwood, in late February 1916 gave them little hope of going anywhere else. According to Rusty, Birdwood told the troops "it was the opinion of those in high circles at home that the Australians, although glorious fighting men, were too ragged and undisciplined to be taken to France". The main concern was that the Australians were "too fond of beer and women to be allowed near the big centres of the French trench lines".

Rusty agreed with the general. "At present the training of the troops is more of a ceremonial nature, such as saluting. Great stress is laid on saluting, and it seems that it is going to be hammered into the men this time. I fancy the Home Authorities have hit it pretty right too when they say the Australian is so hard to control that he is likely to become a danger in France. It is this same high-spirited, don"t care a damn temperament that makes them such glorious fighters and naturally if they lose the former rashness, they will also lose the latter virtue. The Australian is a queer bird right enough."

General Chauvel, commander of the 1st Light Horse Brigade, hammered home the message when he addressed the troops a week later. "All of the three brigades squared up splendidly and in rode the General. He got under way at once, and dealt with the much worn necessity for better discipline. Saluting was so strongly enforced in the European theatres of war that by neglecting the same we would appear a rabble and so shoddy a soldier that very little decent work or any responsible position would be assigned to Australians.

"An English General, seeing the troops wandering so helplessly and undisciplined about Alexandria and Cairo, reported to the English authorities that the Australians were unfit to go to France and mix with the villagers and soldiers there. And now, said General Chauvel, that you have got your chance of testing your mettle beside the continental troops, it is up to you to stand by us and play the game."

It was later revealed the English general was Sir Archibald Murray, commancer-in-chief in the Middle East. Murray had written a damning letter, complaining about the "extreme indiscipline and inordinate vanity" of the Australians. The easily offended knight was irritated that Australian troops were poorly dressed, failed to salute him and were violating military rules by cantering horses, riding in waggons, and causing trouble even in the officers' club. To express how unruly they were, Murray added that of 8858 cases of venereal disease in Egypt, 5924 were Australians.

It was inevitable that there would be friction between the Australian and British sections. The Australians were unimpressed with the airs and graces of the British officers and their rigid army discipline. Many thought the British were wimps and fools. The British turned their noses up at the uncouthness of the Australian colonials. Many thought the Australians were faintly manicured savages.

The eccentric behaviour of the Australian soldiers was also upsetting their own superiors. Chauvel was especially angered that

Australians were "digging up and tampering with dead Turks" buried near the Suez Canal. Chauvel called on those who knew the guilty parties to come forward because the act was "a curse and a crime that Australia will never live down". Rusty wasn't impressed with Chauvel, arguing that the general instead should have taken a lot of the blame for not burying the Turkish bodies months previously.

But it was a minor problem. News from the Western front was that the Germans were making strong gains, and it was time for the Australians, whether or not they had mastered the art of saluting, to come to the aid of the French and British in substantial numbers. The Germans, which had been grinding away at the Allied armies for 18 months, had succeeded in extending their line from Switzerland to the North Sea. The front line, a crazy bloodbath of mud, stretched for well over 560 kilometres.

The Australians headed en masse to the south of France. Most were relieved, including Rusty, who exclaimed in a letter: "Thank goodness we have at last left… the land of Desert and Dirty Niggers".

None realised that for the next two years, they would encounter the most nightmarish of conditions, where tens of thousands would be killed in an often bewildering trench war against the Germans through France and Belgium. The Western front would become synonymous with unmitigated carnage, where in mud, slush and inhumane conditions, thousands of soldiers died like flies while all those who somehow survived never forgot the horror. The land of 'Desert and Dirty Niggers' soon became a yearned for dreamland.

Getting to France was no luxury either. When clambering aboard a ship for Marseilles, Rusty soon discovered rats had overrun the craft. "A cook sets his traps each day down in our hold, and catches as many as 15 in four traps. He saves the tails for which the shipping companies give 1d a tail."

There were hardly any sleeping facilities and he was forced to bunk down on a narrow table in the mess room, until he was able to sneak past a guard, and slept on the lower hatchway.

On 30 March, they were in Marseilles, marching to the railway station for the long trip to the British zone, 200 kilometres north of Paris. "The Frenchmen stood interestedly but unmoved along the route; they were for the most part a very poor looking people, ill clad and slovenly, particularly the womenfolk. Of course this is an inferior quarter of even an inferior town like Marseilles.

"One woman of excellent appearance stood on the roadside watching the march pass when she seemed suddenly moved and, taking a bunch of pansies from her belt, walked unhesitatingly across holding out the flowers towards myself. I stepped out of the column, took the bouquet, saluted and picked up my place again, while the lady was saying 'Good luck Englishman' and something in French I could not follow. It was a very pretty little incident and pleased me very much."

As an avowed Francophile because of his months travelling through the country before the war, he was deeply concerned with how the uncouth Australian would handle the vastly different culture. "The Australian is an awfully arrogant individual; this naturally follows with his isolation from the rest of the world. Our men have heard stories of Paris high life, that they must think Frenchmen live only for wine and sensuality. This may apply to Paris, but it certainly does not apply to France proper. Our men are labouring under the impression that morality is unknown in France and that a fellow is at liberty to accost any woman, invite her to dine and then sleep with her. Therefore, I expect quite a lot of trouble to come about with our men over here."

It was all relatively calm on the northern train. Seated eight to a third-class carriage compartment, in a sixty-five—hour non-stop trip, the Australian soldiers advanced through Arles, Tarascon, Lyon, Dijon, Versailles and Amiens, before a twelve-kilometre trudge over stone-cobbled roads towards Hazebrouck in the north of France, between Lille and Dunkirk. Most of the troops were herded towards allotted villages, slushed-up farmyards and prehistoric barns, already invaded by animals, which would become their temporary home. Rusty wrote: "Our billet is wet and musty and was until just very recently the residence of huge, fat white- coloured pigs. So you can well imagine that we are not pleased with our abode, and there are 47 men sleeping in it. It is about nine foot high to the floor of the hay loft. I slept in a farmer's waggon... anyhow, on putting out the candle I could not go to sleep, there was a suspicion of fowl lice crawling over my face."

Although they were some distance from the front, there were constant reminders of the nearby dangers. "I could hear high explosions all night but now that I am walking in the direction of the firing line I can see hundreds of flashes from bombs and guns. This din continued until bedtime, 10pm, at which time I went to sleep. Star shells lit up the sky showing the layout of the trenches around the district. It was an inspiring sight and an anxious one."

The Australian troops' initiation into France was staid compared to their baptism of fire at Gallipoli. It involved relatively short stays on the front line and ample time well away in the back areas, where in territory known as "the nursery" they trained and were given pep talks, even one from Lord Kitchener who addressed them with the words: "Well, boys, I am very pleased to see you in France. You made your name in Gallipoli."

There was plenty of time to frequent the many *estaminets* (pubs) in the area, imbibe the local beer, wine and champagne, flirt with the French girls, even attend the YMCA picture show and see the latest Charlie Chaplin movie. Rusty caught up with an old 1908 Wallaby colleague, Josh Stevenson, and gossiped about old times and the fate g over old times, and the plight of several of their former teammates, They mulled over suggestions that Peter Flanagan was in financial trouble and Paddy McCue had allegedly "gone to the dogs entirely". Both refused to believe the rumours. During the day their time was taken up with endless marches, growing accustomed to their new flannelette gas helmets, and special drills learning how to walk unprotected through a trench sprayed with invisible weeping gas.

They were usually on the move. By April they were three kilometres from the front in Sailly, where they took over the local hospital, turned it into a dressing station, and attended to Ninth Battalion patients, who had been battered about on the front line by German guns, after retreating behind a brick wall of a billet that collapsed on them. More than twenty were killed.

He was also busy on the inaugural Anzac Day, with a stream of wounded being transported to his station from the front. Fighting fatigue that night, he hid himself away, and let his feelings flow on the diary page.

"One man with a gaping wound in his skull through which his brain bulged persisted in getting into the ambulance car without assistance today. Another fine specimen of Australian manhood is lying in the dressing station on his side in a very awkward position. He has lain there now forbidden to move or ease himself one degree, he was shot through the shoulder, the bullet passing through his lungs and out again at his lower rib on the opposite side to the shoulder at which it entered. His only hope of recovery is to remain perfectly still. Two heroes also lay nearby, one totally blind and the other with his nose and one eye taken away. Terrible sights to see, but oh, how proud these unperturbed, battered and uncomplaining warriors makes one feel for his homeland.

"A country young or old that can breed such diehards might justly be proud of it and need have no fears for its future… Men who can fight so gallantly, bear their pain unflinchingly and die so ungrudgingly for their flag and country are possessed of the mettle that will rise this young nation to a plane amongst nations that has no superior.

"It's Anzac Day today. I did not see nature's spring garb this day last year, but I saw wounded and dying men nursing their injuries in silence. I heard them say when succour was at hand: 'No sonny, I'm done, just give me a drink please, there's some chaps behind those bushes who wants help.' Others said: 'Just tie a bandage around, it might stop the bleeding, then I"ll battle along down to the beach.' 'Oh no my boy, we're going to carry you down to the beach.' 'But you're not,' came the reply, 'there's a lot of chaps worse than me about.'

"Yes, our men are taking their pains and afflictions as well today as they did on those lead-littered slopes at Anzac; but it is gratifying today to find the number of sufferers far less and the facilities to relieve their agony uncomparably superior. Great philosophers have said that is is suffering and hard setbacks that prove the man and bring out the finer qualities that are in him. This is exemplified today as it was exemplified previously, but of course on a much smaller scale.

"However it is not the brave manner in which men suffer that appeals to one as does the wondrous spirit and physical attainment that enabled our born fighters to hang on to the exposed tops of those steep ridges hour after hour and day after day against a formidable and refreshed foe, with the day's heat and the night's cold chill to counteract. These men never for a moment took their minds off their task. They beat off attack after attack, and then dug long holes and scratched away with an entrenching tool between spells to protect themselves from rifle and shrapnel fire. They were fighting for their country's honour and had no time to think of their own hunger and thirst. They were men to the core.

"All that long 25th day of April 1915, cries came down the paths, over the rough virgin scrub and along the winding gorges wet and deep in mud, firstly for ammunition and later for reinforcements. That every part of our front was weakening seemed obvious. As the stretcher bearers returned from the firing zone they were plied with questions from the wounded as to how the fight was going; I saw many men rise up from the narrow rubbly beach with haggard faces pale from the loss of blood and attempt to go back to the assistance of their hard-pressed comrades.

"Yet through all the anxiety and fear there was a whole crowd of fresh soldiers waiting for orders to move up and lend a hand. With their instincts roused and their hearts burning for revenge, those men waited hour after hour for orders to move. They shouted, swore, cursed and even prayed to be allowed to join in the fray and as each depressing cry came back for reinforcements, their blood boiled and their mouths dried up with anger at their own inactivity.

"Late in the afternoon, the order came to 'move up'. This body of tall, gaunt cornstalks came in broken columns over the uneven and bushy country, each man stalking along with tense features. They knew full well what they were going to face, but there was no faltering, their comrades were in need of assistance and no power on earth would hold them back one moment.

"The hillsides tried their breathing, their feet sometimes slipped, some swore, some remained silent. Their time had come to prove their merit and to test their valour. The land they so proudly represented called them forward. The call for help from their line of comrades steeled their determination and forward they went, shrapnel and bullets held no fear for them. They had heard their comrades' cry and felt their country's call.

"These giant cornstalks were our last line, our one hope, we had no reserves in hand now. If the line gave way all was lost, what remained would be driven into the sea, and the cherished name of Australia doomed. At the time, none of us thought of these things, each man was there to do his best. There was no time to consider pros and cons. It was fight, and keep fighting. It was hang on, show no quarter and give no ground, just sit tight.

"Hang on! What it meant to keep fighting and digging in this terrible business of hanging on over those first three days only those who were actually there can ever realise. And it was to the honour of these men amongst men, that with a party of four, I went into a hotel tonight and, in a corner, quietly and thoughtfully, toasted "Our Comrades" of April 25th, 1916."

Rusty"s sentiments were not in the minority. At Gallipoli the Australian troops, in the words of their most admired leader Sir John Monash, proved they were of a special breed. As Monash wrote to his wife a month into the Gallipoli campaign: "I am convinced that there are no troops in the world to equal the Australians in cool daring, courage and endurance." A few days later, Rusty wrote as passionately about the British soldier, otherwise described as a "fragile, weak-hearted, incompetent army".

He could never forgive the British for "the murder of Gallipoli". "Men lying on stretchers aboard a tramp ship en route to Alexandria went green and rotten for want of medical attention, and had to be cut away from the stretcher. 650 patients with two medical men and a dozen orderlies to attend them left Anzac on one ship.

"From Camp Helles came similar reports, so can you, dear reader, think hard of me, or think for a moment that I don't know what I say, when I condemn the British Government (not the British nation, mark you) for their terrible crimes. It is scandalous to think of mere politicians running a war such as this one."

The transport of injured was scandalous. On one ship, where there were almost 500 wounded soldiers, there was only one bedpan, while wounds were often not treated for well over a week. Soon the Australians and British were squabbling over who was to blame for a disgraceful situation where near-dead soldiers were transported from ship to ship in search of accommodation.

At least at the other end was some reasonable medical assistance, and doctors of the calibre of Rusty's old Wallaby captain Paddy Moran, who had been sent to Gallipoli from Aldershot to help with serious medical operations on the hospital ships. Moran marvelled at the supposedly unclimbable cliffs of Gallipoli, and how "men stuck there for months like flies to an upturned plane". Moran eventually left for Malta, suffering with dysentery.

Adding to Rusty's exasperation with the British was his recollection of the 971 Hill battle, where the English "had their bayonets fixed and with the sun flashing on them could be seen fifteen miles away. This is how the Gallipoli Peninsula failed us, through absolute foolery. Just think that if the English anything like played their part, Gallipoli would have been conquered and possibly Germany and her able allies beaten by this time." What angered Australian soldiers most was when the British landed at Suvla, forcing the Australians to act as decoys, culminating in a large number of deaths. The British wasted 48 hours when there was 'an open road to the Dardanelles', doing nothing on the beachfront, while in the words of Monash, 'its leaders were quarrelling about questions of seniority and precedence'."

Rusty was as concerned that poor leadership by the British in France would cause further problems.

"The Australian is the adaptable man possessed of courage, animal instinct and bush resource. The Englishman lacks both dash and resource. He has never been allowed to think and shift for himself. We want the Australians to lead the infantry attacks also. I fear the English will buggerise about, dig himself in when he has the enemy only half routed, as they lost Helles and Suvla Bay (in Gallipoli). The English are damn fool soldiers and I believe that they will yet make an unholy mess of this Somme River fight in which they started off splendidly. They will stop and dig in as at Suvla Bay and Cape Helles just when the day is won. I am afraid of the Englishmen and their shortsightedness."

Rusty's words echoed numerous Australian leaders' sentiments, including those of Monash, who described the British troops as having "no grit, no stamina or endurance, poor physique, no gumption, and they muddle along and allow themselves to be shot down because they don't even know how to take cover". Fortunately, a series of cricket and football matches were played nearby to calm Rusty's unsettled nerves. In an article for the *Sydney Mail*, Rusty said the first football match he saw on French soil, just a few weeks after playing in an Australian-All Blacks match on a stony Lemnos pitch, was a game between the Welsh Engineers and a team of Maoris in the village of Laventie in early May 1916. "About 300 Welshmen and Maoris lined the sides and saw a splendid game. They showed their appreciation towards the close by shouting and cheering that astounded the few remaining inhabitants [of the village], waking them rudely, and causing them to stare in amazement at the excited crowd of dark-skinned Maoris and the uncontrollable Welshmen. These French people shuddered to think what the outcome might be, as they were still well within range of the Germans' heavy guns. But never a thought of the Germans or the power of their guns ever bothered the minds of either player or spectator." The match was a 14-all draw.

The match also confirmed Rusty"s belief that the Colonials were the healthiest of all those fighting the Germans. "The Maoris were in the field waiting quite a long time for the Welshmen. While they were waiting, the Colonials looked physical giants compared to the lean and wiry Welsh. There were other features in the appearances of the two teams that bothered me ... The great self-possession and confidence of the Maoris, also their straight built bodies and big limbs; while their opponents seemed stage-frightened and their ackwardly put together forms bent with hard work and cramped by confinement at the workshop benches.

"The contrast was very marked indeed, and the more notice I took of it the greater and greater became my love for the Colonial, and my mind refreshed as to the difference in appearance of African and English athletes as they stood facing one another in both South Africa and in England. Also the Australians when they faced the Englishmen and the Welshmen in 1908. The Englishmen though always stand up better and finer than the Welshmen, but the Colonial is vastly superior to any of them.

"Football matches have now become common amongst the Australian troops while resting after a spell of duty in the trenches. In the first game I took part in, the playing area was pegged out in the middle of a big paddock. The grass was long, and prevented the marking out of either goal or touch lines.

"A shower of rain made the Flanders mud so slippery that, assisted by the grass, it was very difficult indeed to turn round quickly and keep one's equilibrium, so much so that at times the barrackers shrieked with laughter. A troupe of knockabout pantomime artists would not have been so skilful or half so funny.

"The notable feature of the game on the bank of the River Lys was the length of grass. Before the kickoff, I saw a player stoop down to fix a bootlace, and he was entirely hidden by the length of grass. During the game the men could not follow the ball in dribbling rushes, as they invariably over ran it and stumbled down. I played fullback, and had an excellent view of the desperate attempts to kick the ball, lying half-hidden from the kicker, and also when, after a clean tackle, both men entirely disappeared in the grass for a few moments. A fellow was laid out and one of our players noticed it, he was practically lost in the long grass, the spectators fixed him up after finding him." Adding to the comedy was that to get to the playing field, the teams had to cross the River Lys in "a clumsy raft which wet everybody up to the knees".

Another time, Rusty was the most spirited of barrackers at a 12th Battalion A Company match against the Bombers. "Tomorrow they will be en route for the Somme and the greatest hell ever thought of, greater even than man's imagination is capable of conceiving. But what care they are for the morrow, let's first find out who are the best footballers while there is still time in hand. No international match was more keenly fought out, and as the defeated side came off the field their friends went over and sympathised in the manner of true sportsmen and noble soldiers. They had played a good game. At the bloody Somme any day now both conqueror and vanquished will fight a different fight where rules do not govern the struggle and God alone is the referee."

To ensure the soldiers were as spirited on the front as they were on the football field, around the same time as these football matches, Prime Minister Billy Hughes and General Birdwood, met the First Battalion, to explain that God and Australia were behind them. By their side was the former Prime Minister, Andrew Fisher, now Australia's High Commissioner in London. As Rusty observed, it didn't quite work. Football worked better in soothing souls.

Hughes was brief, explaining that Australia realised they "were fighting and dying for her", "and when you come home, rest assured Australia will welcome and look after you for the rest of your days Today it was strange that Andy Fisher did not say a few words to the boys. More so strange, as he seemed entirely out of his element and just moped along behind Hughes and Birdwood right out of the game altogether.

"The review was held in a paddock that may or may not have been out of range, but to give every possible protection there were some eight or ten aeroplanes flying around to keep off the enemy bomb droppers. The brass band played its best, and when Mr Hughes said that General Birdwood had allowed him to call for three cheers to Australia, they were so heartily given that they could be heard all the way to Berlin. Then one cheer for Birdy was called, and by way of expressing his popularity, the men cheered four or five times. Andy Fisher, also, seemed lost at having to play second fiddle, he was out of it, and to our boys it was rather pathetic."

For the next few months Rusty continued the training drills, ran a dressing station, and explored the war zone wherever possible, usually getting as close to the front line as he could. One day he was in Belgium, the next walking towards Amiens, another day hovering near the Somme, the next observing the ruins of Albert. After a morning sewing up corpses in blankets for burial, Rusty hitched a ride in an ambulance to help any wounded around Albert. "The chief feature of Albert is its immense brick built church with a very high tower," Rusty wrote that night.

"Now, however, the whole structure is tottering to a fall. Shells have riddled it through and through. There was a figure of the Virgin and child. A statue standing perhaps 22 feet in height, it now leans right over the side and is drooping into the roadway. Looking at it from underneath it seems that the Virgin is holding out her child so as to save it from harm in the fall. The child has hands uplifted as though ready to jump into the onlooker's arms. It makes a striking picture. The local superstition is that when the statue falls the war will immediately close."

He was always near the main battlelines, even if at times his adventures were limited by a serious case of lumbago, first suffered when playing for the British Lions in Johannesburg. The guns were forever thundering and German aircraft hovering, but he felt little danger, enjoying the French countryside, which even though "racked and shattered" reminded him of the country around Bathurst, Orange and the Darling Downs. However, he was never able to fully relax. Hell was always nearby.

At the dressing station, each day he observed and helped fellow soldiers, exhausted, battered and bewildered by the frontline warfare. Through July and August 1916, Rusty was near the most horrific of all battlefields, Pozieres, where for miles around "the country was racked and shattered".

After Australian troops had succeeded in taking the small village of Pozieres, a strong German artillery position, during an endless and furious bombardment, they suffered almost as many casualties as they had done at Gallipoli. In less than seven weeks the AIF lost 6842 dead while more than 17,000 were gassed or wounded. The only Australian action to compare took place at around the same time at Fromelles, where more than 5000 soldiers were casualties in just twenty-seven hours of charges through mud and slush, straight at German machine-gun fire.

In the case of Pozieres, a once picturesque northern French village had, in the words of C.E.W. Bean, been turned into "a gigantic ash heap." After the despair of Gallipoli, all Pozieres did was reinforce in the minds of the now deeply resentful Australian soldiers that they were being murdered by their British superiors. As Major Garnet Adcock wrote home: "Everyone here is 'fed up' of the war, but not with the Hun. The British staff, British methods and British bungling have sickened us."

Rusty saw the carnage. On 5 August, he wrote: "I went over to the dressing station before breakfast, and found that the Fourth Division had followed up an artillery preparation and gained possession of the crest of the ridge beyond Pozieres, and regardless of the Germans' costly counter-attacks, our men gave no ground.

It was a far different air the wounded carried from the first attack by the same battalion six days ago. On that occasion everything went wrong, and our men, after struggling with barbed wire while machine guns played amongst them, were forced to return to the trenches without gaining a foot of ground and losing very heavily. Officers broke down and wept when coming through wounded, and the men were strangely silent and heavy hearted. Today, however, it is quite different. Although our men were not smiling, they were just satisfied that they had done their duty and triumphed, but not without carrying with them the burden of their previous smashing up."

All around were the victims. "Yesterday some of them lay out in the garden from 8am until 5pm, waiting to be dressed and sent on to the clearing station. Many a man smiles when he is told that he will never be able to fight again or that he won't be right again for some months. The fellows shake hands with and congratulate their mates and brothers when they find that they have a wound that is not likely to be serious, but will most likely keep them away for a few months. Spotswood, one of our cooks, had his top jaw fractured and as he lay in much pain on the ground, his foster father smiled joyfully and remarked: 'Spotty, you are a certainty for Blighty and a damned good job. You're a very lucky fellow."

'Blighty' was a slang term for a wound sufficient to cause its recipient to be sent to England for rest and recreation leave. "Our wounded, most of whom are driven insane by constantly living under shell fire, are very silent, and speak in a hesitating and bored tone. We used to say Gallipoli was hell unadulterated, but the wounded were more buoyant and willing to talk.

"All night long four doctors were kept working without a break, and several amputations were put through, fingers, hands and even an arm. All these operations were performed without chloroform or anaesthetic of any kind. How these lovely heroes stood it I cannot realise."

Not all were properly treated either. "I went outside and there was a ghastly looking case lying by quite conscious. I spoke to him and found that he wanted to spit and clear his throat. I lifted his head and turned him on his side, he spat out some blood, the poor fellow's lungs were penetrated that was clear. I found that my hand was covered in blood. I turned him again and had a look. To my surprise and horror there was an undressed hole several inches big and every time he breathed the blood just gushed. Again a doctor was brought, but what use was a doctor. But the extraordinary part of it is that this man had been through first the regimental doctor, the dressing station at Becourt, and now had been through the 13th Field Ambulance, and was lying ready for evacuation before so huge and dangerous a wound was even found out and dressed. Seeing the rush that there is, one can hardly blame the doctors, although it is sheer carelessness all the same."

The injuries were not just physical. "One case, Fitzgerald, was most pathetic. He was suffering from shell shock and was quite insane. With his two hands held up, and eyes wide open and staring, he cried all the time, howling loudly with each gun report or flash of a gun. These shell shock cases are awful, and very plentiful. The fellows are quite mad. Their hands shake – it's impossible to hold anything or to find their own mouths. The legs tremble and shake, so that they at times cannot walk without assistance."

Even the uninjured were deeply scarred. "The 19th Battalion came into Warloy last evening looking so haggard and drawn. They were dust begrimed, and their eyes, in many cases, were like those of hunted animals, glassy-like and staring as if their nerves were shattered, and they were silent and frightened. Several I spoke to told me they didn't care a jot what happened, they had lost their pals and felt full up with the whole thing."

But it really hit home when Rusty visited one of his closest Wallaby mates, Australian skipper Syd Middleton, then a captain in the 19th Battalion, who had just spent several weeks at the front, near Pozieres.

"Oh, what a wreck he is, he must be looking ten years older since I saw him last. On being told about it, he said: 'Yes, Cocky, I'm a much older man now, these past ten days have been a terrible strain, yes terrible!'

The whole time he spoke to me he sat on a bed, and looked down onto the floor, and mechanically keeping a cigar alight by short puffs now and again. His voice was low, and like most of the other men, halting."

Middleton was suffering from the strain of being head of a company who had to be on the alert the whole time, but realistically could "do absolutely nothing to help his men, who were "being blown out of their trenches and the others were just sitting around waiting their turn to come, and he could not do a single thing to help them.

"The whole time there were high explosive shells falling around in all directions. One moment there would be a party of men crouching down against a wall jokingly picking out where the next shell will land, and who is the next man to be blown up.

"Captain Middleton looks on at them, passes a word or two, and moves on. Almost immediately he is told that a man is knocked out, he goes back, and there are several of the little party scattered about. The wounded are patched up, and after separating the 'brain from the guts', the identification disc and pay book are found, and then all hands (although many of the dead man's mates fall back and cannot help) throw the body over the parapet to strengthen it. Oftimes a shell will throw a body back into the trench after it has been lying there for some days and is an awful proposition to handle.

"Middleton was practically buried five times in one day, his stars were shot away from his shoulder on one side, the heel of his boot was dinted and his foot wrenched, a piece of shell penetrated his side and made quite a gash. And worst of all for a while was a huge lump of dirt that knocked him down and shattered his mind for a few moments. He thought his time had come to die. Day and night there was no relief, the carnage and toll was more than man could ever realise. Dante and his inferno is a huge joke. It is the real hell."

Death even became a relief, especially when the victim was abhorred. "The fellows in discussion just now were talking of Captain Tozar, who was blown up and killed last Sunday night. Strange, out of the three of them, they agreed that an act of providence must have directed the shell on top of so miserable a man as Tozar seems to be. They say he never would speak decently to anybody at all, and was a curse to walk with."

Not even a visit from King George V to their hospital at Warloy could raise the spirits of the medical staff, or the wounded from various battlefields, including the Somme front, described by all and sundry as a scene of "unmitigated murder." According to Rusty, the King "looked very thin and troubled like, with a beautiful red nose that looked almost suspicious. Inside the hospital the King spoke to none of the patients, nor did he have a consoling work for those lonely nurses working amongst those awful cases, and with men dying to the number of ten or twelve a day out of 50 therein.

"The impression left by the King was very weak indeed. Inside they were all very disappointed, in fact, hurt. Yes, he saluted, but the whole show was miserably formal and cold. Our men are greatly disappointed, many exceedingly annoyed. It is the first time they have seen a King and they wanted to see him show them that he is sorry for all the suffering they have been through during the past weeks, and that he appreciates their efforts in the interests of the Empire. Better by far had he not called at all. He might suit English ideas, but he won't do our democratic Australians. He was too reserved and sober."

All this festered further disillusionment among the Australian troops towards anything English. However, the Australian government remained stoically behind Great Britain, agreeing to virtually all of their demands, including an edict that they provide more troops for the war. While in London, Prime Minister Billy Hughes agreed to this request, even though realising that after the heavy losses on the Somme and the drop in volunteers, the only way to boost the Army ranks was to introduce conscription. Realising that the trade unions, his own Labor

Jim and Joan in Rotorua, New Zealand, on holiday with their father.

Joan and Jim.

Boiling the billy while camping out in the bush.

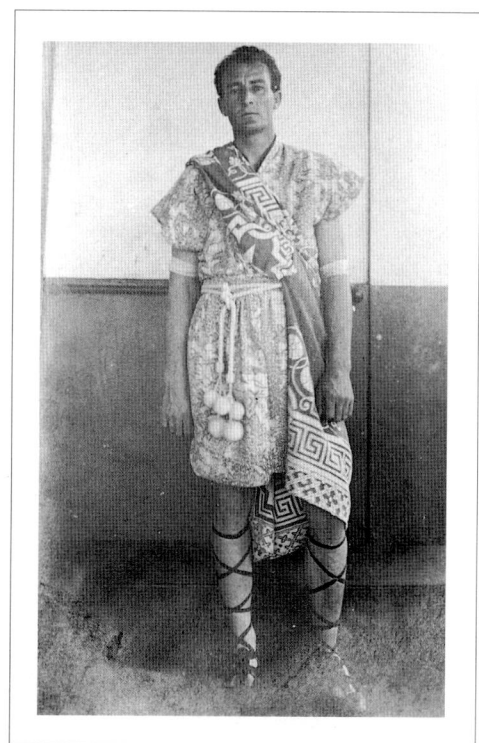

Ready for a fancy dress ball on one of his many boat trips around the world.

This studio photograph shows a debonair man about town shortly after the war.

The dashing Lillian Richards, nee Sandow, the woman Tom knew as 'Snow White'.

In the Pyrenees

A young Lil.

Lil Sandow (left) with two friends, ready for a big night.

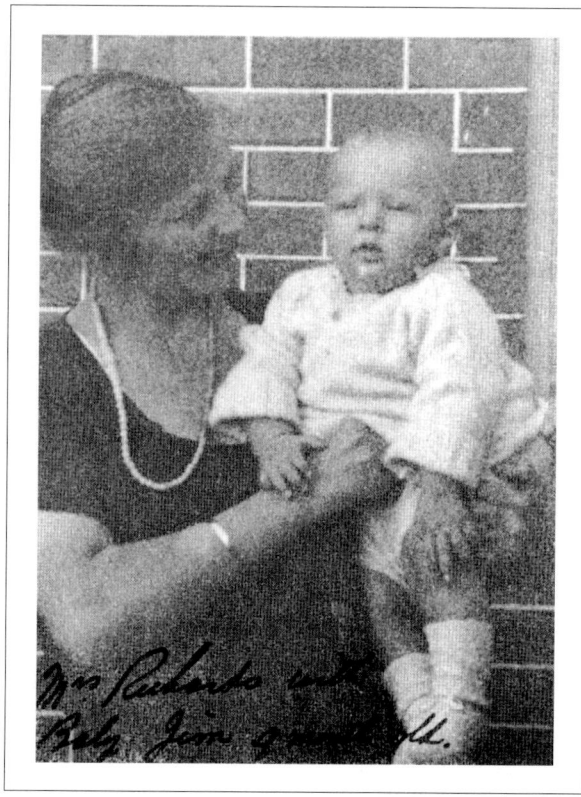

Mrs Tom Richards nursing nine-month son, Jim.

The last photo of Tom Richards, nursing his nephew John.

Party and the Catholic Church were opposed to this, Hughes instead took the issue to the Australian people in the form of a referendum in late 1916. The referendum divided the nation with Hughes, who had the backing of the establishment press, matched up against the equally fiery Irish Catholic Archbishop of Melbourne Dr Daniel Mannix, who vehemently argued the "No" case, primarily because Australia should not conscript its youth to be "cannon fodder". There were violent street fights, eggs were thrown at Hughes, with the fiery PM calling his opponents "scabs".

On the battlefront, a high percentage of soldiers voted against conscription, arguing that if a person is forced into uniform, he will not be of much use. Many argued the merits of freedom of choice, as well as not wanting to push someone else into the hell they had suffered.

Rusty instead sided with the Yes case. "I voted yes not out of any jealous feeling for the chaps at home, but because I firmly believe that every country should be able to call up its manhood in defence of its birthright. The volunteer system to my mind is a ghastly failure because men come away who would be of more value staying at home. Conscription is absolutely essential, not so much, or at all, in fact to force men to come away but simply to regulate the flow and to be thoroughly organised and prepared for the worst." The No vote won narrowly.

Adding to Rusty's concern about an onrush of raw volunteers was that already near the battlefront were perfectly able soldiers who, he thought, should be given the chance to fight, soldiers like himself who were desperate for the chance to prove themselves, who had done the training, and after several years of experiencing the harshness of war, knew what was required.

Rusty was sick of being a bit player, a spectator. He believed his masculinity was under question, convinced that he was a "loafer" because so many of his comrades were, unlike him, at the front. Despite his fearless work behind the lines in Gallipoli and France, he still had convinced himself he was not properly defending his country. That would only happen when he was in the face of the enemy. As usual, he was underestimating his own value. Early in the war, non-combatants had been looked down upon and treated as if they were inferior to the fighting soldier. Those in the Field Ambulance were described as bodysnatchers, linseed lancers, and the medical corps was considered a haven for pacifists and shirkers. However, these derogatory comments soon ceased, following their countless examples of bravery in saving and helping frontline soldiers.

Within days of the Gallipoli landing, the field ambulancemen and stretcherbearers were regarded by the soldiers as saints, with C.E.W. Bean explaining that their work was probably more dangerous than that of the riflemen. Bean believed the stretcherbearer, who sometimes worked for thirty or forty hours without sleep, unarmed and fearless in the line of fire, was the epitome of the spirit of the Digger. They were eventually idolised, tagged as saintly bearers. But this did not satisfy Rusty. Over many months in his diary, there were persistent complaints that he had been under utilised.

Exactly twelve months after joining the Army, he wrote: "The fact that I am not in the fighting line worries me very much and distracts from my conscience the feeling of war achievements. There is the feeling that I have not been much of a warrior. I have seen and stood against all the dangers of war and had narrow escapes with the best of them, but I have not been one of the fighting line."

He could not even find solace in attending Army church services. So disillusioned was he with the calibre of the preachers, and how far-fetched their message, he soon looked for alternative Sunday pursuits. "Bitterness and jealousy are not taught in the Bible and yet one often finds it wrapped around the religions of some peoples regardless of their mere form of worship. It often seems to me that the wrong type of man is engaged in church preaching, the weakling, a man who does not know the world in all its stages… The padre's prayer for the sick, wounded and dead seemed a foolish point in face of what he said concerning all that happens in this world is thought out beforehand and planned by God. If so, why then bother about asking his help and assistance? Nonsense."

At last Rusty, after several restless years of self-doubt, waiting and worried that he was a no-good shirker, was given consent to his demands to leave stretcherbearing and become a fully fledged soldier. On 16 November he was recommended for a commission in the First Battalion. On 2 December he joined A company. He now could do what he wanted for so long: get right in the thick of the battle, head directly to the front.

THIRTEEN

THE HONOUR

RUSTY WAS UNDER NO ILLUSION over what he would encounter. "As I have often said: 'If there's a bullet or a shell with my name and address on it, it's no use dodging it,'" he wrote. These were fearless, near boastful words, but Rusty soon proved them to be no empty statement.

After convincing the authorities he could "command and lead a body of men", Rusty realised he probably would never see Australia again. "I know the danger of the undertaking full well. Eleven officers were shot out of the 1st Battalion during their few days in the trenches at Longueval, some wounded of course. Out of 36 bombers, only six now answer the roll call. I would not have accepted the position only for the fact that I came away to do the bidding of my country. I came to help in any work that those above me saw fit to give me, and now I graciously accept a position of grave danger.

"Some of the fellows say I'm a damn fool, as we all know how officers are cut up, but this I can't help. I've been called upon and willingly I go. The feeling that seems to come over one is akin to a gambler going out with his last punt to make good or die of hunger. Or a thirsty bushman making for the last despairing water hole in drought time… like a man getting a run of heads in a two-up school, they can't go on indefinitely, fate must recoil." Commanding officers "got either Military Crosses or wooden crosses".

Stationed near Pozieres, now a gutted wasteland, Rusty's first ventures to the front in January 1917 amazed him. "While overlooking no man's land with its many dead, Germans as well as our own, I saw two of our Australians waving a white flag. Three minutes later they hopped over, one man carrying a stretcher. They went 30 yards, hurriedly opened the stretcher, put a man onto it, and stooping low hurried safely back into the trench. It was a brilliant sight and speaks well of the German's sense of humour, after the awful things we've heard about him."

A few weeks later, Rusty was firmly settled in the frontline trenches, still pondering the strange behaviour of the enemy. After a superior had remonstrated with Australian soldiers for looking over the top of the trenches and showing themselves so freely, "a moment later I could hardly believe my eyes, for only 30-40 yards away were two Germans waist high over their trench waving a bottle and beckoning to us, at the same time calling out loudly. At first I thought they must be our men having a little joke, but no, they were Germans, much to my astonishment. I have heard a lot of this kind of thing from time to time, but could not believe it. Then again it is said that the Tommies commonly do this sort of thing with the Germans, and in consequence neither side fire at the other. But this is the Australians' first day in the trenches here, so I reckon that in a few days' time, there will be no looking over at one another, it will be war to the teeth."

Rusty's early days were involved in dugout work, carrying sand bags, and improving accommodation up front, especially as France was in the middle of a big freeze. All around were frozen corpses, including hundreds of Germans. "I saw some 20 German bodies lying about in different places, mostly in their prepared positions. They all appeared to have been well looted, and if not soon buried will make a terrible smell. I cut off five buttons from a coat of a dead man to keep."

A month later Rusty and his company were moved to Bazentin, east of Pozieres, to form a fatigue party. On arrival, with a few colleagues, he scouted around the area, visiting several newly taken villages, and discovered the toll of a short advance. "There were bodies of Australians lying thickly about on the ground, some of them in most remarkable positions. One was huddled up on his hands and knees as though in the act of crawling away out of the shell hole in which I saw him. The cold weather had preserved the bodies, and made the scene all the more weird."

In April, after a month in officers' school at Tirancourt on the River Somme, he was directed toward the prime battlefield near the village of Bullecourt south-east of Arras. The Germans had succeeded in retreating behind what was assumed to be the impenetrable Hindenburg Line, a series of trenches reinforced with barbed wire and strategically placed machine gun posts. A pivot of the German defence was Bullecourt, which was ringed by wire and trench systems. Here the Germans, on a low hill, had built a strong fortress with cellars, deep tunnels for reserves to rush to the post and concrete machine-gun emplacements. If an Allied victory were to be achieved, the impenetrable had to become penetrable. It was up to the Australians and British, who went on the offensive, attempting to break through the line near Bullecourt. What followed was some of the most ferocious fighting of the war, for what was essentially a small, near useless piece of ground.

After almost being buried alive on his thirty-fifth birthday when his dugout, tunnelled into the roadside, was blown in, Rusty was involved in the holding of Demicourt, a village taken from the Germans the previous night. He wrote on 9 April: "The shelling today has been awfully heavy indeed, and as we have but litle artillery support it is a trying business. I am sitting in a German shelter where the enemy went to sleep last night, but woke early, and 'beat it' leaving behind everything he possessed, so that our men have today eaten his bread which is a dirty brown colour, very sodden and sour like, but with German jam on the bread the boys barged into it."

On April 10, as officer in charge, he was on duty from 2am in bitterly cold weather. "Every day we had frost, snow or rain, and it's the devil with only our ordinary clothes, as neither blankets or overcoat were allowed to go with us. All we have for protection is a groundsheet. This serves to keep the shoulders dry, but it's an awfully cold thing to sleep with in a damp hole dug down into the ground. Never mind, I have had the pleasure of eating German bread and jam, smoked German cigars, and drank their coffee as well as slept with one of the enemy overcasts in his own sleeping shelter."

Later that day he went to the nearby village of Hermies and witnessed "destruction one could never dream of. It would not shelter a goat as there is not a portion of a roof or a corner of a building left." Rusty's shelter was little better: a two-metre by 1.3-metre by one-metre dugout, covered by "shrapnel-riddled galvanised iron". This was luxury compared to the main trenches, where on 23 April from 3am he was on watch duty, not allowed to move for fear of attracting artillery fire. "I can see the Hindenburg Line plainly. It seems particularly strong in trench systems and wire entanglements. I fear we will require heavy artillery support before we can advance further."

A few days later he was only metres from the Line. Directed towards Bullecourt, on the night of 3 May he was told to be ready to move forward at any moment. For the next three days, Rusty found himself "right into the gaping jaws of hell." The demands were simple. He was in charge of a nineteen-man bombing party, and his directive was that no matter what resistance or enemy numbers were in front of him, the German wall had to be moved, crushed or dismantled.

It was Lone Pine, the Nek all over again. And Rusty was ready. Armed with a limited amount of bombs and grenades, his party marched straight at the enemy line, and when in its shadow, hurled everything at the Germans. The ploy worked, with the Germans immediately retreating, allowing Rusty to lead the men into the German trenches, and despite being fired at from nearly every direction, push the front line back more than 250 metres. Rusty was relentless, continually urging his soldiers on to gain further ground, on the way killing twenty-five Germans with either well aimed bombs or rifle shots. He also took sixteen prisoners.

Rusty's leadership enabled his party to reach an important cross-trench, allowing them to gain touch with the 3rd Battalion and effectively bomb a further fifty metres up the trench. As well, 150 metres of communication trench was won.

In such a short time it was an enormous gain of ground by Rusty and his men, an even more extraordinary achievement considering that early in the fray they ran out of bombs. Instead to reinforce their position, they used enemy stick bombs found in the German trenches to push the enemy further back. As Rusty wrote several days later: "For three whole days we engaged the Germans in bombing attacks and defences and waited until the Hun artillery, or rather, until the devil closed his jaws and crushed us. When the 1st Battalion got into touch with Fritz he got Hell from our rifle and hand bombs also from our snipers. From a personal view it was glorious for me, after leading a bombing party and taking 280 yards of main trench out of Fritz's hand, as well as 200 yards of communication trench, taking prisoners. Splendid specimen of men, right enough, but oh, they were in a pitiful plight from shock, and cried 'Comrade'. They would have willingly kissed me but for my demure and impossible countenance."

When taking enemy ground Rusty immediately built a barricade in the main trench and then linked up with the Third Battalion. For the next seven hours Rusty, perched behind that barricade, thwarted endless heavy artillery attacks."After putting in posts I went back and bustled the fellows to build a barricade, did some good target shooting, and went hanging onto the position with the Germans' own bombs and a very limited number of rifle grenades. It was lovely sport shooting Germans with both revolver and rifle, as well as bombing them down in their dugout. Out of one double entrance dugout nine prisoners were afterwards taken."

Holding onto this precarious position was going to be onerous, considering that their successful charge had led to a substantial bulge in the line, with Germans now flanking them on both sides. As Rusty's party was holding firm, at 7pm he decided to hand over to Lieutenant Howell Price. "I stood with my hand on his shoulder pointing out the German line of trenches ahead when a shell came from behind and smashed his leg above the thigh very badly. He rolled down saying: 'Goodbye Tom old fellow I"m done.' I could not answer, but on cutting away his pants and binding up the wound I felt sure that though he was certain to lose his leg he would do alright. I kissed the boy and tears welled up. We got a stretcher at once, and on being carried away he gripped my hand with a firm hold. A grip of love and tenderness. I went down into the deep dugout at A Coy Headquarters, taken from Fritz that morning, and had a meal. But a little later news came along that Germans had broken through the 3rd Battalion and they were retiring."

This information staggered Rusty, forcing him to sprint back to the front line in a bid to rally his troops, and convince the 3rd Battalion to hold firm. "My heart bled to think that Australians would leave their post and run away from a bombing attack of the Germans. I did not think it possible for a crowd of Australians to throw up the sponge so frightfully. It took a whole lot of coaxing to get 14 of the 50 or 60 to stay with me and hold out. We held out all night in great style but oh I did curse and swear at them, and then pleaded with them in the name of Australia to stick. Had it not been for a few of the 1st Battalion, perhaps we never would have held out. A barrage of Mills bombs turned the tide. I threw bombs with the men, and later settled back, and rallied the fellows with cheers and shouts, like a mighty barracker at a football match, whenever a German assault was launched. We got them every 40 minutes or so until daylight."

Next morning he discovered that the 11th Battalion, also under heavy fire to the right of Rusty's sector, had lost their nerve and were now retreating, jumping out of their trenches before another German bombing assault. Another frantic rush to the battle area was required. Encountered by fleeing Australian soldiers, Rusty crash-tackled several, pushing them back into the trenches. As with the Third Battalion, the 11th were like "cattle stampeding". "I got several boxes of Mills bombs on either side of the trench mouth and pushed some of the 11th into the posts. One 'windy' cove cried that he could not throw bombs. He was too knocked up. But as he trembled with fear I cursed him, hit him a whack on the jaw and shoved him into the post, making him take bomb for bomb with me, and throw it.

"While my cheering and shouting brought several to our assistance, I then ran down and onto the opposite post- got the fellows working there and then back onto the roadside bank, now lined with 170 or more 11th and 12th Battalion men. I called on them to remember they were Australians. 'What will Australia think when she knows you deserted your posts, and let your brother soldiers down!' That shifted some back, and as they passed I gave them boxes of bombs lying about, and cheered long and loudly as they filed back to their trenches. To each three or four men as they passed I gave a box of 12 bombs, assuring him that each of them was guaranteed to drive Fritz back 10 yards, and that each bomb was worth 5 pounds. I saw Lieutenant Bruton at the end with his revolver drawn, and preventing the men from going further back. This they eventually did, but it was an anxious half hour for us."

Others decided on even more drastic action to rally the troops. Corporal Snowy Howell, who was relentlessly holding his position, decided that there was only one way to push the Germans back further, by going straight for their face. All around Howell egg and stick-bombs were raining down, on both sides machine guns were cutting any Australian who pushed too close, while right in front of him eighty Germans, led by two officers, were holding firm.

Suddenly Howell leaped out, scrambling onto the top of an open parapet and then running along it, hurled bombs down at the enemy, who immediately fled. Rusty was close behind, supporting him with a Lewis gun, following along the trench and firing bursts. Howell suddenly ran out of bombs but that did not deter him. He chased after the enemy, jabbing down at them with his bayonet, until he crashed into the trench himself when wounded. Rusty helped get Howell back to safety. After holding their ground for several more hours of intense fighting, Rusty's party were relieved, but not before proving themselves the mightiest of crusaders, the greatest of war heroes.

For his deed, Snowy Howell a builder from the Sydney suburb of Enfield, was awarded the Victoria Cross. The London *Times* even reported on Howell's actions. "It was a fine spectacle," said the *Times*, "and it rejoiced the hearts of the considerable number of men who saw it."

Rusty received the Military Cross. His citation read. "For conspicuous gallantry and devotion to duty. He was in charge of a bombing party, and despite strenuous opposition succeeded in extending the line 250 yards and holding a strong post. He set a splendid example throughout." Just over a week before being informed by General Birdwood of his Military Cross, Rusty was also promoted to Lieutenant.

The honour was high, but the toll was considerable. Rusty could gather only forty-three men to lead from the battlefield. More than 140 from his company were dead. Rusty had taken command of A Company after Lieutenant Yates had fallen back "with his brain protruding into my arms", while his old friend, Howell Price, also died.

"Oh god, when I recall the men that have fallen faithfully by my side, it's so pitiful," he wrote. "First, there was my young Martin, my runner, and a fine lad only 19 years of age. He jumped up onto the bank where I was sniping Huns with my revolver, to get a rifle shot in. A moment later, he fell back onto me, with his head blown in, and blood flowing all over me. I could see he was dead, and raced on around the corner. One moment later, blood poured from a fellow's face. He wanted to stop, but I pushed him back along the trench, and shouting at the top of my voice, went onwards.

"Later Lyle Mackley fell off the communication trench at my feet, shot through the shoulder and lungs. At this moment four Hun prisoners came racing back, shouting mercy, with their hands above their heads. I felt them for firearms, and pushed them on, carrying Mackley between them, and at once linked up with the Third Battalion."

Rusty ended up with a piece of shell in his forearm and knee. After just one day of rest he was informed that he was going straight back to the front. It was disconcerting news, as he had known for the past 100 hours he had been flirting with death. "I am fretting, or am nervous or something. I cannot remember anything clearly. My head is dull and heavy. I take long sighs and broken breaths, like a love sick youth."

Luckily his captain took note of Rusty's edgy state and knew that he had to be rested from the front. There was only so much a person could stand. He was instead directed to attend a "bombing school". His captain thought he was doing Rusty a favour. On the second day at a camp near Albert, after practising throwing dummy bombs and bombing down trenches, the instructors called for a break. They decided that the bombs not yet used would be placed in a sandbag until the afternoon session. "As the bombs were being thrown into the sandbag I heard a stick pin go off, and someone shout out: 'Look out.' Everyone scrambled up and ran, the bomb exploded, and although I was ten to 15 yards away, I felt myself hit on the back in several places."

Although Rusty wrote that he was well away from the bomb, one newspaper stated that he instead "threw himself on the live bomb carelessly dropped by one of his squad. He saved the lives of his men, but was severely wounded." When treated by the 1st Field Ambulance, it was found that he had large pieces of bomb in both shoulders, and if one had gone in a little deeper, it would have penetrated his lung. The following day at the British Red Cross hospital in Rouen, metal was extracted from one shoulder. An x-ray discovered there was further metal under his left shoulder blade, meaning that a transfer to London for further treatment was necessary.

Not even in the relative sedate confines of Wandsworth hospital could he escape drama. In time he regained full feeling in his shoulders, and bored by the lack of activity in the wards, sneaked out whenever he could. He soon found allies in several other adventurous Australian military men, travelling into London, chatting up the local women, playing billiards and generally forgetting what the time was.

One night they arrived after the hospital curfew of 10.30pm, and were forced to scale the hospital walls. However they were caught by a picket as they tumbled to the ground, and were told they would be tried in the morning. Captain Rowley, Captain Osward and Lieutenant Richards were directed towards the hospital colonel, who told them "that our conduct as officers in climbing the wall was extremely bad, and he could do nothing but send us before the general commanding". They were taken to the Horse Guards, where they found themselves standing in front of General Sir Francis Lloyd.

The trio were told to take off their belts, and then one by one the General "gave us a pretty strong blowing up and let us go away". When they returned to hospital, the colonel made a complete about turn, apologised for pushing the matter and ended up shaking hands with the three. The incident further convinced Rusty that the British were strange.

This was confirmed a few days later, when he saw Lady Darnley, the wife of former England cricketer Ivo Bligh, wandering around the hospital. Lady Darnley felt sorry for the Australian soldier and convinced him to follow her to her nearby house for a guided tour. In the library, Ivo, now the Earl of Darnley, was sitting poring through some books, and without any prompting a few minutes later, produced the original Ashes urn, naturally his most prized possession. One minute, Rusty was hospital bound, the next he was holding international cricket's most famous trophy. "I stayed in his library for an hour looking around amongst his books, but alas, they were all printed in old English, Latin or Greek, and though of great value, and intensely novel, and interesting, it was impossible for me to read them." Rusty was as intrigued that the statues throughout the Ivo Bligh household were devoted to either love scenes or nudity. He didn't pay a second visit.

Before returning to France, Rusty even had time for flirtation with a nurse who was the daughter of a parson, mysteriously writing in the diary on 4 July that "before my sister left me at Sole Street station, there were happenings and consequences that will live forever in my mind, and remain at all times an inward and heavy secret." But everything had to be fleeting, as in late August he was heading back towards the front, travelling via Le Havre, Rouen, and on towards Hazebrouck, where General Birdwood and the Ist Division had their headquarters.

It had been three years since Rusty joined up and "it seemed almost a lifetime". His world weariness, was not helped by again being surrounded by devastation. "Hazebrouck, when I was here some ten months ago, was a fine little place with any amount of civilian life, particularly on Sunday afternoon when everybody came out walking. But today there is very few people about at all. Hazebrouck, 14 miles behind the line, has been so bombed and shelled that the people have deserted it. Many buildings are destroyed and thousands of windows broken. It is so sad to see the place so deserted and lonely." He was soon pointed towards Ypres, the scene of the most bloody of battles, where he was attached to battalion staff as a "liaison officer", with his main duty to keep the flanks in touch with one another and organising counter attacks if the enemy pushed back the initial line. It was an important duty but a fleeting one. Within minutes of rejoining the front line a piece of shell struck his forearm, forcing him to be immediately stretchered from the region.

Four days later, he was back in a London hospital, where he stayed for the next five months.

Despite numerous brushes with death, his commitment to return to France and do his duty never dimmed. He was back again as soon as possible, in February 1918. This time, he had unexpected company. When rejoining the frontline south-west of Ypres he passed another battalion, and in the middle of that group was his younger brother Bert. It was a quick but emotional meeting, both delighted that the other had survived thus far. Conversation was cut short as they were soon ducking for cover, being fired upon by German machine guns. Rusty last saw Bert, crouched over heading for safety.

He returned to his pillbox, which was only 1.3 metres high and two metres wide, for " a restless night's watch. A position like this makes one think a whole lot, as we are underneath the Hun, and he could strafe the whole lot of us day or night. The nights are cold, and the walking around in the dark, bogging into shell holes, is trying. It is a long, anxious day, and if the Hun shells or attacks, we are like rats in a trap. If we come out of the pill boxes, his machine guns on the ride in front would clean us out in quick time, and the artillery knock the pill boxes to pieces if we remained inside. The nights are dark, and very cold. We all stand to and strain our eyesight all night long.

"Our grub is short, and the hour of its arrival is very uncertain on account of the ration party getting lost. Hot stew and tea should come about 1am, and rice and tea later on, but a container occasionally gets lost en route. There is no movement of any kind during the day time."

Then came the gas — first sneezing gas, followed by mustard and phosgene gas. All around Ypres a bluish vapour hung over the Flanders fields, with soldiers affected by the gas staggering around as if deliriously drunk. The issued gas masks failed to save the soldiers and by mid March, Rusty was feeling the effects. He could not get rid of a loud, hacking cough, which virtually shook his body, day in, day out. "I am getting quite sick of it all, and find it jolly hard to keep cool and collected. Gas shells of all kinds mixed with high explosive rained down.

"I can"t understand going off like this, and I am beginning to think that I am not as good a man as of old, and the strain of the line is rather too much for me. On reaching camp, my voice was gone. There is no doubt that my trouble, like dozens of others in the Battalion, is caused by gas, a delayed action." He blamed Phosgene gas, which was "sent across in liquid form contained in shells, which upon exploding splashes around, and slowly became gas. It lay in dugouts, out of the wind, for many hours. Men took particles into dugouts on their boots, but it was sufficient to kill them in agony. [There is no doubt] thousands will die in after years from its effects." It soon knocked him around. For several days, Rusty did not have the energy to get out of bed, and sleep was impossible. "It"s the coughing that gets me down, it's the very devil. My cough is mighty bad… it shakes and rattles me to bits, and the Doctor can do nothing at all for me." The only relief was from whisky- at six francs a bottle. Within four days, Rusty had finished off two bottles. It worked as a tasty anaesthetic.

It also gave him the energy for one last fling at the front. After taking the train south to Amiens, he marched to Allonville. "One cannot imagine the dejection and depression of Amiens. All the stores and buildings are deserted. We marched cheerfully through Place Gambette, and passed only a handful of people, whereas we would hardly have been able to get through the crush in ordinary times. It was a sad eyed few people we saw." On his birthday, he was still marching. "The guns seemed fairly busy last night, and I felt afraid that we might be called out these anxious times."

It was impossible not to feel nervous, especially as Australia"' death toll in France was astronomical. The toll at Gallipoli was horrific, with Australia suffering 26,111 casualties before the evacuation. This was still minor, compared to the Western front, where there were 179,537 casualties, including more than 45,000 deaths. Hundreds died by the day. In one twenty-four-hour stretch, Australia suffered 5500 casualties. Soon 60 per cent of the AIF in France had become casualties. By the end of the war, in which more than 61,000 Australians were killed and 155,000 wounded, that figure had risen to almost 65 per cent. A prime reason for this high percentage, when compared to other countries in the British forces, was that Australians were virtually always frontline soldiers. The authorities soon realised that they were no shirkers, and if asked would always lead the charge.

While admired for their fearless, fighting spirit, they were also used and abused, at times being treated as fodder, particularly with the British never able to fully comprehend or appreciate the Australians' free-spirited, anti-authoritarian approach. Their refusal to salute or show what the British considered due respect to their leaders really got up the British nose. And often the Australians were forced to do the dirty work. There was word that the British High Command wanted to used Australians and Canadians in exposed positions to save British troops. This even prompted one brigade who were leaving the battlefield late in the war to refuse to move back into the front line because they that once again they were being unfairly forced to finish off a job the British had failed in.

No wonder Australia's respect for the Tommy soldier and their officers diminished by the day, until by 1918, it was outright contempt. As the Australian historian Manning Clark wrote of Pozieres in his *History of Australia*: "The 'bloody British top brass' had done it again, just as the same inhuman bastards had done it to their cobbers at the Nek and Lone Pine on the Gallipoli peninsula."

But it was not always the fault of the British. Although their ineptitude was rightfully criticised in many flawed battles, it must be remembered that the fateful charge of the Australian Light Horsemen across the Nek, as graphically shown in the movie *Gallipoli*, was instituted by a stubborn Australian officer named Colonel Jack "Bull" Antill, who in the middle of a series of bungles by both Australian and British leaders, caused the third and fourth line of men to rush to senseless deaths.

Australian officers and soldiers blundered, and often. They were not saints, being involved in their fair share of desertions and less-than-heroic retreats. Australians were also inclined to mischief when away from the Western front, which further angered the Tommies.

When he was in Bullecourt, Rusty asked a French female school teacher how the behaviour of the Australians compared to that of the English soldiers. "She replied: 'Oh well, there's not much difference, only when the Australian is sober, he's better than the Englishman, but when he is drunk, he's awful.'

.I am of the opinion that the Englishmen make better guardsmen, policemen and storemen; the Australians being so irresponsible and careless, so generous in fact that they give away too much of the goods they are supposed to be guarding. I have heard the (Australian) police and guards over the potatoes and foodstuffs say to the fellows filling their shirts: 'For Christ's sake, give us a chance to get out of your bloody way.' As guards over prisoners they are just the same careless men."

Naturally Rusty kept worrying that his time could also be up, especially if erratic, senseless orders continued to come from the British brass. British leadership was at its worse during Bullecourt because of poor artillery preparation and reckless attacks, which included failed tank raids. The British tank crews at Bullecourt were regarded by Australians as cowards. General Sir Hubert Gough, in command of the Reserve Army, was ridiculed for being a poor tactician and leader during this period.

In April, Rusty admitted that news of a German victory in the Flanders area was "very depressing indeed. We can hardly see where it is all going to end. We will have to kill off more of the enemy to level them down a bit. Again there has been heavy gunfire around here over night and morning, and it makes one very anxious indeed, as there is a chance of our being called out at any hour. The thing is so uncertain. Early this morning we passed close to Hazebrouck, and it was a miserable sight to see the farmer folk coming along the road with wheel-barrows and bundles. Driven back and away from their farms by the Hun.

"We know nothing as to the situation, only that the enemy is advancing, and we must be ready to hop in and stop him. We came back from wiring at daylight, and though the men had to sleep under a hedge, we four officers got into a house.

"There are batteries all around and the Hun is landing shells all about. It is a sickening feeling. We got into bed and slept fairly well until evening when an artillery officer came and claimed the rooms for his men.

This battery already has four whole houses. Naturally we refused to be turned out. This English one-star officer did not care what became of us as long as his men got the beds. His men carry several blankets a man, and there was floor space for 40 men in the house, but no, regardless of the fact that we never even had an overcoat, he wanted to turn us out.

"He was the meanest and most inhuman man I've yet met. We ended up by laughing at him. Later he brought his Major, but it was hardly likely we were going to shift; more especially as it was English troops that let the German through, and we were hustled up to hold on and cover up the Tommys' weakness." The Australians held their ground, and the Tommies moved on.

In April 1918 the Germans were advancing again, with Field-Marshall General Haig demanding that the Australian troops cover Hazebrouck. Rusty's role was to help lay bared wire around the village of Strazeele near Hazebrouck. An onerous task, especially as it had to be done in the middle of the night. Rusty wrote on 16 April: "Strazeele is the key to Hazebrouck, and the 1st Australian Division have sworn to defend it to the very last. It is awfully dark laying down barbed wire, and a little disconcerting when the Huns put down his barrage at intervals. We got back to bed at 2.30am, but was disturbed by gas until 'stand to' at 4am. At 2pm we moved 400 yards away into a field, and at 5.15pm, after the boys have their sleeping positions good, we have withdrawn their coat and blanket, rolled them in bundles, given out two bombs and three bandoliers of ammunition each man, 280 rounds altogether, and are ready to move into action at five minutes' notice.

"The church tower at Vieux-Berquin is a good observation point for the enemy. We heard our artillery were going to knock it down this afternoon, and sure enough the tower disappeared at 4pm.

"We moved out at 6.30, a Battalion in artillery formation, over the fields with the intention of attacking on the flank of a French Division that was taking Meteren. We came under heavy shell fire and lost men but reached some reserve trenches, and lay down there in the cold until nearly 4am, wondering what was going to happen to us, and we as cold as it is possible to be. We were roused up just before daylight and rushed up to a system of outposts where we relieved the Scottish Rifles, and at daylight we were sniping at Huns wandering about in large numbers. I don't know what happened to the French attack, but nothing eventuated at all last night." Rusty discovered the following day that the French attack did not begin because the English captured the French runner who had the complete operation order and held him for two hours, believing he was a spy.

17 April was another "cold night of anxious waiting, but we have had some good sport shooting Huns today, as they seem to be hopping about aplenty. The enemy planes have been especially active, they came down low and fired upon our posts. They also brought down two of our machines, and have been fighting and hovering about all day. McGill shot through the head 1.10pm. My batman Lucas also killed at my side. Clarkson shot through the helmet, slightly wounded."

"We have had some tough sniping set tos, but I reckon we killed a number of Huns. I think I got four for certain with my own rifle. I only have a Lewis gun, and nine riflemen as a platoon now. A number of Germans extended out in front, the SOS went up from the adjoining posts on either side, this move provided us with more shooting. It seems the enemy is attacking strongly on our right. At nightfall we had the Hun as tame as a caged canary, and afraid to look 'over the top' at all. It has been damp with light rain all day, and it is cold tonight with frost. The enemy seems to be working in front ... I can see numbers of them, we are also digging in so, alas, I cannot fire on them."

The next few days fighting was restricted because of hail, snow, sleet and howling wind, enabling Rusty to bury two of his colleagues, McGill and Lucas, whom he called "good lads". He could ill afford any more losses. As he explained on 23 April: "It is a bit rough when a man has to hold a platoon post with 12 men all told, including Lewis gun post, and then receive orders that there must be no retiring. Fight on and on. When asked had I an SOS signal in my post, I replied, 'No, we deal in 303 (rifle ammunition) only.'

"And although in both posts on my right and my left put up the SOS for artillery support, my platoon laughed and went on killing Huns, who seemed to be preparing for attack."

Rusty was also forever grateful that the men next to him were Australians, and not English. In the same diary entry, he wrote: "Some awful stories of the English troops funking and running away are being told on every hand. Both the French soldiers and civilians on the Somme and here at Meteren say they (the English) were demoralised and broke. Something damned bad must have happened, or the enemy could never had got outside of his artillery range, and I fear that the English reputation of being bulldogs is entirely lost. Both here and on the Somme, a few Australians restored the line the moment they got into position, and had the finest sport of their lives.

"Without artillery no troops can possibly push back the opposition if they will fight. It is hard to believe, but it seems quite clear the English refused to fight, and ran away."

The following day, he reiterated: "It seems doubly hard to have to give good lives to regain a high vantage point like Meteren when the Tommy ran away and left it without firing a shot. It is frightfully disheartening to us."

On Anzac Day 1918 there was no time to reminisce. He was told to pack up, track down "the odds and ends left over from the Battalion to form the framework of a new Battalion should it be wiped out in the line.

We walked for an hour amidst shellfire and bomb dropping. We have a very rough sleep in a thin wooden hut."

However his body eventually gave in on him. For several years, he had been suffering from lumbago, but his back condition had become chronic after he was blown away with a section of trench while defending Hazebrouck. He could hardly walk, bend over, do anything. His days in the front line were numbered.

Again, Rusty worried about what his fellow soldiers would think. "It is a miserable kind of trouble as a fellow has nothing to show for it, and could easily be malingering. It is remarkable how a fellow hopes and longs for a smack from a shell or bullet, so as to get away from this business for awhile. This is not my case as much as the fact that I cannot get well."

He was taken to hospital in Boulogne, where it was discovered he had osteoarthritis of the lumbar vertebrae, and was in no fit state to continue fighting. Back to London and hospital one more time.

On 31 May relief came at last. General Charlie Ryan sent him to the Board for a full examination, and "talks of Australia for me." Rusty was not going back to the front. He was going home. His back was gone, his shoulders damaged, his coughing from the gas incessant. He was ill. But he sank to his knees, and thanked whoever or whatever was watching over him for looking after him. He was one of the lucky ones. A survivor. Millions of others weren't so fortunate.

Like so many other Australians, he left the war zone disenchanted, and knowing whom to blame. One of his last war diary entries read: "These Englishmen beat the world for sham and waste. If they win this war it is a 1,000 times more than they deserve."

As he headed for safety, he sang…

> Goodbye Billy Birdwood
> Farewell Douglas Haig
> Since we've joined the Army
> We've been your bloody slaves
> Gallipoli was a failure
> France a bloody farce
> You can take the whole of the AIF
> And shove it up your arse.

FOURTEEN

HAPPY EVER AFTER ?

RUSTY NEVER GOT OVER THE WAR. It invaded his thoughts, affected his decisions, dampened his outlook on life, plagued his body. The effects of the gas, and his perennial back complaints, caused him unending pain. But he wasn't as scarred as some other serving Wallabies, including 1908 tourist Darb Hickey who was so disgusted with what he had been through that on returning from the front he threw his war medals into Sydney Harbour.

Still Rusty soon had other distractions to occupy his forever wandering, often wearied mind. Not for the first time he was lovestruck... the victim of yet another Manly ferry romance.

For so long he had known there was something missing in his life, and that after years of wandering, it was time to settle down. War had stopped that for four years, but even in his diaries from the front there are repeated entries about lost loves, missed opportunities, comments that maybe it was time for him to think of becoming a husband and father. He knew this would never happen until he could settle in one spot. He didn't know whether he would ever overcome his adventurous streak. But at thirty-seven he could no longer act like an irresponsible, homeless pup.

Nonetheless his wanderlust rose to the fore yet again when he was allowed to leave England in August 1918 and return to Sydney. Not surprisingly, he did not choose the most direct route. Instead he took six months to get home, travelling via Cape Town, Johannesburg, Victoria Falls, Stellenbosch and Bloemfontein, visiting family, friends, and sightseeing whenever possible in a neverending 10,000-kilometre train trip after again setting foot in South Africa. As usual, he could not stay in one place for too long. When peace returned in November 1918, Rusty was in Pretoria.

By February 1919, Rusty was again striding down the Corso in Manly, agreeing to coach the local football side, meeting up with his old mates at the Manly Surf Club and flirting with an assortment of old girlfriends.

Even bent over by his back complaint, in pain and obviously aged by his war experience, he was still among the most handsome men around Manly, a war and sporting hero whose physique was still impressive. Adding to the attraction was his reserved manner; Rusty was not the usual cocky local, all show off and no substance. He was polite, shy even, forever serious. Someone you could easily mother, if you can get close enough. There were complexities. And many women loved complexities. Rusty was never short of female company.

He had a short spell in Randwick hospital for further tests on his back, onto Macquarie Street and a nasal operation to overcome sinus problems where he "actually watched the doctor cutting, breaking and tearing pieces of bone away from my nose", followed by a few weeks on the road as a travelling salesman. All these gave Rusty ample time to think over his options, and to convince himself that a more solid base to his life had to be found.

A proper job would also help. That came in April when he was made officer in charge of the employment section of the NSW Repatriation Department, which involved helping returned servicemen get jobs. In charge of a staff of sixty, having to deal with as many 3,600 returned soldiers per day, his annual salary of 400 pounds was substantial. He was able to secure a reasonable flat in Manly, within sight of the ocean, enabling him to enjoy a dawn bodysurf before a quick breakfast and a leisurely ferry ride into town each day to work.

Not before long he noticed a striking blonde-haired, seductively built woman, who also caught the 8.10am Manly ferry to town every morning. She was confident, outgoing, always with a boisterous group of friends around her, nattering away over the next half-hour or so until the ferry berthed at the Quay. She was attractive and she knew it. There was nothing self-conscious about this lively, impulsive, obviously headstrong woman. Brash even. Opposites attract.

She knew who he was. Rusty was one of Manly's favourite adopted sons, and he was repeatedly stopped down the Corso by acquaintances and admirers. After all, he was as big a catch as she was. It took a little more time for Rusty to find out something about her. He made the right enquiries, and found out that she worked in the blouse department of Robsons, a city store right opposite Mark Foys in Liverpool Street. She later moved to Farmers department store, where she was involved in advertising.

After numerous ferry rides, where they cast sometimes shy other times bolder glances at each other, Rusty eventually summoned the courage to front her. She responded straight away. Yes, she knew exactly who he was, and would like to walk around Manly with him. Yes, she would love to go to the theatre with him. He was smitten with Lillian Effie Jane Sandow. And she seemed just as interested in him.

She was what he wanted. Someone to bring some life back into him. Argumentative, opinionated, outgoing, a proper character. She forced him out of his shell and soon they were inseparable. Life for Rusty was at last starting to get some sort of solid foundation. There was at least one solid link: both their fathers were passionate Methodist preachers. Like all her other male friends, he called her "Snow White." His princess. But as much for her striking blonde hair and fair skin.

She had a way of continually surprising him. She was forever making him blush with her outrageous views or actions. She was a livewire. She loved the high life. She loved partying, going to the races on Saturday, playing cards, playing for money. She always seemed to have money, and like many people with money, was self-assertive, with a certain assurance in her stride. He loved being around her. He could show her off, and he did. Lil, of Danish descent, originally came from the Mallee region of Victoria, where her family were farmers. She lost her parents early and was brought up by her stepbrother Bert, who agreed to be her guardian.

But late in November, 1920, after Lillian and Rusty had been going out for some months, she told him that she might not be able to see him for a while as she was actually engaged to someone else, the local barrister Cornelius Alexander (Alec) Haley. He had never practised at the bar, however, as he had a comfortable income from his deceased father's estate. He had impressed Lil with the trappings of wealth, and poor impoverished Rusty could never match that. Haley, twenty-three years older than Lil, had been pursuing her for nearly a decade, ever since she was a young teenager and had moved into Manly with her stepbrother.

Haley, a fine billiards player and rifle shooter in his youth, had even trekked as far as Melbourne to win the hand of this dashing young teenager. For many years she had resisted, realising she was too young for marriage, knowing it was important to play hard to get in front of a rich legal man who already boasted a healthy list of girlfriends, including several he had lived with, much to the shock of his conservative neighbours. If the news of the unexpected engagement was not a big enough shock, Lil told Rusty the following week that she had secretly married Haley at a Methodist church in Leichhardt, and they were about to move into a flat at Kirribilli Point, so they could live together.

The story got crazier by the week. On the way home from the wedding, Haley had stopped off at his solicitor's office, signed the will, and then when hopping back into his car, said to his bride of a few minutes: "Snow, I hope that this will is never, never used… because it's not the way I want it."

Finally an official wedding was organised so two of Lil's brothers could attend from Melbourne to give their blessing. Then just before that proper wedding in February 1921, Haley took ill at the Pacific hotel in Manly. Three days later, Cornelius Alexander died in St Ronan's private hospital.

Haley's death certificate reveals that he died of lobar pneumonia after a seventy-two-hour illness. His occupation was listed as grazier, with his brother, Barclay, the informant of the death, in charge of their property, Wetalabah near Yass. He had been married before, twenty-four years earlier, to Eleanor Atchison in Melbourne.

Naturally, Rusty was in a state of shock. The story was too bizarre, too unusual, but after checking it out, everything was true. Lil was secretly married. Her husband of a few weeks was dead, and he had already been buried in Boroondara cemetery in Kew, Victoria.

Rusty felt duped, used, confused and devastated. To overcome his pain he went walkabout, heading for far-flung parts of new South Wales. As he explained in a diary, written some years later for his children: "I was so upset and dejected that I resigned from the Repatriation Department and wandered around the country, staying at Breiza station, near Werris Creek." He said he did not care where he went or what he did.

He had been burnt one too many times: First the promises of Zelda and now the two-timing of Lil. The only way to forget was to indulge himself in something else, far away from the original scene. After his country jaunt, Rusty headed for Newcastle with two of his brothers, Bill and Bert, where he made axes and pick handles at a factory. The aim of the exercise was to see whether the three brothers were sufficiently attracted by the exercise to buy the actual factory, and "settle down as a tool handle makers".

It was a quick exercise. After only eleven days they found it too much of a grind. The boiler had to be stoked at 5.30am so that there was enough steam for everyone to start work two hours later; and there was a shortage of good young spotted gum wood required for the handles. The brothers headed back to Sydney, while Tom looked for another excuse to go elsewhere. Next he was on a fishing trawler off Eden, catching leatherjacket, flathead, john dory and skate. Then he was at the Christmas Gift goldmine at Cootamundra. Eventually three months after disappearing, he returned to Sydney.

And someone was waiting for him.

Lil had also fled Sydney after Haley's death. She headed to the ski slopes at Mount Kosciusko, before a spell with friends out west at Barmedman, near West Wyalong. She now had money; Haley had generously made over half the income of his substantial estate to her. Each week, she received 20 pounds from the estate, a large sum of money that enabled her to live like a princess. She was one of the first women in the Manly area to have her own car- a stylish Morris Cowley, which she had spray-painted the same colour as her favourite green suede coat.

Rusty's family, after years in Johannesburg, also returned to Sydney, and moved to Manly. His mother bought a large block of units on West

Esplanade, close to the Manly ferry, the local baths, the Corso, everything. Rusty moved in, a move that coincided with the return of Lil from Barmedman, who with ample cash, was able to reside into the plush Earl's Court boarding apartments nearby.

With Lil a free woman again, Rusty returned to the chase. To convince her that he was now a solid upstanding citizen who could support her, he took up a job again as a travelling salesman, selling electrical goods for an old north Queensland mate, and also selling motor tyres throughout New South Wales for the Perdriau Rubber Company. At the time Perdriau, a Sydney-based family firm that owned the steam ferries running between the city and Balmain, was one of the main competitor to Dunlop, specially catering for sportsmen, making their own tennis shoes as well as importing Slazenger tennis rackets and balls from Europe.

Rusty"s full-time employment with a successful company enabled him to convince Lil that they should get married, by August 1921. But his plan was almost ruined when he took Lil home to meet his mother. Mrs Richards was a crusty, grumpy, argumentative woman, who through the wide, unforgiving travels of her wandering mining husband, had learnt about life the hard way. The meeting of bride-to-be and future mother-in-law was a disaster. As Lil later told her daughter, Joan: "After leaving the house that day, I honestly and truly thought, 'I mustn't marry him, I really mustn't. That Ma is an old bag.' I went against all my instincts in agreeing to marry him."

But right from the start, Lil showed she would always be her own woman, and the marriage would be on her terms. Forever headstrong, before her marriage she had organised with a group of American friends a trip on the *Marella* to Java, and nothing was going to change that, not even a wedding to Manly's most eligible bachelor. There was even a possibility that she might go on to the USA. She didn't want Rusty to go with her – and Rusty was so besotted with her that he agreed. Prior to leaving for Java, Rusty "persuaded her to marry me quickly" on 27 August before Rev John Ferguson at St Stephen's Presbyterian Church in Phillip Street, with close friends Les and Hilda Macqueen as witnesses. The wedding breakfast took place at the Carlton hotel, and the party went to the Tivoli Theatre afterwards. breakfast at the Carlton Hotel, Castlereagh Street, and went to the Tivoli Theatre afterwards.

Just two months later Lil was off to Java, starting off one of the most unusual of marriages. Rusty was back in Manly, alone again. During the three months Lil was away Rusty joined the local Masonic Lodge, as well as the Manly Golf Club. He continued to flit around the country, including a trip to Brisbane, but was home in time to greet Lil, only to be told she would not be around for long, having decided to go on a holiday to Hobart, with her friends Mr and Mrs Tommy Foster. He also discovered why she had also returned from Java early, and had not proceeded to the United States. She was desperately ill with malaria, and needed to go to Tasmania to recuperate.

Several months later, Rusty agreed to meet her halfway in Melbourne, and before three of her brothers they were officially married at the Punt Road Methodist Church on 25 March 1922. At last the pair could have a proper honeymoon, leaving for Sydney that night to spend a fortnight in the Blue Mountains before returning to live in Manly.

The opening weeks were idyllic, but soon married life began to sour. There was friction because Rusty was away for lengthy spells as a travelling salesman, while the couple living so close to his mother did not help. Mrs Richards persisted in each night making her favoured son dinner, and getting Bill to deliver it to their apartment high up on the hill above Manly. There was never any food for Lil because Ma detested her.

One evening, with Bill and food on the doorstep down below, Lil opened their first floor window, and called down to him: "Bill, if Ma sends that to me again, the next time I"ll drop it down on you." Bill, who liked Lil, laughed it off and returned the following night, only to have the previous evening's food dumped on him. He never returned.

As well, the pair's vastly different characters were bound to lead to clashes. As daughter Joan explained: "Daddy was much older. Mother used to say he was twenty years older, which he wasn"t. He was fourteen years younger, because Mother had tampered with her age a few years to make herself sound younger." (Their first wedding certificate indicates it was actually a fifteen-year difference, Rusty stating his age as thirty-nine and Lil twenty-four.)

"Daddy was very earnest, and always wanted to better himself, whereas Mother was looking for the gay, bright lights. She wanted to go to the races, gamble, play cards, go to parties, have a good time. He didn't like that. They obviously weren't really going to get on.

"But he thought she was wonderful, divine, gorgeous. And she was. Daddy was gorgeous too… everyone thought that. Women were always swooping, hovering around him, talking to him, and fussing over him, and Mother hated that. She liked being the kingpin.

"You would see them playing at card games. Mummy wanting to bet big, and Daddy exclaiming: 'I only play for matches.' That"s all very hard when you are a young woman years younger than your husband — she couldn't stand that. And he couldn't stand her playing for money. It went both ways.

"Sometimes I wonder now how he and Mother ever got together. Yes, he was handsome looking. But Mother was everything I think he thought wasn't a good thing. Really, they were opposites."

While Lil, with her wild streak, was always going to be taxing, Rusty would have also been difficult to live with. So long a loner, he was not used to being penned in. As well, he was irritatingly fastidious, methodical and overly moralistic.

His meticulously kept diaries reveal so much, and one can see through them how he could grate on others.

Apart from copious amounts of intense detail on his personal life they show that he was obsessive in keeping records on everything. In one diary, Rusty kept a record of his weight, recording each year between 1902 and 1935, how he hovered between 11st 4lbs and 14 stone 2 lbs. He jotted down every letter he sent, and every letter he received by name, date and destination. He wrote diaries in the name of his son and daughter, trying to describe their adventures through their eyes. In others were copious notes on lectures he had attended at Sydney University, where he had taken a special interest in psychology. Then there were precise details of trips he had made, both working and on holidays, meals he ate when convalescing from various ailments, bonuses he had made while on the road, shares he had bought and sold. He did not leave much out.

He was at his most enthusiastic though when talking about his children, though his tone was sometimes possessive and stifling. His desire to be at the head of a growing family came to fruition in November 1923, when a son James Jarman Richards was born, followed in June 1925, by Joan Anne. As his diary indicated Rusty, while indicating the looming storm clouds, had never been happier. A solid base had at last come to his life. On the birth of James, he wrote: "I went up to the hospital and I found your mother jubilant and happy, and you, my son, clean and so bright as though you were days old. It was a proud and delightful moment for me, as it was to you, both of us looked to brighten up our home and make us both happier.

"Your mother is some 14 years younger than myself, and up to this point, our lives had not been very happy, at the same time there was no serious quarreling or bad trouble, it was just that we did not understand one another and our form of mental, as well as, physical vocation lay in different directions. But we are both as happy over your coming and proud of you, not only being a boy, but of your apparent good health and excellent disposition."

Despite Lil's money from the Haley estate, there were neverending financial problems. Lil would spend the money as soon as she received it. With Rusty away and with a nurse and cook to help in the house, Lil could enjoy the high life: playing bridge, going to the races, and meeting friends were all part of her daily regime. And Rusty could not really police the situation because he was forever on the road, sometimes months on end, travelling through the north of the state, selling motor tyres and anything else to ld ensure a reasonable income. Within a few months, the marriage was only in name.

"We are poor," wrote Rusty, "I am about 10 pounds in arrears at the moment, and I have never been to a theatre or spend on drink or tobacco. It seems like money being badly wasted somewhere. We have some furniture but no home of our own. I never go out, seldom to the picture show, partly to try and save a few shillings, and also because I don"t get enough rest."

By the end of 1926, Rusty"s diary had turned forlorn. "Wife and I hitting it pretty badly just now. She is frightfully discontented, and loves getting about never doing a hands turn. The kids' clothes, pyjamas especially, have no buttons on and gross carelessness is evident everywhere. She is living well above her income of 20 pounds a week too!"

Adding to the despair was that Rusty was again sick. His war experiences, especially in France, were coming back to haunt him. His back was again stiff and sore, not helped by long trips driving the back roads around Walcha, Armidale, Glen Innes, Tenterfield, Inverell, Moree and Mungindi, hopping in and out of the car to open and close farm gates. But more seriously, his rasping cough had returned, forcing him to spend three weeks in Prince Alfred hospital. The fear was that he had tuberculosis.

"The only other cough I ever had like it was when gas was plentiful in France in 1918. The Army doctors thought that my war service and the effects of gas was having a serious effect on my lungs. Hundreds of fine healthy young soldiers are now developing T.B from the German gas inhaled on service.

"But I don't agree with them at all. I am not a happy man regardless of my glory in and for my children, and I think my worries are just pulling me down now. I have not seen my two children or mother for eight weeks, and the time has been almost torture.

"Day and night I fret and long to see your smiling faces and to have a little play. I cannot put on any weight. I fear I worry far too much about you all. Ah, how I would love to be with you, my children. I have a disposition that makes friends and gets me every comfort at the various hotels I stay at, and my work is easily carried out, and fairly profitable for a man who had has to battle through life, and who has no money making profession. If only my wife and children were near me, I would be so happy.

"Oh! I do miss the children. It"s hard not having them about. It will be terrible being away in the northern part of NSW for months and months without them. It is, and will be so lonely, and I have never been lonely in my life."

So concerned was he about having TB that he visited ten different doctors, including his old Wallaby captain Paddy Moran, meeting him at his Darling Street practice in Balmain. No one was certain of his exact ailment, and a series of tests, failed to show up any positive TB results. His demeanour was also not improved, by the death of his Test-playing brother Bill in June 1928, "after a long, sad illness. He never gave in at any stage. Miner's complaint got him, aged 47. We buried good old Bill at 3pm at Manly Cemetery. Good hearted and staunch; not a really big outlook on life, but he was honest, clean and sincere, and if God loves a fighter, Bill will be right."

His brother's death also made him consider their differences, and how Bill's influence was crucial in making Rusty the complete footballer.

"When I was about 16, my brother, who was captain of a first-grade team, said I was not worth a place in his team, but I succeeded in getting in another team. Within two years, I was leading my team to victory against all comers, including my own brother's side.

"Bill was a big-boned, strong man and powerful, as kind as a child at heart, but relentless in his regard to his latent power. He was afraid that someone might accuse him of shirking, so he did three men's work in the rucks and a further man's work in open play.

"I wasn't as robust as Bill and as I wanted to play real international Rugby I had to build up a system different to Bill. A system which I know was going to bring criticism upon myself for being a loafer and afraid of the rough stuff.

"And this certainly did follow, and had I remained in north Queensland, or even in Australia, these accusations may have prevented me from winning high honours. So my loose open style of game was developed in spite of criticism and in defiance of popular prejudice."

To overcome his general gloom, hastened by the departure of a close ally, he hoped that the homefront would improve. In January 1928, he received a letter from Lil, saying she wanted to leave him. He pleaded with her to keep the family stable for the sake of the children. His trips to Manly were short, and usually tense. He wrote in March 1928 that when in Sydney to pick up a new Buick car, he "enjoyed the days with the children, but did not see much of my wife. I kissed her upon my arrival, and she turned me down. I stayed with my mother and went up for the children every day. Fate has been unkind to me in not providing a wife to come along earth's stony path with me. I do want a mate, a pal, a friend. All through life I have had to go alone; when I was young it was good battling, but now it's mighty hard."

In a valiant to save the family base, he suggested to Lil to head up north with him for a short while, and travel around with him. She might be sick of him, but might at least enjoy the beautiful scenery. He attempted to convince her that he was in nirvana. After all, he had just given Wally Hammond, another Bristolite, a lift from Warwick to Glen Innes, and the touring English Test cricketer loved every minute of it. If the lugubrious Hammond liked it, surely so could Lil, even to the extent of enjoying the simple life of camping. Lil did try, agreeing to spend some time sleeping under the stars. But as daughter Joan explained:

"Mother camping? That was not my mother's scene at all."

Or as Rusty wrote: "Relations are very strained between your mother and myself, strained it seems beyond repair, and it breaks my heart. I can"t see any way of us getting together again. The suspense is cruel, and for the children's sake it's terrible. It shakes my health almost to breaking point. I have always disliked failures in life and had no sympathy with them, and here I am situated with a wife and two of the best children in the world, and I can't enjoy the happiness that should be mine. Perhaps I take life too seriously.

We made off to Mungindi where I did my business and we then camped. Mother and I slept inside the 'camping car' and you children slept one at each end on a camp stretcher. You were very excited and took some time to get to sleep. Mother did quite a lot of driving on the trip, but she did not enjoy it a bit, which disappointed me intensely. I can't get on with my wife."

But Rusty persisted, convincing Lil that the family should move on to Inverell, and then Lismore. Somehow he was able to get her to agree. It worked for a few weeks. The children moved into the local schools, and joined Rusty when he went on the road, Jim revelling in learning how to fish, shoot pigeons, emus and kangaroos, catching rabbits for their skins, while being taught the wonders of the bush by one of its most rabid enthusiasts, his dad. Joan, meanwhile, was "the picture of health and activity". Country life worked for both of the children. At the end of year play at the Inverell Grammar School, Joan was an impressive bluebell.

Not so impressed was their mother. One minute Lil and Rusty were getting along better "than for years", being regular theatre goers, but then, as Rusty wrote in May 1929, "she is still very self opinionated and does not see the future welfare of us all very clearly. But I still have hopes of some domestic happiness as time goes on."

After six weeks in Inverell, Rusty thought he had saved the marriage, with the children revelling in country life, and wife relatively content. But one afternoon Lil told him that she "hates me like poison, simply (if she is telling the truth) because I have spoilt the kids who are a 'disgrace and a horror'. I can't understand such unworthy conduct. I can't imagine myself an angel to live with, but why my wife should be viciously fighting me I can't even imagine. Certainly the children are a little fresh. All their lives they have been tied down to flats and boarding houses; in their present atmosphere of health and happiness, with a father to play with, and a father that loves every minute he spends with them…. I feel like throwing up the whole thing and moving off to New Guinea. Why she hates and fights me is beyond my imagination."

Then a few days later, Lil fronted him with the claim that for some time he had been unfaithful. "I am told by my wife today that I had Miss Dunn at the Hotel Inverell, and that several people have told her (Lil) I was playing about with women. She states she has intercepted a letter from Sacka Dunn to myself, and that it has gone already to her solicitors and that use will be made of it.

"The letters I have at times received from this girl would certainly create suspicion, but she is very young and treats me as a father, and loves to tell me stories, and say suggestive things. I wouldn't mind brightening my wife"s life if it were possible to do so without blighting the children. They are all the world to me. My wife should be also, but she never has gone with me, she has always gone 'upstream', and the hours of peace we have experienced together have been few indeed."

Lil, believing that Rusty was going to Brisbane to meet Miss Dunn, made out that she was off to Sydney- but instead headed in the opposite direction. She "motored to Brisbane evidently expecting to catch me with another woman in accordance with a letter of mine she intercepted, which was stolen out of the post. But I had no intention of meeting any woman in Brisbane, though I do want to see Brisbane again.

"Perhaps I have played around a little (very little really) but then what is a neglected man to do months and months on end living isolated and lonely. I have been in the country 3 1/2 years and see my wife at big intervals, and for small and mostly disagreeable periods."

Lil's suspicions had originally been raised four months previously, following what appeared the most innocent of incidents. Rusty had decided to drive the extended family from Inverell to Bellata for the day, inviting a certain Mrs Booth with her three children and a maid for the outing. "I asked her (Mrs Booth) to get into the front seat, and when Mommie saw her there, she declared that was her seat, and that I had insulted her beyond words."

Eventually Lil said she had enough. She packed up the two children and drove off, wishing to move right out of Rusty's life. "The wife informs me that she is clearing out and taking the two children to Melbourne to live. She is fed up, and finished with me for good. I told her that she has always pleased herself what she did and how she did it, and I wouldn't stand in the way of anything she wished."

To add to the pain, Lil showed off a new star studded diamond wedding ring, because "mine wasn"t good enough".

The day of the departure was horrendous. No goodbyes were said. Only a note was left, giving her address to a boarding house in Cremorne. A week later Rusty rang the boarding house. The caretaker had not heard of Lil or of the children. Rusty was bereft. He was again a solitary, barren rock.

FIFTEEN

THE BREAKDOWN

EVERYTHING BECAME TOO MUCH. In Rusty's words, he had a "complete breakdown". He was in the depths of depression, suffering coughing fits, while his back was agony. He tried to avoid admitting the obvious — that he was dying of the gas. Instead he placed a lot of the blame on his disastrous personal life. As he lay in Randwick hospital for weeks, attended by military doctors who continually probed every part of his body, especially his chest, he mulled over his life. It failed to improve his gloomy demeanour. He gave up work for a time, believing he could not do it justice, as he was "forlorn and dejected". He eventually found his family, who had moved on to Melbourne from Cremorne, but that was little consolation.

In his diary, kept for Jim and Joan, he wrote at the end of 1930: "I shouldn't have breakdowns; but then you children have been away from me for two months, and I don't see any hope of my ever getting back with you. Mother makes a lot of serious accusations against my honour and fidelity. There is no doubt some grounds for suspicion, but absolutely no breach of fidelity on my part, and I have suffered nearly 3 1/2 years of desertion and forlorn loneliness, and Mummie now declares she will never see me again. It's a free country, I suppose, and she can please herself. But it's very hard and very bitter. I have not questioned her right to have possession of the children. She is your mother and bore you, though you are both part and parcel of my very life. Mother gave you your life, Jim and Joan, and I have to stand down and take my chance in 'blazes'."

His personal diary was even more depressing and he wrote in November 1930 that his latest medical

examination had led to an increase in his pension. "This money is all very well, but it means that I am badly gassed, TB has set in, and my days are numbered. The heartbreaking experience and the loneliness of being separated from my children is truly terrible, and will hasten the development of TB. Wife says Jim is coughing violently, and probably has whooping cough in Melbourne, and I am helpless and hopeless. It's just hell."

He kept trying though, travelling to Melbourne after being released from Randwick hospital to spend some time with his children. For two weeks it was eternal bliss, father, son and daughter, travelling around Victoria and through the Daylesford and Hepburn Springs region, as well as a day on the historic Ballarat minefields. Joan vividly remembers those outings.

"Daddy was tremendous with both of us, and doted on us. He was fanatical about teaching us, and always so eager to show us everything. When we were away together, it was one long adventure. He was always wanting to better himself, and us. He was as fanatical about health. I remember he bought Indian clubs for Jim to swing around, because he didn't feel that Jim's chest was developing properly. Jim was only six at the time.

"But even though Daddy and Mummy weren't together, my brother and I would have had no idea that they fought. He never spoke against her to us, or vice versa. They hid their problems away from us. However, Mummy once said that Daddy as a street angel but a house devil."

They must have picked their time to throw barbs at each other, undoubtedly when the children were well away or tucked up in bed, as when they returned from Hepburn, Lil made it very plain to Rusty where he stood. "I spent half an hour with Mummy. She is hard and bitter. Wants a divorce. Says she would sooner live with a snake."

Rusty would also make secret trips to Melbourne to ensure his children were getting a proper education. Lil's extra income enabled her to place Jim and Joan in two of the most exclusive schools in Melbourne. Jim was at Melbourne Grammar, while Joan went to St Catherine's School for Girls in Toorak. Rusty helped out with the school fees, but reluctantly, as he could not believe how exorbitant they were.

"While Daddy was so education-orientated, he was not happy with the schools we were in in Melbourne, because they were private, and he hadn't been brought up that way. We were in the best schools in Melbourne, and he had left school when he was very young. He came down to Melbourne and without telling mother, quietly went to our schools, making appointments with our headmaster and headmistresses. The day he arrived at my school, I was doing flag drill out on the oval, and he was enthralled.

"From that day on, he turned completely round. He first thought mother was throwing her money away, but now realised she was on the right track. From then on, he devoted all of his money to our education."

Not long afterwards, he wrote a personal note to Jim and Joan, to convince them of the importance of study and learning. "An educated man or woman can hold their own before the world. We are all born with a certain amount of brain power, but they who can develop it by study and concentration will surely lead the world." And referring to himself: "Want of education is a terrible hardicap in life."

He also devoted himself to getting his records in order. He was uncertain how long he had to live.

In early 1931, Rusty had his soldier's pension increased to the highest rate, which "warns me that gas will yet beat me. This being so I am now preparing to meet the slow torturing death by getting my records up to date, sorted and properly filed so that when my 'lingering time' comes I will be able to occupy my mind by reading and writing, and preparing to take whatever the gods provide for me. I am not looking forward to my end in terror, no, far from it. But I want to meet it fighting all the way."

His chief exercise was to write a series of lucid, entertaining and colourful articles on his footballing career for the *Sydney Mail*. It was a popular nineteen-part series, chronicling his early life in Charters Towers, but devoted primarily to the 1908-09 Wallaby tour. The series, which ran over several months and shared column space with articles by A.B. 'Banjo' Paterson on horse racing and L. O. S. Poidevin on cricket, remains one of the most vivid and accurate sources of early Australian Rugby history.

It also showed that Rusty, despite being so self-conscious about his lack of education, was a natural writer. He even wrote an article about Taronga Park Zoo, which portrayed his love for nature and animals. He rated the hippopotamus his favourite animal, "with his complete lack of 'make believe'" and was distressed to see an overworked elephant forced to take hundreds of children for rides around the zoo. "Jumbo is everybody's friend, but I thought he continued round and round his tortuous circuit with a crowd of children packed on his broad back in a spirit of passive protest against his loss of majestic bearing and unkind humiliation." The *Sydney Mail* received a multitude of congratulatory letters from readers, most stressing that Rusty's "descriptive writing was almost on a par with his football." While the series did not make Rusty rich, it did enable him to pay some bills. But he was still broke. He didn't even have enough money to attend his Battalion officers' reunion in 1931. "I would really love to be there, but six shillings to go, and probably a few drinks besides at the bar at the Imperial Services Club gave me a feeling that I could not afford to go. I stayed home, but my soul was with those glorious soldiers and wonderful men."

Missing such a reunion hit Rusty hard, as he was the proudest of servicemen. He did not talk much about his war experiences, especially about what happened to him on the Western front, but was proud that when Australia called he responded. But even he was surprised by the mythmaking that surrounded the Anzac legend, especially the overblown portrayal of John Simpson Kirkpatrick as the ultimate Australian war hero.

Rusty had known Simpson, working with him in the opening days of the Gallipoli campaign, where they were both carrying wounded soldiers to dressing stations. Rusty mainly carried soldiers on his back or with the aid of a stretcher. Simpson instead used a donkey to transport injured Anzacs, until he was killed less than a month after landing at Gallipoli. Simpson and the Donkey soon became the image of Gallipoli.

After seeing Simpson described in a Melbourne newspaper as "the Australian spirit personified" Rusty was moved to write in his personal diary: "Simpson had an outstanding personality, he had initiative and imagination and successfully brought these qualities into operation when he saw a loose donkey on Gallipoli. Simpson has become a 'national hero' not altogether because he was brave or that his donkey did any extraordinary work, but because his work was brought into prominence by its originality.

"In actual work done, that is hard, physical toil, he didn't do anything like as much as ordinary stretcher bearers, but he certainly brought in more patients than they did. That is, patients who could sit up. The stretcher bearer had to carry the badly wounded man. He was brave and had to expose himself, but there is no evidence that there was any special demonstration of valour. No, his initiative appealed to the popular man and he died at his post. Certainly a worthy hero." It was still many decades after Rusty's diary entry that it was publicly revealed a great part of the Simpson story had been cleverly fabricated.

Rusty's *Sydney Mail* articles eventually provided him with an opening. W.M. Early, one of those who wrote to the paper applauding Rusty's football series, agreed to finance a trip to New Guinea, on the undertaking that Rusty write a series of articles on what he observed there over two months, especially on its goldfields.

This offer could not have come at a better time, as Rusty had been made redundant from the recently merged Dunlop Perdriau company after working unsuccessfully through the north of Queensland selling tyres for them. The company were "dissatisfied with my work, and plainly told me so."

In a letter tucked away in his diary, Rusty, at the time of his dismissal, feared he was a "misfit. The pettiness of the tyre traders, particularly in Townsville, is beyond me to fit in with. My health gives me concern as my wind is bad and I kind of think there is a mental dullness existing also. This may be imagination, or it may be due to my chest condition or perhaps to the fact that I am lonely and feel the loss of my children for over 12 months very severely that I fear it all tends to make me indifferent to others and short in patience.

"It is an awful position to be faced with at my time of life, nearly 50 years of age. Adrift, an outcast without hope of any kind…. It's my own hopelessness that appals me."

So depressed in not seeing his children for most of 1930-31, he tried to convince himself that they were actually with him when he went bush. He often sang to them "imagining you are sitting beside me in the car as I run along the roads. Being separated from you (Jim and Joan) is breaking my heart; it keeps me dejected and the folk pity me. I don"t want pity. I have always been proud and independent, accountable for and responsible to myself only. I have always lived within myself and will manage it severely than ever now as all I really want in life is to be near my children to watch to train and to teach them." His and the children's favourite song was 'Pack up yoiur troubles in your old kit bag'.

He was also beset with financial problems. Lil was constantly asking for money, pleading hard times and that she was in debt because of a moratorium which had cut her income in half. One day he sent off 20 pounds, only to cry that he was "a big mug as money cannot help her out of debt".

A wild adventure was required to clear the cobwebs, and New Guinea fitted the description perfectly. In a near impenetrable frontier, Rusty was given the task of heading to its most remote areas to describe the country, the natives, the gold mining pioneers and the hangers-on for inquisitive readers back in Australia. As his four-part series in the *Sydney Mail* so aptly described it, Rusty found himself in a "land of gold, stone age customs and daring flying men". His companion for part of the trip was Ray Parer, whose background was as colourful as Rusty's.

Parer was the most daring of flying men. The cousin of the renowned war cameraman Damien Parer, Ray had made his name shortly after the war when he and friend, Lieutenant J.C. McIntosh, had been the first to fly from England to Australia in a single-engined aircraft. They had been lured by the Commonwealth government's offer of 10,000 pounds to the first Australian to fly from England to Australia within thirty days. The greatest surprise was not that they made Australia, but how they actually survived the dangerous 260-day flight. They blew a tyre in France, the engine caught fire over Italy. The engine again exploded near Baghdad, forcing them to land in the desert to repair it. No easy task, as they were hassled by local tribesman. There was an easy solution — they threw a Mills bomb at them, which dispersed the mob. The aircraft caught fire a third time over Malaya, forcing them to crash-land, smashing their propeller, undercarriage and radiator. They also almost crashed in the Dutch East Indies, while between Timor and Darwin the plane struggled to get airborne because of too much additional petrol on board. Although they failed dismally in beating the thirty-day deadline, the Australian government felt sorry for them, giving them a 1,000-pound consolation prize because they had arrived home as heroes.

A wild, swarthy character, Parer was soon lured by the discovery of gold in the New Guinea hinterland, prospecting for a while before getting back in the pilot's seat to pioneer the inland airways of this wild country. He was the perfect man for New Guinea, a swashbuckling, larger-than-life character from a fascinating family, which included Damien's father, a compulsive gambler who would disappear at times from Australia to try to win a fortune at the roulette wheels in Monte Carlo, only to lose it all. Parer senior ended up running a pub in the New Guinea village of Wau.

Ray agreed to fly Rusty around parts of New Guinea, and they soon hit it off during a journey that went from Salamoa, Wau, Bulolo, Bulwa, Kiandi and even a walk along the Bulolo River from Wau to Bulolo.

They found themselves in crocodile country, in crowded bar-rooms where "bushy-headed natives, dressed in lap-laps, waited upon the luncheon tables", in mountains and clouds that enveloped their plane completely, in wild jungle, on mountainous zig-zag tracks, and in cannibal territory.

"From the grass-roofed mess at Bulwa I could see miles and miles of rugged mountain, as wondrous a panorama and as magnificent a scene as may be viewed in the Rocky Mountains of America, with the added thrill that away up there somewhere the wandering tribe of Kuku Kukus organised their raids upon the native labourers employed along the Watut River. They are cannibals, upon whom the white man's laws have had little effect.

"The Kuku Kuku men are real killers, and nobody appears to have established friendly relations with them. Only recently they carried off and ate a "boy" from a miner"s camp nearby, putting terror into the hearts of other natives."

The gold miners were almost as wild. One of Rusty"s great attributes was that he could mix it with the highs and lows of society. He had that common touch, which came in handy when surrounded by crazed pioneers trying to make their riches in the primitive New Guinea backblocks.

In a letter to an old Bristol teammate, Rusty wrote: "The other night a temporary room mate on mine at the Hotel Bulolo came in at 2.30am. I asked him if he had had a good night, and whether he was ready to turn in, at which he became a little indignant and explained that he had only come in to put on a pair of shorts as he was going to fight a fellow for a tenner.

"I got up and there were a number of incandescent hand lamps on the verandah rail, lighting up a patch of grass on which the fight was to take place. The contestants shook hands and assured each other that there was to be no ill-feeling after the fight, which was to be of four two-minute rounds and one minute intervals, during which there was to be no malice shown.

"No quarter was given, and being good fighting men no chances were given away; body punches were terrific and the battle was declared a draw at the end of the fourth round.

"There were 32 men looking on and being a good, satisfying fight, drinking was enthusiastically continued until 4am when the remnants turned in. But at five the contestants met in my room and round after round of "gin slings" were served and the night voted a great success. One of the fighters declared that he had had a wonderful night. He won 48 pounds, had as much grog as any other man, and a real good fight thrown in.

"Of course this type of man is always found on far away mining fields, and although they drink and fight, they also have the pioneering spirit that sees them through hard and dangerous times midst isolation and indifferent food supplies, surrounded by malaria and fever and untamed natives. It seems to be nature's strange way when selecting men for the hardships of pioneering in jungle and hostile lands."

Rusty met the owners of goldfields and plantations, who also knew how to rough it.

These included Doris Regina Booth, the author of *Mountains, Gold and Cannibals*, and the Bayliss family, who were attempting to grow tropical fruit, including pawpaws, bananas and melons, near Bulolo.

"One afternoon, while out walking, her native attendant was bitten on the foot by a snake. There was nothing at hand with which to make an incision until Mrs Bayliss's presence of mind suggested breaking a button off her dress; the sharp edge was used to cut the tough skin, and with her mouth she drew the poison from the wound and saved the native's life."

Even the flight back from Wau to Port Moresby to catch the boat home was tense. It took the pilot almost two hours to decide whether to start the aircraft as he was concerned that his heavily laden plane would not rise quick enough to get over the mountains.

Eventually the pilot summoned the courage, and the passengers "scrambled hurriedly into the small cabin, and in great haste raced roaringly down the runway. Suddenly the plane tilted forward from its upward angle in a distinct downward direction. We looked anxiously from one to the other; the luggage shifted, and the passengers adjusted their balance and smiled as it was realised that the mountains were successfully crossed and the plane was making down on to the flat delta country beyond."

The country had "changed from a merciless, inhuman character to a more composed and hospitable nature, even if crocodiles, malaria fever and semi-savages were our nearest neighbours. We circled over Port Moresby to warn the Papuan authorities of our arrival. A health officer and a Customs representative eventually gave a clearance. A little later the Macdhui steamed out over the reef into a thousand fathoms of blue ocean where flying fish left pretty patterns on the smooth surface."

Rusty wasn"t surprised to hear that his pilot that afternoon, Frank Drayton, later crashed and was killed in the mountains near Wau.

This short trip revitalised Rusty, convincing him that he had to continue travelling while he could, and not be so reclusive. Shortly afterwards, Lil gave him permission to take Jim and Joan to New Zealand, with the two children travelling from Melbourne to Sydney on the S.S *Mariposa*, under the care of the ship's captain, joining their father for the trip across to New Zealand.

While delighted to be with his children for two months, he was also pleased that his footballing conquests were still remembered in New Zealand. While he was in Auckland, the *New Zealand Herald* sought an interview, and Rusty nobly explained that Rugby was now a better game than when he played. Back play had definitely improved, even though he was concerned that the work of the forwards had deteriorated.

A highlight of the New Zealand tour was when the three on Christmas Day went on a ten-shilling joy-flight above Rotorua. It was no ordinary joy-flight as the pilot was Charles Ulm, Charles Kingsford-Smith's right hand man in several famous adventures, including the 1929 record flight from Australia to England, the first flight across the Tasman Sea, and the first Trans-Pacific flight between America and Australia.

The joy-flight was in Ulm's plane "Faith in Australia." A short time later, Ulm disappeared on a flight between San Francisco and Hawaii on the first leg of a trans-Pacific flight to Australia. His body was never found.

Rusty was even swayed to attend the twenty-fifth anniversary reunion of the famous 1908-09 Wallaby team at the Tattersall's Club in Sydney. Although the team had split after the tour in acrimonious circumstances, with many moving across to Rugby League, it was a rollicking evening, attended by sixteen original members, including Paddy Moran, Chris McKivat, Bob Craig and Phil Carmichael, who travelled from Brisbane for the function. Four had died — Wood, Murnin, Barnett and McCabe, while several were either overseas or interstate. Each member was asked to speak of the trip, with Charles McMurtrie summing up the Wallabies as "five per cent tenacity, five per cent sheet lightning and ninety per cent guts". McMurtrie attributed his distinct memories of the trip to having been a teetotaller all his life.

The function ended with the players presenting through Stan Wickham, an inkstand "of beautiful polished Australian wood with two upstanding Wallabies in silver" to their captain Moran. Even twenty-five years later, Moran was still idolised by his players. Shortly after Moran left for Italy and the eternal city, where he had already been received by Benito Mussolini, and where he later wrote a sympathetic pamphlet called "Letters from Rome", which expressed how Australia "did not justly appreciate" the achievements of the Italian Fascist leader.

Rusty was more interested in simply staying alive, especially as the New Guinea trip had taken its toll. Over Christmas he discovered he had malaria, and just after overcoming that, had a second attack in March.

On top of that, the cough had returned. He returned to Randwick hospital for further tests, which revealed the inevitable. He in fact had tuberculosis, and that "the gas I swallowed during the war is beating me down steadily". He could not walk without puffing. Strolling up a hill was near impossible.

His breathing was getting seriously "worse and worse, and it must continue so, only more rapidly than in the past, until I will lay up, weaken and die after having lived a splendid life full of excitement and achievement for the humble miner's start in life But alas my marriage overcomes and blots all. My children whom I have nursed and loved are cut off from me. I have really failed at the greatest point of all. A failure."

He tried fasting in Cairns. Then, struggling now to even climb one flight of stairs, he was directed to Lady Davidson hospital in Turramurra, on Sydney's North Shore. This private hospital was controlled by the Repatriation Department, and specialised in caring for returned soldiers suffering from chest complaints, especially tuberculosis.

Rusty gradually improved, helped by long stretches of walking, going as far as Bobbin Head, but the doctors decided it was no time dodging the issue. Rusty was told he had six months to live.

For a week, he was in a state of shock. He was alone, living on a relatively meagre pension, and was a shadow of his former self. He did not want to depart a loner. As demoralising was that he realised he could not live with his mother any longer. At the time, he wrote despairingly of his mother: "I am sorry and distressed that I can't get along satisfactorily with her. Her outlook upon the world is most unkind. She condemns and runs everybody and everything down. She is not good company for me… I can't live with her."

He eventually summoned the courage to go to Melbourne to throw himself on the mercy of his estranged wife. Despite their enormous differences, he still believed she had a heart of gold, and in this time of need, she might help. After a leisurely sea trip to Melbourne, where he kept all his fellow third class passengers awake with his monotonous hacking cough, he arrived at the footsteps of Lil"s house.

Lil answered the door, and was aghast at what she saw. The once proud, stout, statuesque, handsome sportsman was doubled over, gasping for air, coughing intermittently, desperately hanging onto the side verandah railing to keep his balance. His clothes were too big for him. His eyes were cloudy. His hair patchy. His demeanour sad. He had aged twenty years.

"Snow… just listen me out for one minute, please. Don't slam the door on me. I am sick, dying. I've been told by the medical doctors that I have only six months to live. I know you hate the sight of me. But I would be appreciative if for the final months of my life, my wife and children are with me. Then I will never trouble you again. I do not want to die alone."

That night, when the children arrived from school, they were staggered to see their father in the living room.

Lil announced: "We're going... we're packing up and going with Daddy." Rusty returned to Sydney two weeks later, followed shortly after by the rest of his family, who decided to go by sea on the *Kanimbla*. Lil had her faults, but she still had an enormous heart.

Joan recalled: "Mother moved into the Australia Hotel; and the rest of us went to say at grandma's at Manly. Grandma was tremendous to both Jim and myself. The doctors had told Daddy that he had to go to the Blue Mountains, believing the air would settle the effects of TB." He wasn't eating well, was not being fed properly, and needed someone like Lil, an excellent cook, to look after him.

"One day, Mother simply hopped onto the Blue Mountains train, and when she saw a station which looked pretty, got out, went across the road to the estate agent and agreed to take over the lease of the house belonging to the local doctor, who was away for a year."

The next day the family followed. They were now living in Wentworth Falls, in a sprawling house, including an outdoor verandah, where Rusty lived and slept.

"As he was dying of TB, Mum made Dad swear that he would never kiss us, or fondle us. Mother was concerned that whatever Dad had could be passed on to us children. And Daddy agreed to the request. He never touched us, and lived out on an enclosed, glassed-in verandah."

The move worked. Within months, Rusty had improved. He was breathing more easily, was able to walk around with little discomfort, drove the family car to pick up Jim and Joan at the local state school and even made them a canoe out of corrugated iron. "Daddy got so much better. Mummy basically brought him back to life," says Joan.

While Rusty and Lil were hardly the loving couple, he was indebted to her generosity. He honestly had not thought she would help him in his time of need. But Lil's unselfish attitude, caring spirit and clinical belief that she could improve his health had overwhelmed him. One day, with the children sitting nearby, he sat her down, and said slowly: "Snow, you're pure white, white all through."

He was pleased that he had been remembered. He bought C.E.W. Bean's fourth volume of his official war history, which is devoted to the A.I.F in France 1917. Rusty is mentioned twice — his charge of the cross-trench at Bullecourt and his critical involvement in Snowy Howell's action, which won Howell the Victoria Cross.

"I believed after reading of the many bombing attacks, and the wins and losses thereof, that the show I put over on 4th May was the most complete, we killed a lot of Huns and took a number of prisoners, and with very few casualties in my party, which fact is not commented upon in the book. Anyway it's quite an honour to be mentioned twice," he wrote.

After ten months, the Richards family moved on. Following a hazardous Christmas-New Year, where Rusty was laid low with pleurisy, he was again healthy enough to believe a move to the warmer climate of Brisbane would improve him even further.

Following almost a year in the mountains, in April 1935, the family, and a dog called Friday (all of Lil's dogs were called Friday as they were invariably bought that day at the Prahran market), crammed into their second-hand Hupmobile for the five-day drive to Brisbane.

They moved into a bungalow in Ascot, and for some weeks Rusty continued to brighten. Lil was so confident that their time in Brisbane would be lengthy that she even sent for her long-time maid, Frances, to move up.

However, by May Rusty was struggling. He had seen the local military doctors, and was told "my case is now well advanced and the odds of living very long seems short, but I will fight to a finish". He was weak, but had not lost his spirit, or sense of anger. Lil was also starting to get at him again. Among his private papers was this succinct note, written in July- "We have been living here in a furnished flat for four weeks. So that my wife won't suffer from loneliness, we have a motor car, a maid, wireless set, a girl companion (not on the pay roll), and two fine children, as well as a sick husband. Yet she is from four to six afternoons, and two or three nights each week out playing bridge, which averages fully $3\frac{1}{2}$ hours a day each week. What a weak, cheap world some of these women make of this immense and beautiful universe."

As well, he was concerned about the family finances. "I"m not contented, and worry at the cost of 10 pounds each week to live. In addition my wife will be telling me again as before that the least I can do is to provide a home for the children, or at any rate 200 pounds worth of furniture to them. This hurts when she sold up and to pay her debts the furniture they had, and at the present moment spends her life rushing round to tea and bridge parties in a big Hupmobile car, spending fully 3 pound a week on fudge and waste. She wastes a house full of furniture every 18 months, and then puts it back wickedly upon myself. I tell you it hurts."

By the end of July, Rusty was took weak to stay at home, and was admitted to Rosemount hospital. Joan remembered: "In those final months, Mother devoted her attention to him. There were certainly no parties in the Brisbane household. Out would come the egg flips at 9am, 11am and so forth. She fed him up. But he eventually became too sick, and had to go to hospital. We would visit him every second day. He was still not allowed to kiss or fondle us. I used to sit beside his bed, and we would play a game called Casino for hours on end. As I was on the right hand side of the bed, it basically turned me into a lefthander, as that was the hand I used to play cards with.

"When we were sitting there, he was tireless in wanting to get the message through. He continually talked about the importance of education. He was scathing about men who just drank and talked about women. He wouldn't deign to speak to them. He was a very one-eyed person. And then he thought mother was marvellous. He had no time for the ignorant. He'd say: 'They couldn't hold a conversation. They never read a book. All they do is drink and talk sex.' He hated that. He had very strong views, and imparted them to me."

Rusty was quickly deteriorating. Joan recalled, "He didn't want us to see him with his oxygen mask on. He thought that would frighten us. As soon as we were coming down the walkway of the hospital, the oxygen mask would go away. But as weeks passed, the oxygen mask stayed on. He was now too ill."

Considering the gravity of Rusty's condition, Lil sent for his mother to Brisbane. Lil hated the sight of Mrs Richards, and the feeling was mutual. Their relationship, which from day one had been rocky, had hardly been improved when the family had moved to the Blue Mountains. One day, Ma Richards, who according to her granddaughter Joan had a way of angering everyone because she was a "never-ending stirrer", so antagonised Lil's maid Frances that she dropped the Christmas roast turkey onto the floor.

And every time she went to the mountains to visit her son, Ma would badger her about how much she wanted one of Lil's fur coats.

"Nan kept saying that she wanted this fur coat, until eventually my mother said: 'For God's sake, take it.' The next time Mother saw Bert's wife Aunty Elsie, she was wearing the fur coat. Mother was furious."

But in Brisbane, Lil and Ma attempted a truce. It was short lived. "One day at the hospital, the sisters came up to Mother and said: 'Something is upsetting Mr Richards… and it's all happened since his mother has visited him.' Mother strode to Daddy's bed, and said: 'OK, Tom, what is it? What"s happened?' And he said: 'Grandma wants me to sign a new will, that Bert (his younger brother) will look after the children, while leaving the Manly property to my brother and myself.'

"Mother was blind with rage. 'Right Tom. The moment you sign that will, you"ll never see me again, and you"ll never see your children again. We"ll get in the car and go straight back to Melbourne.' Shortly after, grandma was on her way back to Sydney on the train." Rusty left everything to Jim and Joan.

Knowing there were only a few days left, he wrote to an assortment of friends. One letter read: "Don't be sorry or sympathetic. I have no requests or regrets, and have well fortified myself so that I can still smile and play to the whistle."

In his final letter to his brother Bert, Rusty wrote: "Sleep, one of my best friends, has turned and deserted me. I am taking sleep dope now, and it juggles a fellow's mind a lot, but there is a steady improvement set in. But come what may I am prepared to meet it. I have built and fortified myself to meet a crisis, and I have lots of spirit left to fight it, so I am alright."

Tom Richards died on 25 September 1935, content that his family were around him, but ever unsure whether he had fulfilled all his dreams and aspirations. The final line of his last letter was: "I sometimes fear my children will never get the chance in life they should."

How wrong he was. Could one gain enough satisfaction from being an international footballing hero, and Australian war hero, when his private life was tarnished? Unlike everyone else, who were understandably convinced and tried to convince him of his boundless worth, he thought not. The ultimate perfectionist, he believed he had endured the imperfect life.

Joan explained: "In the end both Rusty and Lil achieved for their children what they both wanted. I feel Daddy would have approved."

AFTERWORD

THAT OLD BAG OF A MOTHER-IN-LAW thought she got Lil back in the end. Ma Richards would not allow Lil to attend the ceremony at Manly cemetery when Rusty's ashes were placed next to those of his elder brother Bill. Lil laughed it off. After attending a military cremation for Rusty in Brisbane, Lil couldn't be bothered arguing with Ma Richards. Ma Richards was demanding her son's ashes. Lil passed the ashes on, clambered into the Hupmobile and headed for Melbourne with Jim and Joan.

Rusty was not forgotten. Over the years, he received many accolades. When alive, he was described as the first person who would be picked by Earth to play Mars and when he died, the words were as impressive. In one obituary, P.F. Rowland described him as a "man of intrinsic nobility ... Born at Oxford, he might have been a professor; for he had an acute brain, a fine memory, and quite a professorial turn of mind; born a Towers miner and the son of a miner, it was in Rugby football that he pegged his claim to immortality," Rowland wrote.

"Of ideal physique and temperament, always abstinent, always in finest trim, always firm, always tolerant, always observant, with the instinct of genius for doing the right thing, however unorthodox, at the right time; he was a type of which any country might be proud. He spoke with a fine sympathy and charity, but I noticed some quiet scorn for the snobbery prevalent in Australian social life, where to have been to the right school and knowing the right people counts for so much more than originality or merit. I can only say that no man in my life has more impressed me as intrinsically noble; one of God's gentlemen."

One report, written by 'Cestus' began with: "That great Rugby Union footballer 'Rusty' Richards has died. It is hard to realise that so vital a person as Rusty should have passed on. He was such a live individual, so eager, so fit and strong. At least he was in the days of his vanity, the days when his prowess on the football field acclaimed him as one of the great players of his time."

In 1953, G.V. Portus, Rhodes Scholar, England International and friend of the 1908-09 Wallabies, wrote his autobiography *Happy Highways*. In a rambling text, Portus selected his greatest Rugby lineup. Rusty was one of five Australians selected, alongside Jack Ford, Eddie Bonis, Chris McKivat and A.P. Penman. The lineup also included Rusty's Lions teammate 'Cherry' Pillman, the legendary New Zealand fullback George Nepia, and fellow All Blacks Cliff Porter, Maurice Brownlie and Mark Nicholls, plus South African winger Attie van Heerden.

A 1990 book on the British Lions, written by John Griffiths, wrote that Rusty was "probably the most interesting Rugby player to win Test caps for the Lions". Sporting historian Jack Pollard, in his book *Australian Rugby Union: The Game and the Players*, described Rusty as "one of the most colourful Rugby players the world has known" and "among the greatest loose forwards Rugby has seen".

In 1999, the Miller's Guide asked a group of Rugby writers to select their ten best Australian players. Acclaimed author Spiro Zavos listed Rusty in his group alongside David Campese, John Eales, Mark Ella, Ken Catchpole, Phil Kearns, Col Windon, Trevor Allan, Johnny Wallace and Dally Messenger.

As expected, Ma Richards refused to depart quietly. She kept going and

AFTERWORD

going until after her ninety-sixth birthday. Her wish was to be buried above Bill's body, and Rusty's ashes. This was respected. The only problem was that on the day of the burial, it was discovered the hole for her casket was too small, forcing some last-minute frantic digging by the cemetery attendants to avert embarrassment. It was still a tight squeeze. Until the end, Ma Richards was forever demanding her space...and getting it.

Lil resettled in Melbourne, frequented Flemington racecourse, joined Kingston Heath golf club, and re-enrolled Jim and Joan in Melbourne Grammar and St Catherine's. She was soon back on the party and bridge circuits. Four years after Rusty died, Lil remarried another war veteran, another Manly surfer, another man substantially older than she. Her third husband, Sid McAuliffe, was an old mate of Rusty's. Like Rusty he returned from the war scarred, but with more noticeable complaints. One of his legs was blown off, as was the kneecap of his other.

It was a happy marriage where Lil still kept up a cracking social pace. Joan recalls: "I don't remember mother actually being up when I went to school. She was always in bed until her maid brought her breakfast."

After Sid's death Lil returned to live in Sydney, to be near her daughter, who had married a wine and spirit merchant, Clive Menck, after World War II. The Mencks were a well-known Victorian sporting and business family, with their moment in the sun occurring when their horse, the 33-1 outsider Colonus, led all the way in atrocious conditions to win the 1942 Melbourne Cup. Clive Menck's father, L.O. Menck, was reputed to have won over 60,000 pounds by backing Colonus, which had been 200-1 overnight, 66-1 early in the day, before shortening to 33-1 at starting time. Colonus then revelled in the mud. L.O. Menck never revealed how much he won, but press reports of the time stated that he presented his trainer, Frank Manning junior, with the deeds of the Mentone property — stables and land — that Manning had been renting. Menck had promised Manning that if the horse won the Cup, he could have as a gift the rented property. Shortly after, Colonus, which cost Menck only 150 pounds, was sold to a wealthy American woman for 10,000 pounds.

A doting grandmother and great-grandmother, Lil never lost her impulsive streak. For several years, she lived on the upstairs floor of one of Sydney's best known hotels, the Greengate at Killara. The back room of the Greengate soon became a haven for Lil's many friends, who turned it into the spot on the North Shore to have a quiet game of cards and a chat. Gambling was feverish. Lil was a demon at the local bridge club, astounding her new son-in-law when she came home after the first night with more than 300 pounds from winnings. Clive forbade her to go back there. Even in her final years, she was immaculate in her appearance and grooming, forever the lady. Before Lil died in her mid eighties, she suffered a heart-rending tragedy.

Jim was so much like his father. An enthusiastic sportsman, who played cricket, football, tennis, rowed, swam and boxed at school, he loved nature, loved to explore. Unlike Rusty, whose delight was to travel and learn, Jim's passion was flying. He joined the Royal Australian Air Force in 1942 just after turning 18. Within a year, he was a fully fledged pilot. By 1944, Sergeant Richards was flying Vultee Vengeance dive bombers in New Guinea. In the cockpit Rusty was with him; when Rusty died, his Military Cross had been passed on to his younger brother, Bert. When Jim was about to leave for overseas, Joan wrote to Bert, asking for the medal to be given to her brother as a momento. The request was first refused, with the excuse that Jim was too young to be given something so valuable. However a second letter from Joan, which explained that someone old enough to fight for his country was also old enough to look after a valuable medal, saw the Military Cross back in the hands of Rusty's children. Each time Jim flew, he pinned the Military Cross inside his helmet, near his right earpiece. Joan and Lil received numerous letters from Jim in New Guinea. It was like reading Rusty's letters all over again, as he talked about the butterflies he had caught in the mountains, the panoramic views, the different climate.

Then on March 5, 1944, he took off in one of those cumbersome, heavy bombers, out over the sea off Madang. The plane never returned. Jim's body was never found. He was not even twenty-one. It was assumed that Rusty's Military Cross had also gone down with the plane. However some months later, Jim's personal effects were returned to the Melbourne family home. Among his belongings was the Military Cross in its original box. That day, Jim had decided not to fly with his father's medal. Maybe he knew something.

AFTERWORD

Joan continues to thrive, with three sons, nine grandchildren and one great-granddaughter. She has the eyes and determination of her father; the fire and frolic of her mother, the energy and mind of a twenty-year-old. Like her dad, she is a consummate competitor. Like her dad, she always wanted to learn, believing in many of his moral values, the importance of education, worldly travel and experiences. Joan still plays No 1 pennant bowls, and in her prime hit a mean golf stick. Like her mother, she is an enthusiastic bridge player. One can see Rusty and Lil in her. A tantalising mix.

Even Joan was unaware of the vast depth of her father's achievements, especially the football triumphs, the accolades from his peers, the extent of his travels, or his bravery at the front. Obviously Rusty was too modest to admit to it all or talk about it, even to his own daughter. Maybe he thought it was too unusual and fanciful a story. Children are imaginative, but there is only so much they will believe.

On a hill above Manly, in the same cemetery where Australia's first rugby captain Frank 'Banger' Row is buried, Rusty's grave is in a poor state. It is weatherbeaten, stained, in disrepair. The headstone is leaning to one side, its base having slipped. A flower vase in the middle of the grave has not been used for some years. The base is streaked by pools of water, mould and black muck. No one has stood in front of the grave or attended to it, for a long, long time. Someone has slept next to it, a smashed beer bottle to one side giving away the remnants of an inebriated night. Some years after Rusty died, Lil and Joan found the grave. Lil was disgusted by what she saw. "That's typical... look what's on the grave. She (Ma Richards) hasn't even mentioned me."

Obviously there has been some work done since. Lil, Jim and Joan's names are now on the headstone. There is no mention of Rusty's footballing conquests. No mention of his war glories, except for the initials M.C. after his name. Even the date of Rusty's death is wrong, by exactly one month. Rusty died in September. The headstone says October.

Nothing can kill off Rusty's spirit. Not even death.

ACKNOWLEDGMENTS

THE SEEDS OF THIS PROJECT WERE SOWN when I read Rusty's collection of articles in the *Sydney Mail*, a marvellous series that describes so poignantly the early days of Australian Rugby. With them in mind I began researching those involved in the first Wallaby tour of 1908, but I was always struck by the actions of one individual. Afer discovering so many extraordinary facts about Tom Richards, I kept asking myself: "Surely he couldn't have done all this? It's humanly impossible." But everything Richards claimed to have done was proven over and over again.

There is a small group of people who made this project special and enriching. One of the most important is Rob Urquhart. When I telephoned him to say I was researching the first Wallaby tour and would appreciate a quick glance at Rusty's scrapbook — probably Australian Rugby's most important single document — his immediate words were: "Mate, after you look at this, you won't be writing a book about the 1908 Wallabies, you'll be writing a book about Tom Richards. You will not believe what's in this scrapbook. You won't believe what a man he was."

He was 100 per cent correct. I am still astounded at the

ACKNOWLEDGMENTS

thoroughness with which Rusty chronicled all parts of his life, and I am deeply indebted to Rob Urquhart for letting me be the one to find out.

When I discovered that Rusty had been a decorated World War I soldier, and knowing his eagerness to write and take photographs, I knew he must have kept war diaries. Finding them was a chore, prompting countless drives from Sydney to Canberra to visit the Australian War Memorial archives, before the Richards family came to the rescue.

It took some time to track down Rusty's descendants, but every difficult step was fruitful. Firstly, his nephew and niece, John Richards and Hazel Young, were contacted, and both were immediately willing to help. John had heard a great deal about the idolised Rusty from his father, Tom's younger brother Bert, while Hazel had conducted her own research about her illustrious uncle. John provided me with the actual personal diary Rusty had on the day he landed at Gallipoli and that he had by his side until he died about twenty years later. It is a treasure trove of information. Hazel, meanwhile, was the guardian angel who provided me with her copy of Rusty's extensive 1914–1918 war diaries, and a personal diary he left for his two children.

Hazel revealed that Rusty's daughter Joan was still alive, but knew little more, not having seen or heard of her since the 1930s. I eventually found Joan and after her initial surprise that someone was eager to write about her father, she became the most enthusiastic of allies, devoting endless hours to tracking down old diaries, mementos and medals, and offering advice, reminiscences and anecdotes about members of her family, including her mother. She kept remembering more and more, fleshing out the story with countless details. She also gave me permission to use her father's war and personal diaries, for which I am grateful.

I received important support from several other sources, particularly the tireless Judy Macarthur at the Australian Rugby Archives, and *Sydney Morning Herald* colleagues Spiro Zavos, who kept spurring me on, and Sam North who, with a pressing deadline, provided the title for the book. Like so many other writers I am also indebted to those anonymous staff members of libraries from Cape Town to Sydney, who put up with a persistent researcher.

Special thanks must go to the Australian Rugby Union chief executive John O'Neill for granting me permission to use photographs in Tom Richards's second scrapbook, housed in the Australian Rugby

Archives. These photographs, as well as those in my possession and from Joan Menck, adorn this book.

My father-in-law Trevor Chard kept probing, forcing me to ask further questions about the more obscure facts in the book, while my wife Elizabeth and children Anna and Angus endured those times when I had to hide away from civilisation to get the manuscript finished.

My deep and abiding belief is that Tom Richards kept such extensive records and wrote so deeply and passionately about his life and times in the hope that someday, somewhere, someone would read his words and believe them worthy of more than being stuck in the bottom of a drawer or hidden away in an attic.

I was the lucky one who found it all.

To you, Rusty!